o
ご
ぞ
ど

ぼ
ぽ

	ya	yu	yo
k	きゃ	きゅ	きょ
s	しゃ sha	しゅ shu	しょ sho
c	ちゃ cha	ちゅ chu	ちょ cho
n	にゃ	にゅ	にょ
h	ひゃ	ひゅ	ひょ
m	みゃ	みゅ	みょ

r	りゃ	りゅ	りょ

	ya	yu	yo
g	ぎゃ	ぎゅ	ぎょ
j	じゃ ja	じゅ ju	じょ jo

b	びゃ	びゅ	びょ
p	ぴゃ	ぴゅ	ぴょ

o
ゴ
ゾ
ド

ボ
ポ

	ya	yu	yo
k	キャ	キュ	キョ
s	シャ sha	シュ shu	ショ sho
c	チャ cha	チュ chu	チョ cho
n	ニャ	ニュ	ニョ
h	ヒャ	ヒュ	ヒョ
m	ミャ	ミュ	ミョ

r	リャ	リュ	リョ

	ya	yu	yo
g	ギャ	ギュ	ギョ
j	ジャ ja	ジュ ju	ジョ jo

b	ビャ	ビュ	ビョ
p	ピャ	ピュ	ピョ

JAPANESE FOR BUSY PEOPLE

Kana Workbook
for the Revised 3rd Edition

Association for Japanese-Language Teaching
AJALT

KODANSHA INTERNATIONAL
Tokyo • New York • London

The Association for Japanese-Language Teaching (AJALT) was recognized as a nonprofit organization by the Ministry of Education in 1977. It was established to meet the practical needs of people who are not necessarily specialists on Japan but wish to communicate effectively in Japanese. In 1992 AJALT was awarded the Japan Foundation Special Prize. AJALT maintains a website at www.ajalt.org.

Illustrations by Shinsaku Sumi.

CD narration by Yuri Haruta and Howard Colefield.

CD recording and editing by the English Language Education Council, Inc.

PHOTO CREDITS: © Sachiyo Yasuda

Distributed in the United States by Kodansha America, LLC, and in the United Kingdom and continental Europe by Kodansha Europe Ltd.

Published by Kodansha International Ltd., 17–14 Otowa 1-chome, Bunkyo-ku, Tokyo 112–8652.

ISBN 978–4–7700–3037–5

First published in 1992 under the title *Kana for Busy People*
Second edition 1996
Third edition 2007
18 17 16 15 14 13 12 11 10 12 11 10 9 8 7 6 5 4

CONTENTS

INTRODUCTION

The *Japanese for Busy People* series focuses on teaching Japanese for effective communication. It is the aim of this workbook—designed for students at the beginner level—to help you to master kana (hiragana and katakana) as painlessly and as efficiently as possible. It is hoped, too, that by learning kana you will feel encouraged to foray even further into your studies of the Japanese language.

By teaching the basics of the kana syllabaries, this book will enable you to better acquire the rhythms and sounds of Japanese speech, thus improving your oral command of the language. The reading and writing abilities gained through the study of kana will, moreover, help to enhance your overall communication skills.

Many of the vocabulary items and expressions in this workbook have been taken from *Japanese for Busy People I: Revised 3rd Edition*. You can use the *Romanized Version* of that text in tandem with this workbook, or you can complete the workbook before embarking on the *Kana Version*. In any case, a mastery of hiragana and katakana is essential for anyone planning to use either *Japanese for Busy People I: Revised 3rd Edition, Kana Version* or *Japanese for Busy People II: Revised 3rd Edition*, since those books use kana and kanji exclusively—that is, without the aid of romanized Japanese.

Overview of the Book

Before going straight into the workbook itself, you may find it worthwhile getting a general idea of its contents. The remainder of this introduction is devoted to that. Note first of all, however, that there is a kana table on the inside of the front cover, showing all the hiragana and katakana along with their pronunciations.

Introduction to the Japanese Writing System

This section gives an overview of the Japanese writing system, providing some cultural background to capture your interest, while also showing how the kana that you are about to learn fit into and function within Japanese orthography as a whole.

Introduction to the Japanese Sound System

Here you will be introduced to the sounds of Japanese along with the hiragana and katakana used to represent them. Samples of each sound may also be heard on the CD.

Hiragana

This part of the book explains how to write Japanese sounds in hiragana, proceeding from voiceless and voiced consonants to p-sounds, contracted sounds, long vowels, double consonants, and combinations of contracted sounds and long vowels. Lessons on each category of sound move step by step from recognition, reading, and writing of individual characters to reading and writing of entire words. In this way, the book allows you to acquire hiragana logically and efficiently.

Both in this hiragana section and in the katakana one that follows, spaces for practicing individual kana come with reference lines to help you get a feel for the proper size and shape of each character. By thus learning the correct angles and spaces between strokes, you will be able to master even confusingly similar-looking characters and make full use of them in reading and writing.

The Reading Challenge sections starting on page 38 present labeled, picture dictionary–like illustrations of place names, foods, familiar items, and other vocabulary related to daily life in Japan. These pages are intended to provide you with a fun way to practice reading hiragana. Answers can be found at the back of the book.

Starting from page 48 are short reading exercises that present elementary Japanese sentences written in hiragana. Practice reading the sentences, paying particular attention to the irregular readings of hiragana used to write particles.

Katakana

The lessons on katakana open by introducing several katakana with shapes similar to their hiragana counterparts, followed by an overview of the entire katakana syllabary that uses the kana table to relate the characters to the hiragana learned earlier.

As with hiragana, discussion of katakana proceeds from voiceless and voiced consonants to p-sounds, contracted sounds, long vowels, double consonants, and combinations of contracted sounds with long vowels, moving you efficiently from recognizing and writing individual characters to reading and writing whole words.

One function of katakana is to transliterate foreign words into Japanese. As you look through the vocabulary in the lessons, you will gradually come to see what katakana are used to correspond to what sounds in English or other foreign languages. Listen to the CD to familiarize yourself with how the transliterations alter the original sounds to fit Japanese pronunciation.

Illustrated Reading Challenges appear in this part of the book, too. Here, however, different types of words are taken up—mostly loanwords taken from Book I, including country and city names, words for articles of clothing and foods, and other familiar items brought into Japan from the West. Again, the answers are at the back of the book.

Also provided is a section that invites you to learn about and guess at the meanings of various interesting types of katakana words, for example onomatopoeic and mimetic words, contractions, and Japanese-coined words based on English.

The final page of the book, Comprehensive Reading Challenge, will call upon you to bring together everything that you have learned by practicing reading words and sentences written in both hiragana and katakana.

Note: All exercises recorded on the CD are marked with a  icon.

INTRODUCTION TO THE JAPANESE WRITING SYSTEM

Four Types of Characters

As you walk around Japan or leaf through Japanese books or newspapers, you will notice that Japanese orthography employs several different sets of characters, including the Latin alphabet as well as some others of differing degrees of complexity.

Kanji (Chinese characters): Most complicated in appearance

Kana: Simpler looking than kanji and made up of two sets, hiragana and katakana

Hiragana: Curvilinear characters

Katakana: Angular characters

Romanization: Written using the Latin alphabet

Kanji, the oldest of the four, comes from China and is logographic, with each character representing one unit of meaning. Kanji were introduced into Japan sometime around the sixth century.

Hiragana and katakana were developed in Japan based on kanji, in order to represent the sounds of Japanese. Pure syllabic symbols, they carry none of the meanings originally conveyed by the kanji from which they derive.

Japanese today uses a mixture of kanji logograms and kana sound symbols. The bulk of Japanese writing is done in kanji and hiragana. Katakana is used primarily for words borrowed from foreign languages, though it is also used for onomatopoeia, mimetic words, and scientific names of animals and plants as well as for indicating emphasis.

Finally, romanization, while at first glance much like English, is a system for transliterating sounds in Japanese according to set rules.

In Japanese prose, hiragana typically takes a supporting role as *okurigana* (suffixes that show the inflected endings of verbs or adjectives) or as particles indicating sentence structure. Kanji, meanwhile, are used to write nouns and stems of verbs, adjectives, and adverbs. Hiragana can also be written alongside, above, or beneath kanji to indicate reading, making it a convenient tool for helping learners grow familiar with different characters. Hiragana used in this way is called *rubi* or *furigana*.

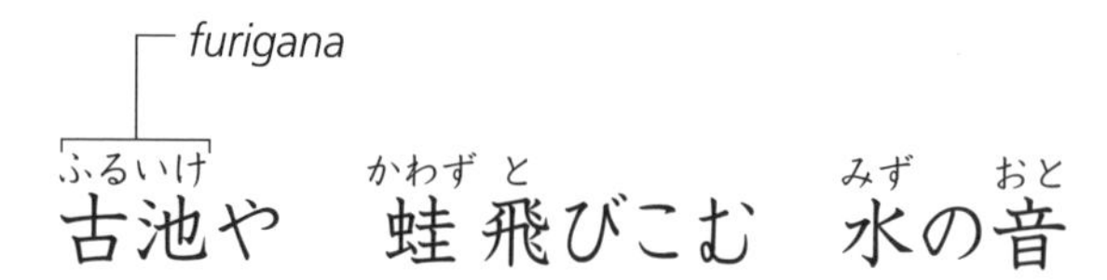

Japanese was traditionally written vertically, from right to left. Along with the influx of Western writing, however, it also came to be written horizontally, from left to right. Today, both systems are equally well used.

Typing in Japanese

On computers with Japanese word-processing functions, users first type in words through keyboards set to accept input either in hiragana or in romanization. After entering a word, users select from several screen options to convert the word as desired into kanji, hiragana, katakana, or romanization. Complicated as it may sound, this method is the one most commonly used for writing e-mails or instant messages in Japanese.

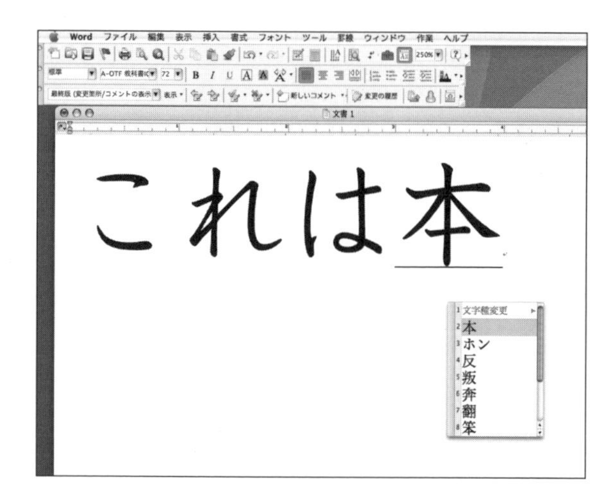

Learning Characters

In Japanese elementary schools, children first learn hiragana, then katakana, then gradually move on to study kanji. As they begin to learn kanji, they start writing what words they can, using the characters they know. Children study about one to two hundred new kanji a year, meanwhile sounding out and learning unfamiliar characters with the aid of *furigana*.

The following pages will introduce you to the two syllabaries of hiragana and katakana as a first step to learning how to write in Japanese.

INTRODUCTION TO THE JAPANESE SOUND SYSTEM

The Japanese phonetic system is composed of five vowel sounds and a number of consonants that combine with these vowels. Each vowel or consonant-vowel combination is one syllable in length, and can be written in either hiragana or katakana.

BASIC SYLLABLES

The Vowels

a	i	u	e	o
あ	い	う	え	お
ア	イ	ウ	エ	オ

The first line of the syllabary consists of the five vowels: *a, i, u, e,* and *o*. They are short vowels, enunciated clearly and crisply. Pronounce the English sentence below, making all of the vowels short, and you will have the approximate sounds.

Ah, we soon get old.
a i u e o

The *u* is pronounced without moving the lips forward. The *o* is similar to the initial sound of "old" but it is not a diphthong, so do not round your lips when you pronounce it.

Consonant-vowel combinations and *n*

The rest of the syllabary consists of syllables formed by a consonant and a vowel. Most Japanese consonants are pronounced with the lips or the tip of the tongue more relaxed than in English. For example, if the *t* in *kite*, as in *kite kudasai* (please come), is pronounced too strongly and with a good deal of aspiration, it will be heard as *kitte* (stamp), an entirely different word. So be especially careful to pronounce *p*, *t*, and *k* with less aspiration than in English.

	a	i	u	e	o
k	か	き	く	け	こ
	カ	キ	ク	ケ	コ
g	が	ぎ	ぐ	げ	ご
	ガ	ギ	グ	ゲ	ゴ

The consonant *k* is pronounced more softly than in English.

At the beginning of a word, the *g* in *ga, gi, gu, ge,* or *go* is hard (like the "g" in "garden"), but when occurring in the middle of a word or in the last syllable, it is often nasal, as in *eiga* (movie). The particle *ga*, too, is usually nasalized, though nowadays many people use a hard *g* when pronouncing it.

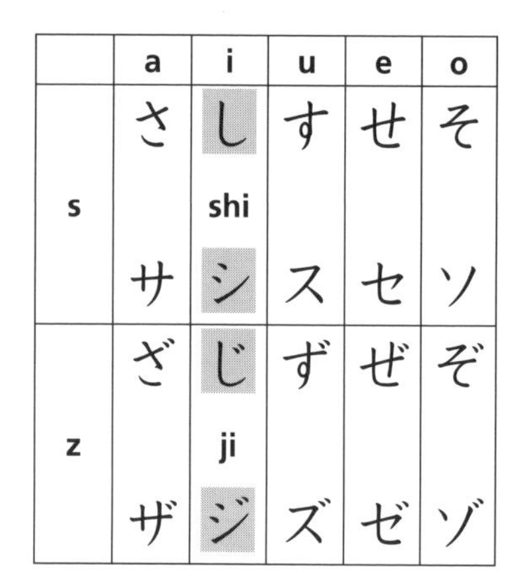

	a	i	u	e	o
s	さ サ	し shi シ	す ス	せ セ	そ ソ
z	ざ ザ	じ ji ジ	ず ズ	ぜ ゼ	ぞ ゾ

The breath is expelled less forcefully when pronouncing this consonant in Japanese than in English. *Shi* is a near equivalent of the English "she" but is enunciated with the lips unrounded. Note that there is no Japanese syllable *si*.

The breath is expelled less forcefully with this Japanese consonant than with the English one. When *za*, *zu*, *ze*, or *zo* come at the beginning of a word, the *z* is affricative, sounding like "ds" in "kids." In the middle of a word or in the last syllable, however, it is fricative, sounding like the "z" in "zoo." *Ji* is an affricate at the beginning of a word, like the "je" in "jeep," but fricative in a middle position, like "si" in "vision." Note that Japanese does not have the syllable *zi*.

	a	i	u	e	o
t	た タ	ち chi チ	つ tsu ツ	て テ	と ト
d	だ ダ	ぢ ji ヂ	づ zu ヅ	で デ	ど ド

The aspiration of this consonant is weaker than its English counterpart. *Chi* is pronounced like "chi" in "children." *Tsu* is pronounced with the consonant *ts* similar to the "ts" in "cats." Note that Japanese does not have the syllables *ti* or *tu*.

ぢ and づ are pronounced *ji* and *zu*. (The syllables *di* and *du* do not exist.) In general, *ji* and *zu* are written じ and ず, respectively, but in a few rare cases custom calls for ぢ and づ.

	a	i	u	e	o
n	な ナ	に ニ	ぬ ヌ	ね ネ	の ノ

This consonant is similar to the "n" in "nice" but is less prolonged.

	a	i	u	e	o
h	は ハ	ひ ヒ	ふ fu フ	へ ヘ	ほ ホ
b	ば バ	び ビ	ぶ ブ	べ ベ	ぼ ボ
p	ぱ パ	ぴ ピ	ぷ プ	ぺ ペ	ぽ ポ

The breath is not expelled as strongly as in English. In *fu*, the consonant is not made the same way as the "f" in the English word "foot." It is produced by expelling air through lightly compressed lips, much like blowing out a candle.

This consonant is pronounced nearly the same as the English "b."

This consonant is pronounced with less aspiration than the English "p."

	a	i	u	e	o
m	ま マ	み ミ	む ム	め メ	も モ

This consonant is similar to the "m" in "mind," though not quite as long.

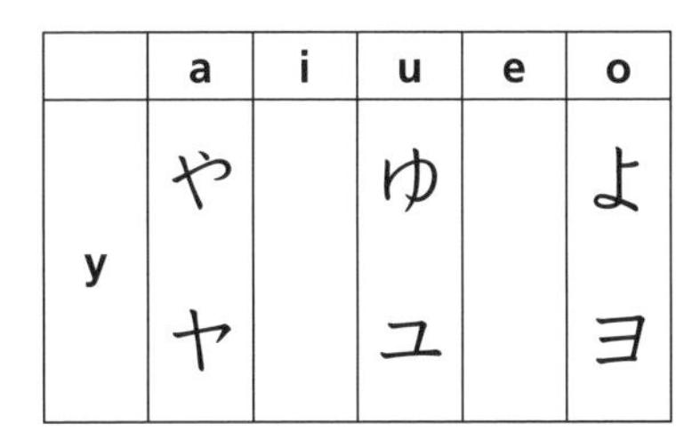

	a	i	u	e	o
y	や ヤ		ゆ ユ		よ ヨ

The Japanese *y* is pronounced with the tongue in a more relaxed position than for the "y" of "year."

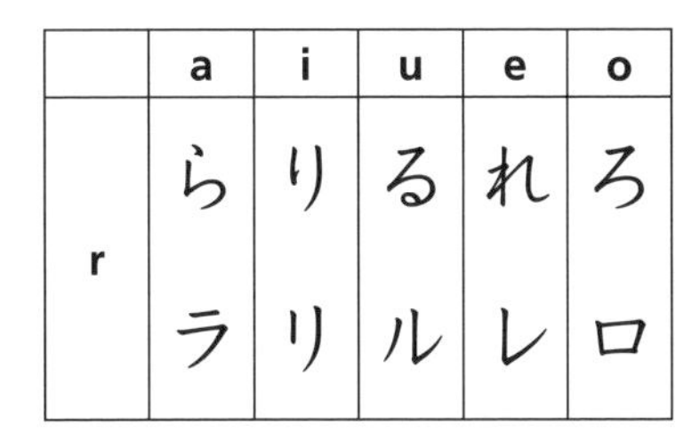

	a	i	u	e	o
r	ら ラ	り リ	る ル	れ レ	ろ ロ

The Japanese *r* is produced by tapping the tip of the tongue lightly against the teethridge. It is never pronounced with the tip of the tongue curled back.

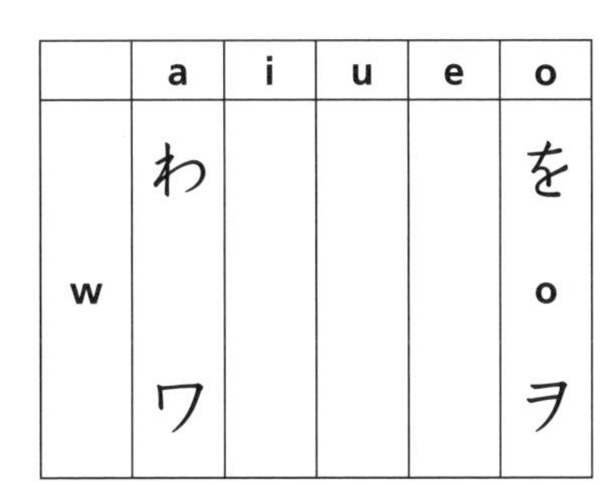

	a	i	u	e	o
w	わ ワ				を o ヲ

W is pronounced with the lips rounded, but not so tightly or forcefully as for the "w" in "wait." を and ヲ used to be pronounced *wo* but are now pronounced *o*.

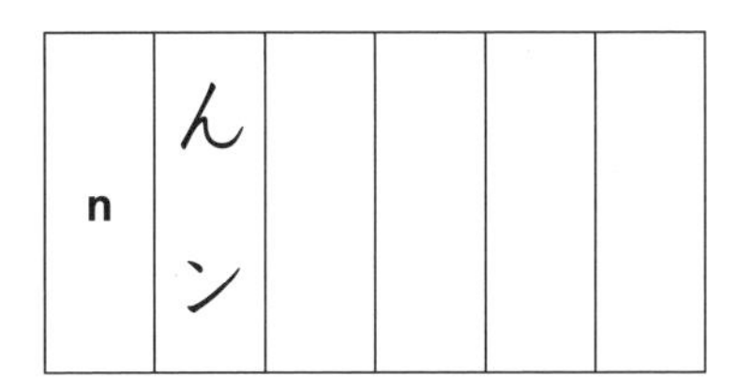

n	ん ン				

N is the only consonant not combined with a vowel. Occurring at the end of a word, it has a somewhat nasal sound. Otherwise it approximates the English "n." If it is followed by syllables beginning with *b*, *m*, or *p*, however, it is pronounced more like "m" and accordingly is spelled with "m" in this book.

Special care is needed when the syllable *n* is followed by a vowel, as in the word *kin'en* (*ki-n-en*, "no smoking"). Note the difference in syllable division between this word and *kinen* (*ki-ne-n*, "anniversary").

MODIFIED SYLLABLES

Consonants plus *ya*, *yu*, or *yo*

Although the following are each written with two hiragana or katakana characters, they are pronounced as single syllables. The *y*, which sounds like the "y" in "year," is pronounced between the initial consonant and the following vowel.

	ya	yu	yo
k	きゃ キャ	きゅ キュ	きょ キョ
g	ぎゃ ギャ	ぎゅ ギュ	ぎょ ギョ
s	しゃ **sha** シャ	しゅ **shu** シュ	しょ **sho** ショ
j	じゃ **ja** ジャ	じゅ **ju** ジュ	じょ **jo** ジョ
c	ちゃ **cha** チャ	ちゅ **chu** チュ	ちょ **cho** チョ
n	にゃ ニャ	にゅ ニュ	にょ ニョ

	ya	yu	yo
h	ひゃ ヒャ	ひゅ ヒュ	ひょ ヒョ
b	びゃ ビャ	びゅ ビュ	びょ ビョ
p	ぴゃ ピャ	ぴゅ ピュ	ぴょ ピョ
m	みゃ ミャ	みゅ ミュ	みょ ミョ
r	りゃ リャ	りゅ リュ	りょ リョ

OTHER SYLLABLES

Long Vowels

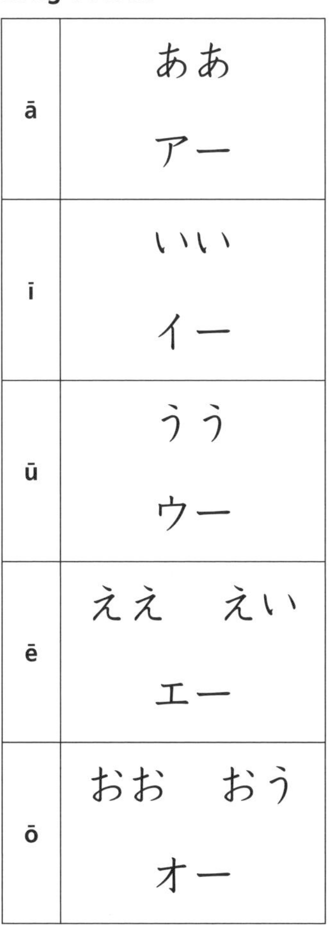

ā	ああ アー
ī	いい イー
ū	うう ウー
ē	ええ　えい エー
ō	おお　おう オー

Long vowels, indicated in romanized Japanese with a macron [¯], represent a doubling of single vowels. Be particularly careful to pronounce them as a continuous sound, equal in value to two short vowels. The way long vowels are written varies from case to case. With *ā, ī, ū,* the single vowel is simply doubled: ああ, いい, うう. *Ee* is most often written えい, though ええ is also seen. *Ō* is generally おう, but some words customarily demand おお. The same rules apply when a consonant is followed by a long vowel: e.g., *kā* (かあ), *kī* (きい), *kū* (くう), *kē* (けい, けえ), *kō* (こう, こお).

Double Consonants

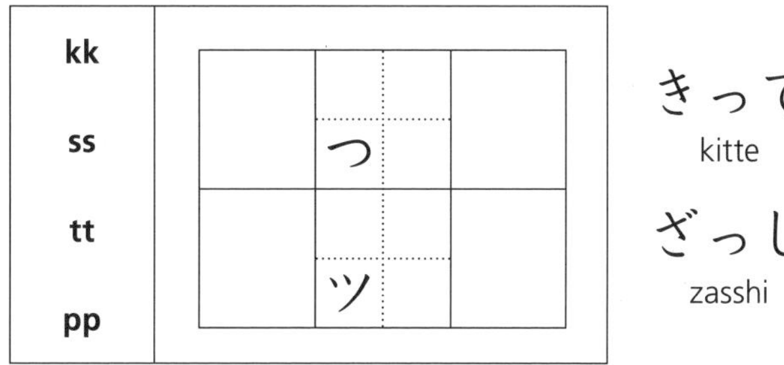

きって
kitte

きっぷ
kippu

ざっし
zasshi

サッカー
sakkā

The first consonant of the double consonants *kk, ss, tt,* and *pp* is written with a small っ. The っ here indicates a one-syllable pause, during which the mouth prepares itself for the pronunciation of the next syllable. Take *kitte,* for example. After pronouncing *ki,* pause for the length of one syllable, shaping your mouth for the pronunciation of *te,* and then pronounce it—*te.* With *ss,* as in *zasshi,* see that a small amount of air is emitted between the teeth before pronouncing the following syllable.

HIRAGANA

BASIC SYLLABLES

Recognition of Forms

あいうえお　かきくけこ　さしすせそ

Identify the syllables in parentheses from among the ones listed to the right.

I. (あ) a　ゆ お よ あ ぬ お
(い) i　い に こ い り い
(う) u　え う ろ ら う ら
(え) e　ん え よ ん く え
(お) o　あ よ は お ま お

II. (か) ka　が か け が あ か
(き) ki　ま さ き ざ き ぎ
(く) ku　し へ く ぐ し く
(け) ke　は け ほ げ は け
(こ) ko　こ い に い ご こ

III. (さ) sa　き さ ざ せ さ き
(し) shi　く し へ ん じ し
(す) su　ま す む よ す ず
(せ) se　せ さ や ぜ さ や
(そ) so　え そ ろ ぞ ら そ

IV. (あ) a (い) i (う) u　あ り こ い あ ろ う ら こ お い う お あ い
(き) ki (く) ku (え) e　さ し え き ぐ ん ぎ く へ く き さ え べ き
(す) su (そ) so (お) o　ま ろ そ よ す あ ず そ お ろ す お あ そ す
(せ) se (け) ke (か) ka　や せ は け ほ が か お に け ぜ か け や せ

Reading (answers given below)

1. あか　2. いえ　3. かぐ　4. しお　5. かぎ　6. あお

1. **aka** (red)　2. **ie** (house)　3. **kagu** (furniture)　4. **shio** (salt)　5. **kagi** (key)　6. **ao** (blue)

たちつてと　なにぬねの　はひふへほ

Identify the syllables in parentheses from among the ones listed to the right.

I.
(た) に こ た な に こ
ta

(ち) ろ う る ち ら ち
chi

(つ) し う つ く て つ
tsu

(て) し で こ て く て
te

(と) を と て と ち と
to

III.
(は) ば は ぱ け ま は
ha

(ひ) ぴ ひ び ひ ぴ ひ
hi

(ふ) そ ふ ぷ へ ぶ ふ
fu

(へ) つ へ ぺ く へ べ
he

(ほ) は ま ほ ば ほ ぼ
ho

II.
(な) た な ば な は な
na

(に) に た こ に い こ
ni

(ぬ) ね め ぬ ぬ な わ
nu

(ね) め わ ね れ ね わ
ne

(の) め の ね の め の
no

IV.
(た) (な) (は) に な ほ ば た は け ぼ な た は な た な は
ta na ha

(で) (ど) (べ) と で へ を ど し べ ご ぺ て へ で と ど ぺ
de do be

(て) (に) (の) た の て で に の こ く て に め の に で た
te ni no

(つ) (ぬ) (ち) し め つ ち ら ね へ つ ぬ め し く さ ち ぬ
tsu nu chi

Reading (answers given below)

1. はな　2. おかね　3. さかな　4. いぬ　5. ちかてつ

---

1. **hana** (flower)　2. **okane** (money)　3. **sakana** (fish)　4. **inu** (dog)　3. **chikatetsu** (subway)

まみむめも　やゆよ　らりるれろ　わをん

Identify the syllables in parentheses from among the ones listed to the right.

I. (ま) よ ま き ま ほ ま
ma

(み) ゆ の み み お み
mi

(む) ぬ す め む す む
mu

(め) の ぬ め あ ぬ め
me

(も) も ま し と も ほ
mo

II. (や) せ や せ さ や せ
ya

(ゆ) の ゆ る ゆ ひ の
yu

(よ) ま ゆ よ ろ す よ
yo

III. (ら) ろ そ う る ら ち
ra

(り) い り こ り い り
ri

(る) ら る ろ り ら る
ru

(れ) れ わ ね れ わ め
re

(ろ) そ ろ ら ち ろ ら
ro

IV. (わ) れ わ ね め あ わ
wa

(を) と を と を て を
o

(ん) ん え て ん え ん
n

V. (ま) (よ) (も) お ま ほ も ば よ す よ き ま も お も ま も
ma yo mo

(ら) (ろ) (る) る そ う ら ろ ち る え ら み ろ ら お ろ る
ra ro ru

(め) (わ) (れ) れ ぬ め ね わ む め ま ろ わ を れ め ね あ
me wa re

(を) (と) (て) さ と つ て を き へ て で と ど を て ど へ
o to te

(く) (し) (つ) く ぐ じ つ へ し け じ く つ へ て づ し ぐ
ku shi tsu

(は) (ほ) (ま) ぼ ま は は よ す ほ ば ま け に は ま よ ほ
ha ho ma

Reading (answers given below)

1. やま　2. かわ　3. むら　4. よる　5. みんな

---

1. **yama** (mountain) 2. **kawa** (river) 3. **mura** (village) 4. **yoru** (night) 5. **minna** (everyone)

Writing

The gray lines are aids to accurate style. In writing hiragana, the stroke order is, as a rule, first from top to bottom, then from left to right. To be sure, follow the arrows.

あ	a
い	i
う	u
え	e
お	o

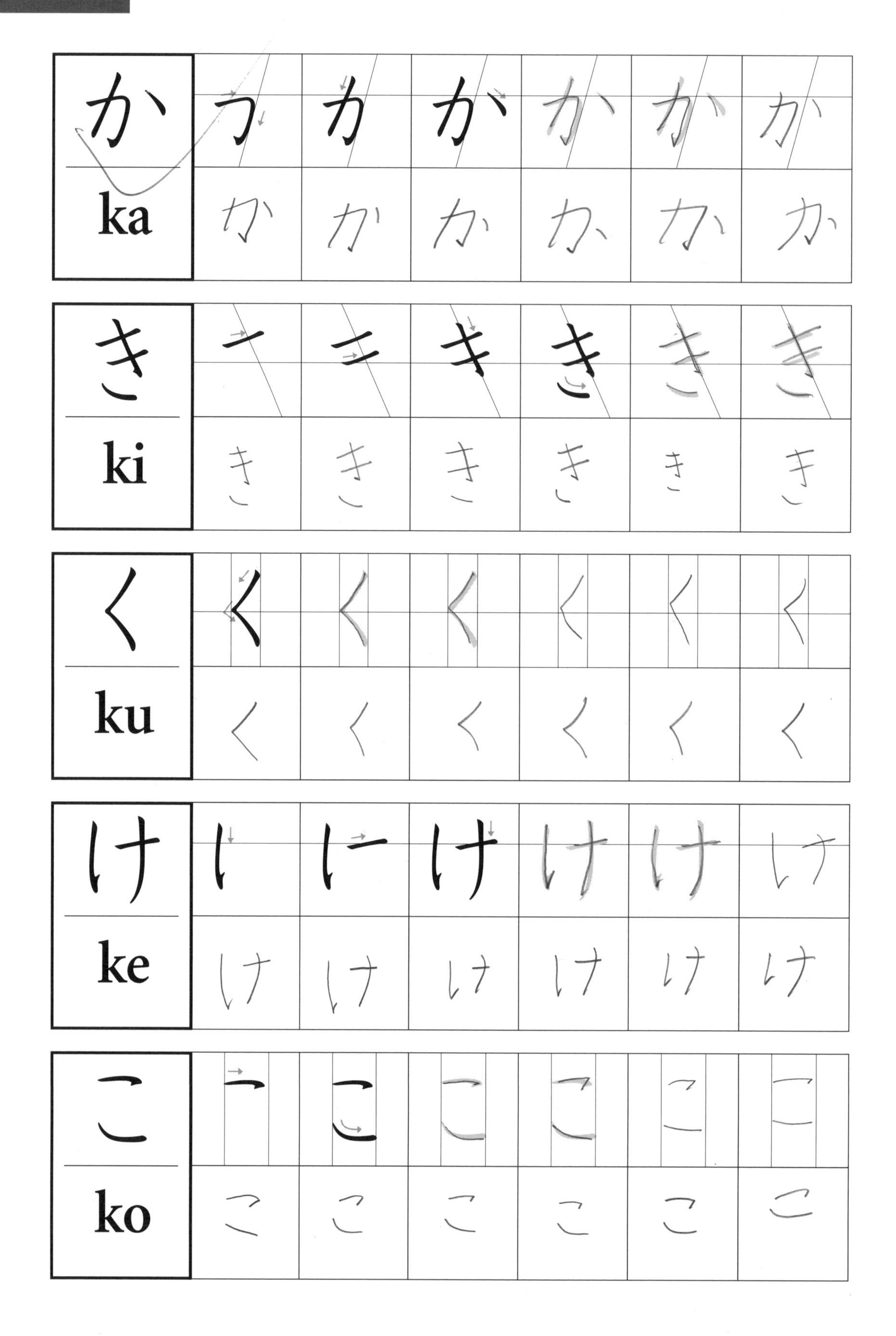
か
ka
き
ki
く
ku
け
ke
こ
ko

さ
sa
し
shi
す
su
せ
se
そ
so

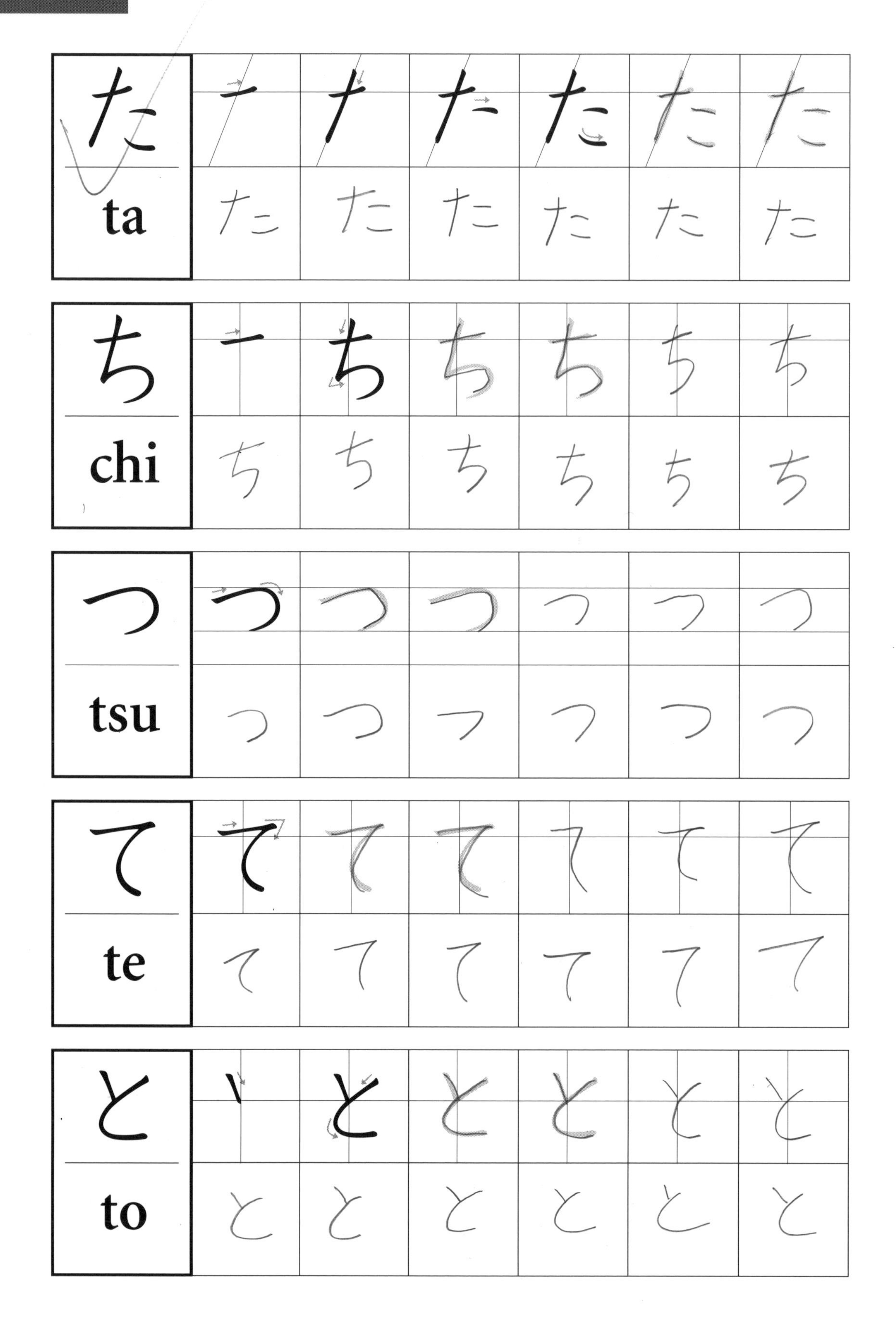
た
ta
ち
chi
つ
tsu
て
te
と
to

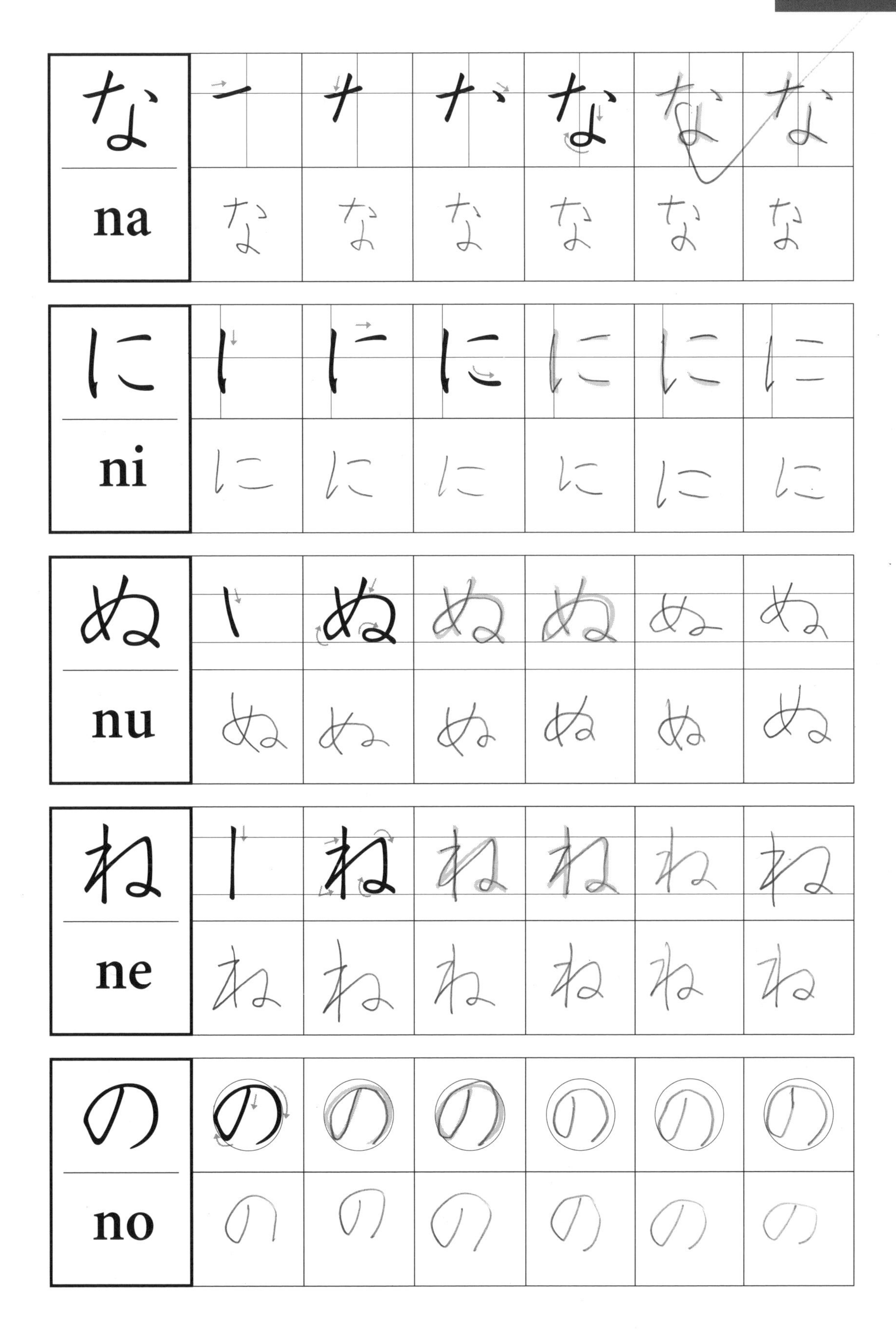
な
na
に
ni
ぬ
nu
ね
ne
の
no

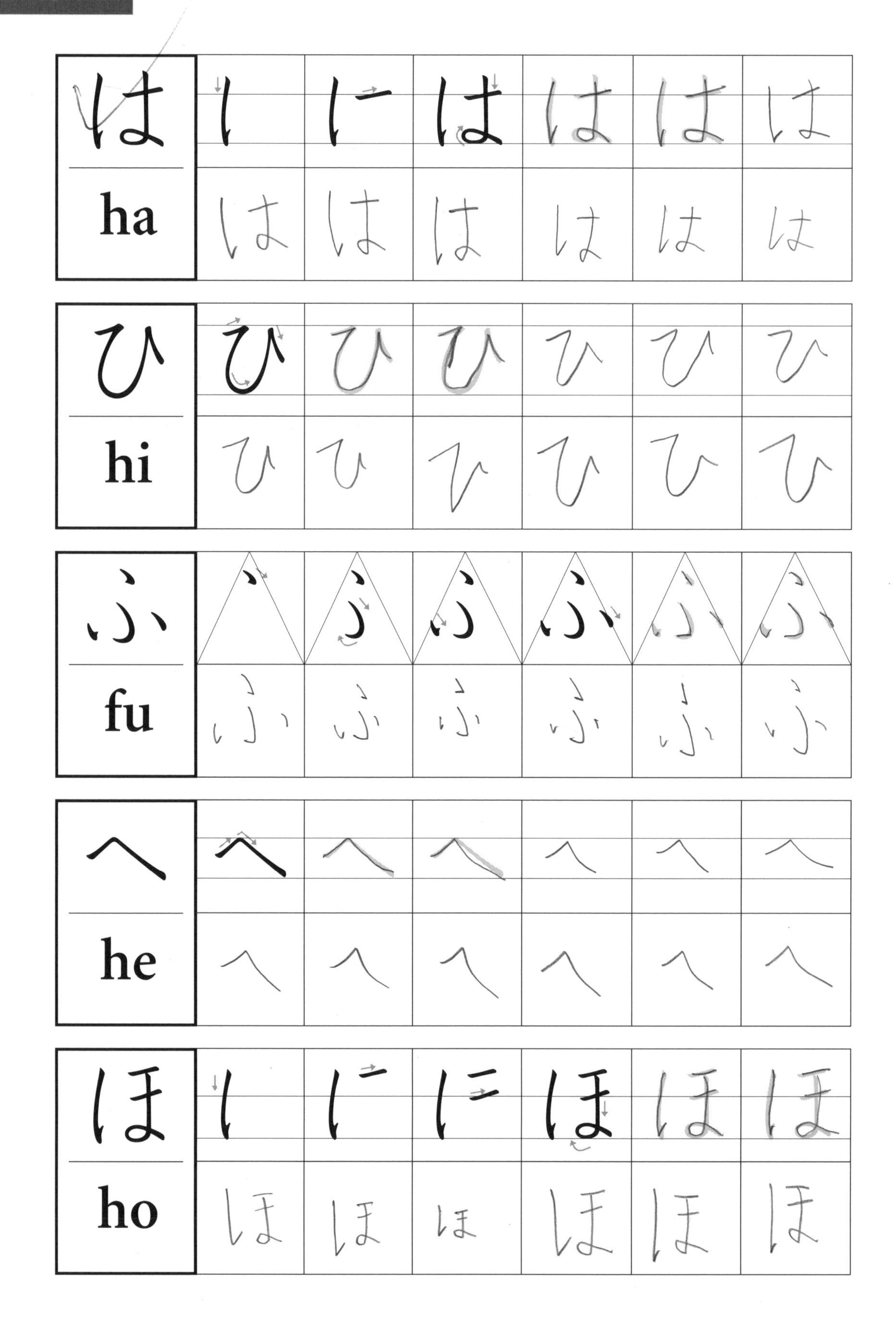
は
ha
ひ
hi
ふ
fu
へ
he
ほ
ho

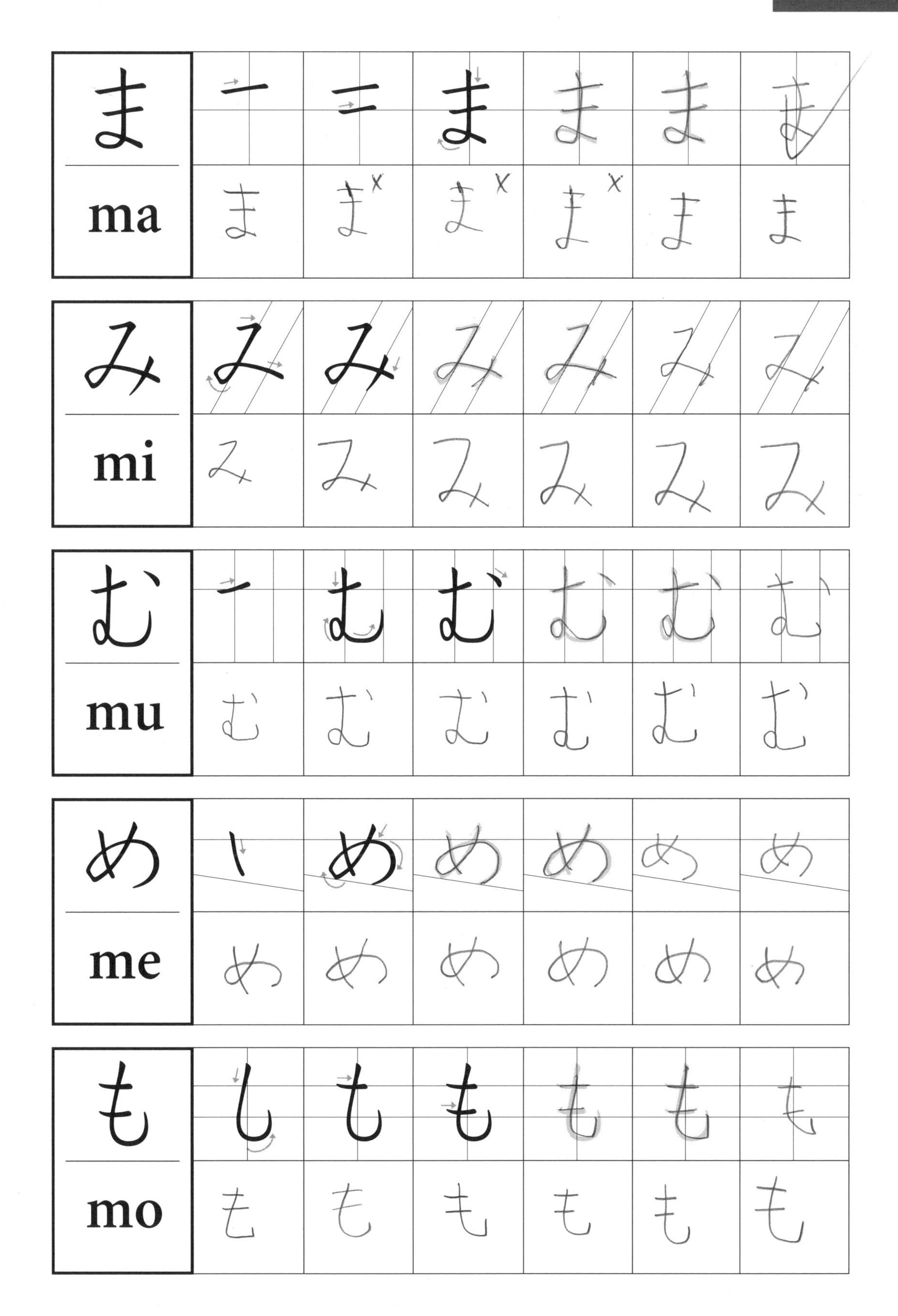
ま
ma
み
mi
む
mu
め
me
も
mo

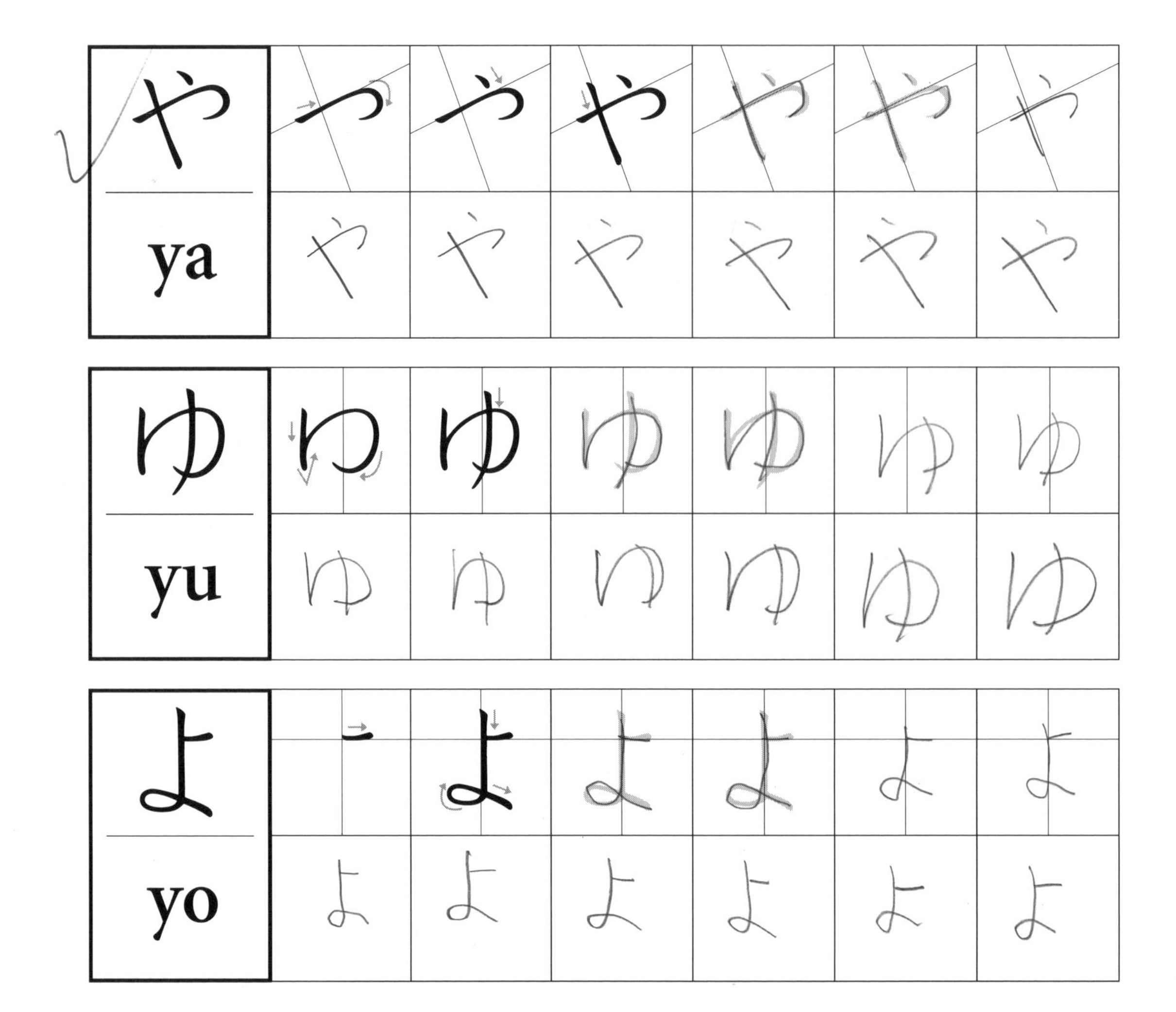

や
ya
ゆ
yu
よ
yo

ら ra						
ら	`	ら	ら	ら	ら	ら
ra	ら	ら	ら	ら	ら	ら

り ri						
り	､	り	り	り	り	り
ri	り	り	り	り	り	り

る ru						
る	る	る	る	る	る	る
ru	る	る	る	る	る	る

れ re						
れ	｜	れ	れ	れ	れ	れ
re	れ	れ	れ	れ	れ	れ

ろ ro						
ろ	ろ	ろ	ろ	ろ	ろ	ろ
ro	ろ	ろ	ろ	ろ	ろ	ろ

わ
wa

を
o

ん
n

VOICED & SEMIVOICED SYLLABLES

The (゛) and (゜) in が, ぱ, etc., should be written in the upper right-hand corner of the syllable. Write the following hiragana, following the examples.

Reading & Writing

First read the words, then write them.

1. うち
2. くるま
3. かさ
4. しごと
5. みず
6. かぎ
7. べんごし
8. なつ
9. ひと
10. ほん
11. でんち
12. みかん

1. **uchi** (home) 2. **kuruma** (car) 3. **kasa** (umbrella) 4. **shigoto** (job, work) 5. **mizu** (water) 6. **kagi** (key) 7. **bengoshi** (attorney) 8. **natsu** (summer) 9. **hito** (person) 10. **hon** (book) 11. **denchi** (battery) 12. **mikan** (tangerine)

LOOK-ALIKE HIRAGANA

Some hiragana look alike. Read, write, and distinguish the following pairs of look-alike syllables.

1. あ お
2. き さ 
3. ぬ ね 
4. て こ 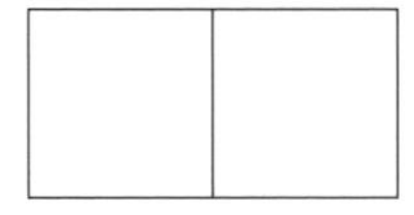
5. し も 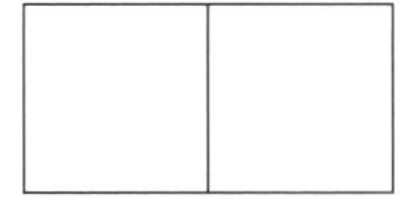
6. る ろ 
7. ほ は
8. た な 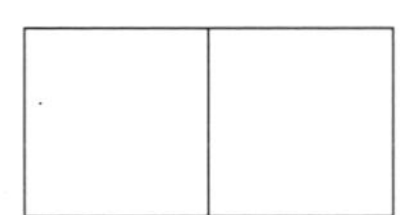
9. つ と 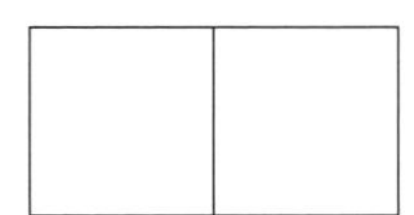
10. う つ 
11. こ い 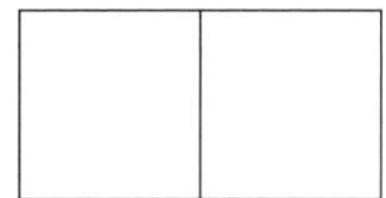
12. ま ほ 
13. め ぬ 
14. へ て 
15. り い 
16. す む 
17. え ふ 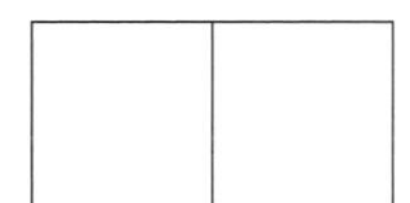
18. そ て 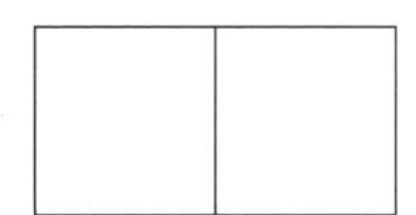

---

1. **a o** 2. **ki sa** 3. **nu ne** 4. **te ko** 5. **shi mo** 6. **ru ro** 7. **ho ha** 8. **ta na** 9. **tsu to** 10. **u tsu** 11. **ko i** 12. **ma ho** 13. **me nu** 14. **he te** 15. **ri i** 16. **su mu** 17. **e fu** 18. **so te**

MODIFIED SYLLABLES

Recognition of Forms

As you have already learned, a consonant plus a small ゃ, ゅ, or ょ is pronounced as a single syllable.

きゃ **kya**	きゅ **kyu**	きょ **kyo**	ぎゃ **gya**	ぎゅ **gyu**	ぎょ **gyo**			
しゃ **sha**	しゅ **shu**	しょ **sho**	じゃ **ja**	じゅ **ju**	じょ **jo**			
ちゃ **cha**	ちゅ **chu**	ちょ **cho**						
にゃ **nya**	にゅ **nyu**	にょ **nyo**						
ひゃ **hya**	ひゅ **hyu**	ひょ **hyo**	びゃ **bya**	びゅ **byu**	びょ **byo**	ぴゃ **pya**	ぴゅ **pyu**	ぴょ **pyo**
みゃ **mya**	みゅ **myu**	みょ **myo**						
りゃ **rya**	りゅ **ryu**	りょ **ryo**						

Identify the syllables in parentheses from among the ones listed to the right.

(きゃ) きゅ　ぎゃ　ちゃ　きゃ　きょ　みゃ　きょ　きゅ

(しゅ) じょ　しゃ　りゃ　じゅ　ひゃ　ちゅ　しゅ　しょ

(ちょ) ちゅ　にょ　みょ　しゅ　ちょ　ちゃ　きゅ　ひゃ

(にゅ) しゅ　ひゅ　にょ　びょ　にゅ　にゃ　みゅ　みょ

Reading (answers given below)

1. かいしゃ　2. おちゃ　3. ひゃく　4. りょかん　5. うんてんしゅ

1. **kaisha** (company) 2. **o-cha** (green tea) 3. **hyaku** (one hundred) 4. **ryokan** (traditional Japanese inn) 5. **untenshu** (driver)

Writing

A consonant plus a small や, ゆ, or よ is written with two hiragana characters and occupies the space of two characters. Small や, ゆ, and よ are written approximately one-forth the size of a normal character. In horizontal writing, they appear small in the lower left quadrant of the square.

ja	じ	ゃ	じ	ゃ	じ	ゃ	じ	ゃ
ju	じ	ゅ	じ	ゅ	じ	ゅ	じ	ゅ
jo	じ	ょ	じ	ょ	じ	ょ	じ	ょ

cha	ち	ゃ	ち	ゃ	ち	ゃ	ち	ゃ
chu	ち	ゅ	ち	ゅ	ち	ゅ	ち	ゅ
cho	ち	ょ	ち	ょ	ち	ょ	ち	ょ

nya	に	ゃ	に	ゃ	に	ゃ	に	ゃ
nyu	に	ゅ	に	ゅ	に	ゅ	に	ゅ
nyo	に	ょ	に	ょ	に	ょ	に	ょ

hya	ひ	ゃ	ひ	ゃ	ひ	ゃ	ひ	ゃ
hyu	ひ	ゅ	ひ	ゅ	ひ	ゅ	ひ	ゅ
hyo	ひ	ょ	ひ	ょ	ひ	ょ	ひ	ょ

bya	び	や	び	や	び	や	び	や
byu	び	ゆ	び	ゆ	び	ゆ	び	ゆ
byo	び	よ	び	よ	び	よ	び	よ

pya	ぴ	や	ぴ	や	ぴ	や	ぴ	や
pyu	ぴ	ゆ	ぴ	ゆ	ぴ	ゆ	ぴ	ゆ
pyo	ぴ	よ	ぴ	よ	ぴ	よ	ぴ	よ

mya	み	や	み	や	み	や	み	や
myu	み	ゆ	み	ゆ	み	ゆ	み	ゆ
myo	み	よ	み	よ	み	よ	み	よ

rya	り	や	り	や	り	や	り	や
ryu	り	ゆ	り	ゆ	り	ゆ	り	ゆ
ryo	り	よ	り	よ	り	よ	り	よ

LONG VOWELS

Reading

ā	ああ	ī	いい	ū	うう	ē	ええ　えい	ō	おお　おう

Sound out the following words, being careful to pronounce the long vowels correctly.

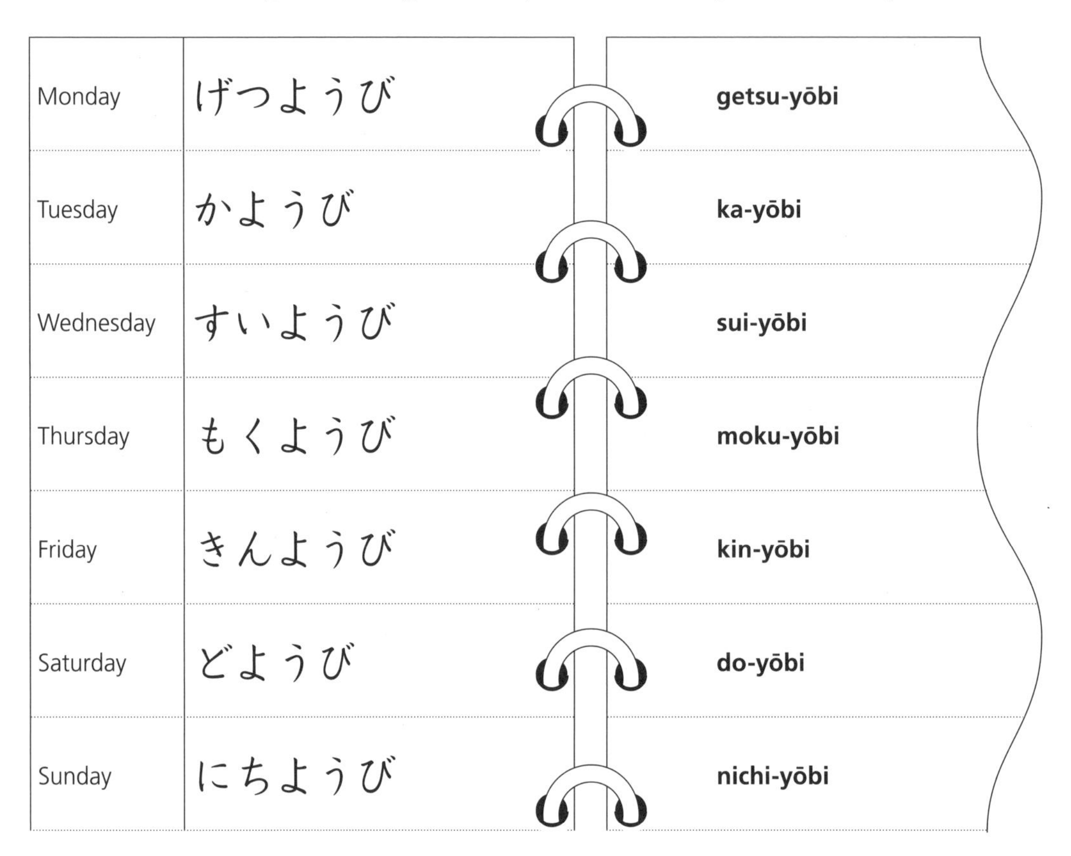

Monday	げつようび	**getsu-yōbi**
Tuesday	かようび	**ka-yōbi**
Wednesday	すいようび	**sui-yōbi**
Thursday	もくようび	**moku-yōbi**
Friday	きんようび	**kin-yōbi**
Saturday	どようび	**do-yōbi**
Sunday	にちようび	**nichi-yōbi**

Reading

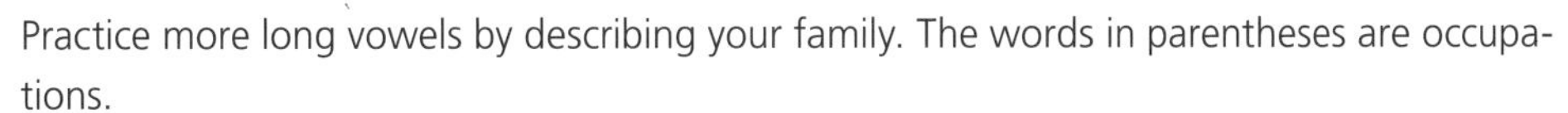

Practice more long vowels by describing your family. The words in parentheses are occupations.

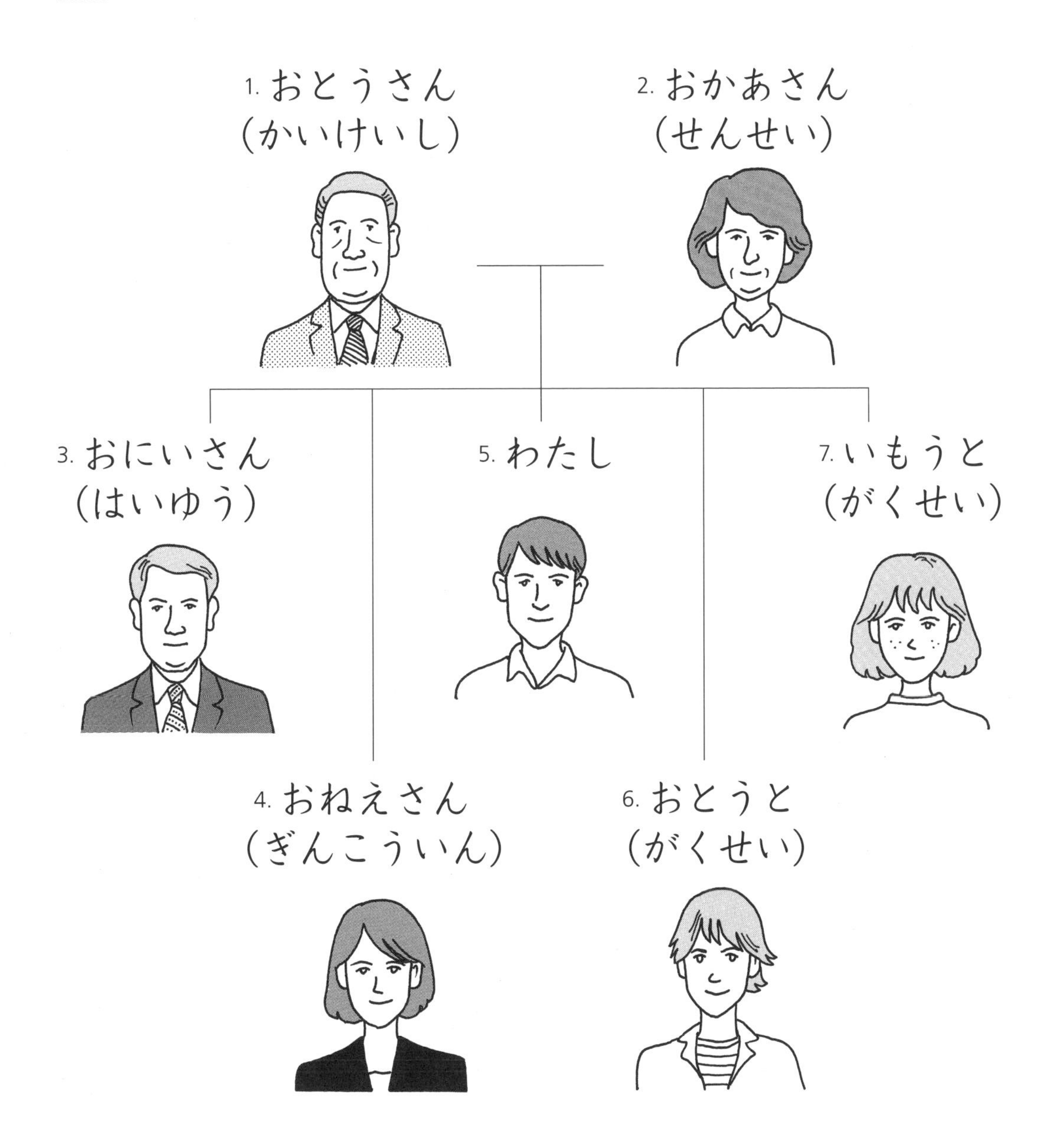

---

1. **otōsan** father (**kaikeishi** accountant) 2. **okāsan** mother (**sensei** teacher) 3. **onīsan** elder brother (**haiyū** actor) 4. **onēsan** elder sister (**ginkōin** banker) 5. **watashi** me, myself 6. **otōto** younger brother (**gakusei** student) 7. **imōto** younger sister (**gakusei** student)

Writing

1. げつようび
2. かようび
3. おとうさん
4. おかあさん
5. おにいさん
6. おねえさん
7. せんせい
8. ひこうき
9. とけい
10. とお

1. **getsu-yōbi** (Monday) 2. **ka-yōbi** (Tuesday) 3. **otōsan** (father) 4. **okāsan** (mother) 5. **onīsan** (elder brother) 6. **onēsan** (elder sister) 7. **sensei** (teacher) 8. **hikōki** (airplane) 9. **tokei** (watch, clock) 10. **tō** (ten)

DOUBLE CONSONANTS

Reading

kk ss tt pp	っ

As you have already learned, the first consonant of a double consonant (*kk*, *ss*, *tt,* or *pp*) is written with a small っ. Read the words below, taking care to pronounce the double consonants properly.

1. ひとつ 

2. ふたつ 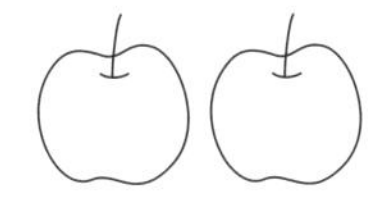

3. みっつ 

4. よっつ 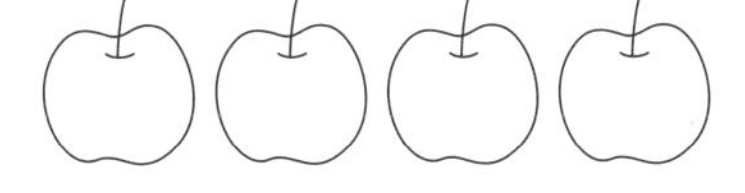

5. いつつ 

6. むっつ 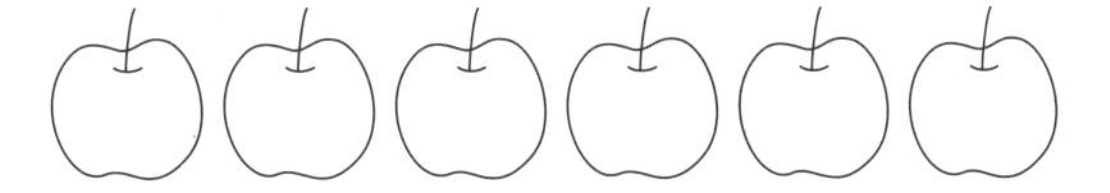

7. ななつ 

8. やっつ 

9. ここのつ 

---

1. **hitotsu** (one) 2. **futatsu** (two) 3. **mittsu** (three) 4. **yottsu** (four) 5. **itsutsu** (five) 6. **muttsu** (six) 7. **nanatsu** (seven) 8. **yattsu** (eight) 9. **kokonotsu** (nine)

Writing

1. ひとつ
2. ふたつ
3. みっつ
4. よっつ
5. いつつ
6. むっつ
7. ななつ
8. やっつ
9. ここのつ

10. いっぽん
11. いっぷん
12. ざっし
13. きって
14. きっぷ

---

1. **hitotsu** (one) 2. **futatsu** (two) 3. **mittsu** (three) 4. **yottsu** (four) 5. **itsutsu** (five) 6. **muttsu** (six) 7. **nanatsu** (seven) 8. **yattsu** (eight) 9. **kokonotsu** (nine) 10. **ippon** (one [when counting long, slender items]) 11. **ippun** (one minute) 12. **zasshi** (magazine) 13. **kitte** (stamp) 14. **kippu** (ticket)

COMBINATIONS OF MODIFIED AND OTHER SYLLABLES

Reading

1. きょう
2. てちょう
3. りょうり
4. しゅうまつ
5. じゅうしょ
6. ゆうびんきょく
7. とうきょう
8. ちゅうごく
9. しゃちょう
10. りょこう
11. びょういん
12. たんじょうび
13. しゅっちょう
14. りょうしゅうしょ
15. ちゅうしゃじょう

---

1. **kyō** (today) 2. **techō** (datebook) 3. **ryōri** (cooking) 4. **shūmatsu** (weekend) 5. **jūsho** (address) 6. **yūbinkyoku** (post office) 7. **Tōkyō** (Tokyo) 8. **Chūgoku** (China) 9. **shachō** (company president) 10. **ryokō** (trip, travel) 11. **byōin** (hospital) 12. **tanjōbi** (birthday) 13. **shutchō** (business trip) 14. **ryōshūsho** (receipt) 15. **chūshajō** (parking lot)

Writing

1. いっぷん
2. じゅうしょ
3. しゅっちょう
4. りょこう
5. ひしょ
6. でんしゃ
7. たんじょうび
8. とうきょう
9. 5じ10ぷん

い	っ	ぷ	ん

じ	ゅ	う	し	ょ

し	ゅ	っ	ち	ょ	う

り	ょ	こ	う

ひ	し	ょ

で	ん	し	ゃ

た	ん	じ	ょ	う	び

と	う	き	ょ	う

5	じ	10	ぷ	ん

---

1. **ippun** (one minute) 2. **jūsho** (address) 3.**shutchō** (business trip) 4. **ryokō** (trip, travel) 5. **hisho** (secretary) 6.**densha** (train) 7. **tanjōbi** (birthday) 8. **Tōkyō** (Tokyo) 9. **go-ji juppun** (5:10)

VERTICAL LAYOUT

The small ゃ, ゅ, and ょ in modified syllables, and the small っ that indicates a double consonant, are written in different quadrants according to whether the text is horizontal or vertical. As we have seen, in horizontal writing they appear in the lower left quadrant of the square. In vertical writing they appear in the upper right quadrant.

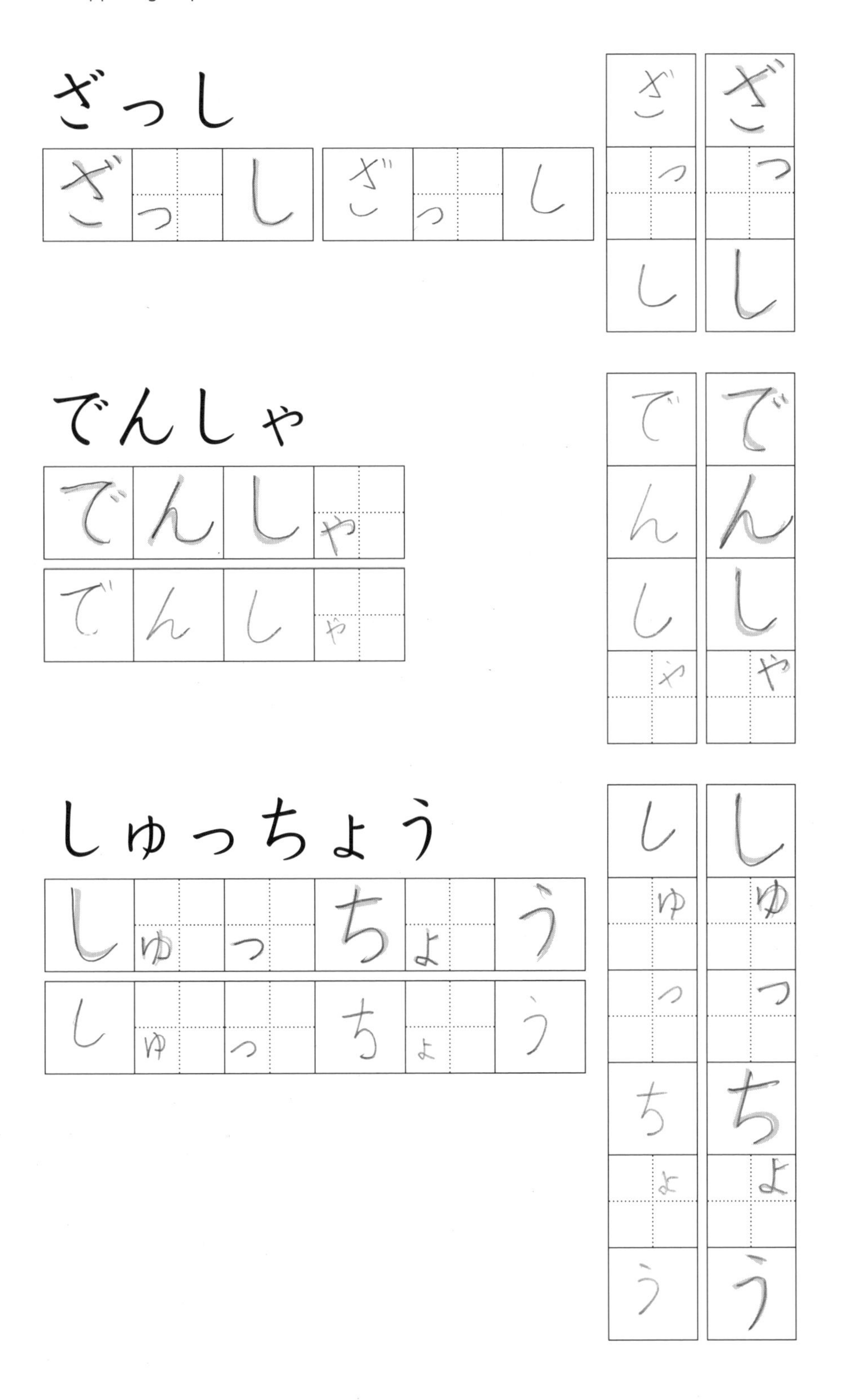

READING CHALLENGE 1: Japan

(answers on p. 85)

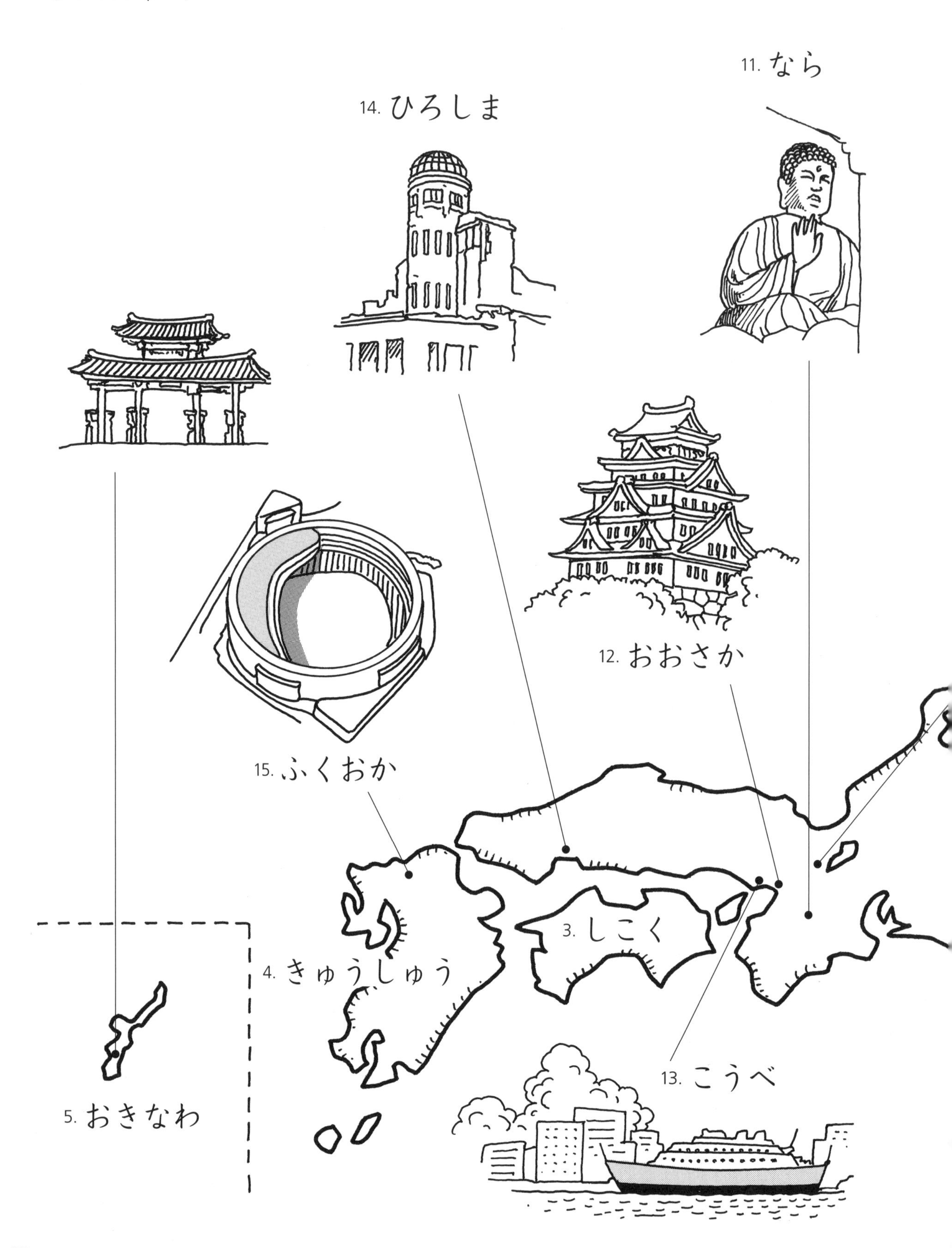

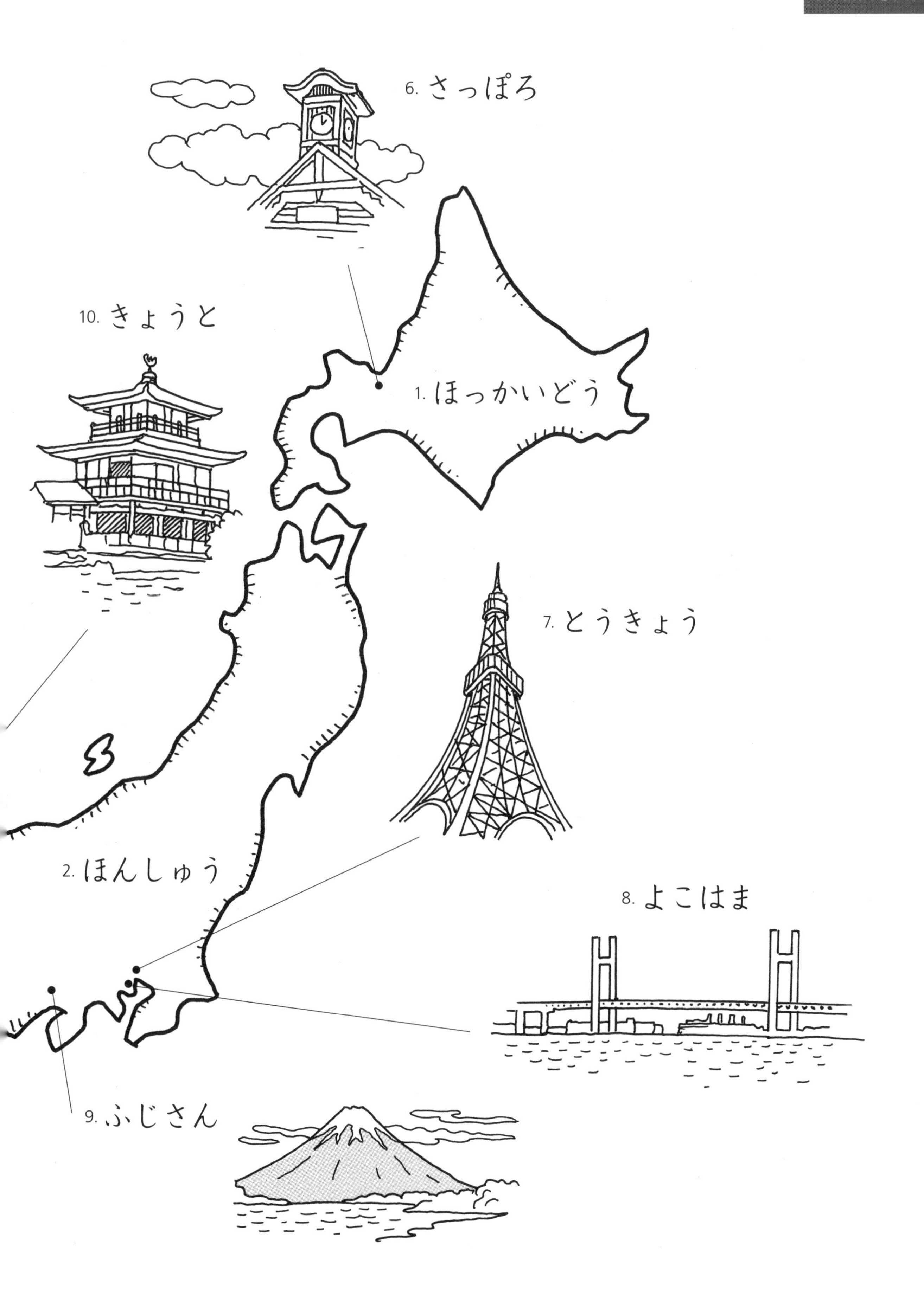
6. さっぽろ
10. きょうと
1. ほっかいどう
7. とうきょう
2. ほんしゅう
8. よこはま
9. ふじさん

READING CHALLENGE 2: Tokyo

(answers on p. 85)

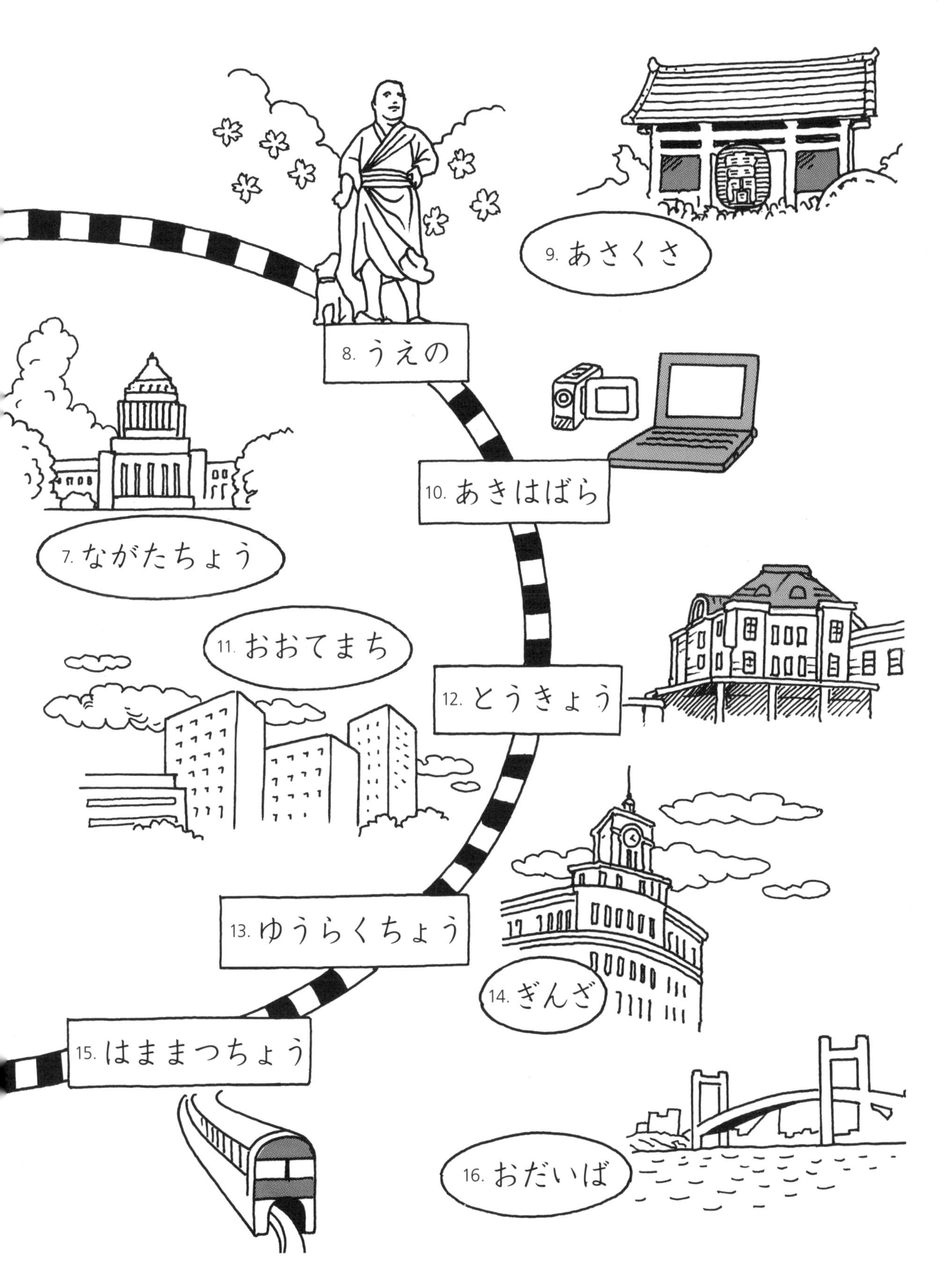

8. うえの
9. あさくさ
10. あきはばら
7. ながたちょう
11. おおてまち
12. とうきょう
13. ゆうらくちょう
14. ぎんざ
15. はままつちょう
16. おだいば

READING CHALLENGE 3: Japanese Food

(answers on p. 85)

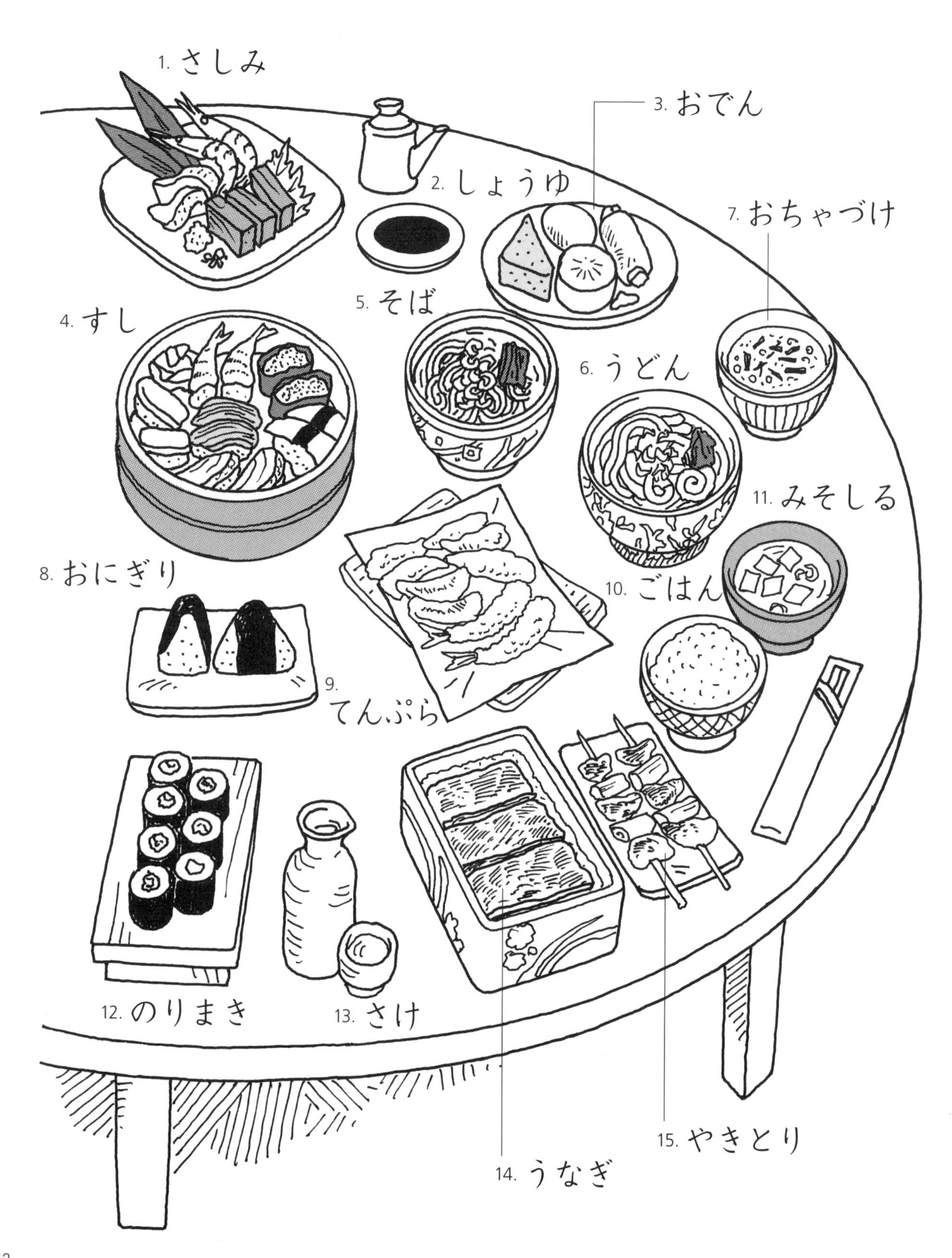

16. しゃぶしゃぶ
17. すきやき

READING CHALLENGE 4: A Japanese-style Room

(answers on pp. 85–86)

8. とこのま
9. かけじく
10. つぼ
11. しょうじ
12. ゆき
13. ものおき
14. にわ
15. ほうき

READING CHALLENGE 5: Daily Expressions (answers on p. 86)

Note: Japanese uses a (。) for a period, and a (、) for a comma.

1. おはようございます。

2. おやすみなさい。

3. いただきます。

4. ごちそうさまでした。

5. おめでとうございます。

6. どうも　ありがとうございます。

7. どういたしまして。

8. いってきます。

9. いってらっしゃい。

10. ただいま。

11. おかえりなさい。

12. おげんきですか。
    はい、げんきです。

Writing

Practice writing greeting cards.

1.

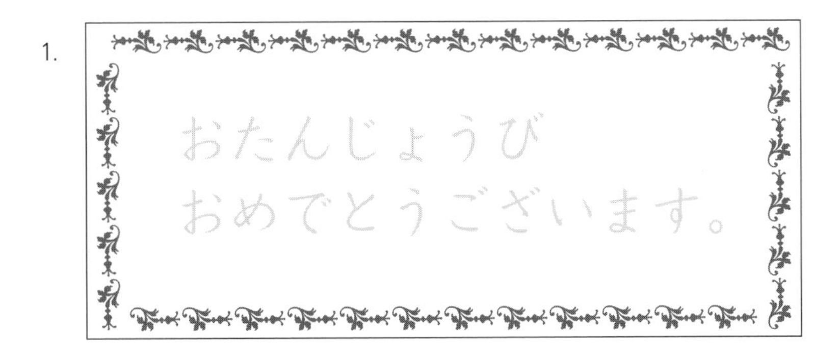

2.

いつも　いろいろ
ありがとうございます。

3.

あけまして
おめでとうございます。

ことしも　どうぞ　よろしく
おねがいします。

20XX. 1. 1

---

1. **O-tanjōbi omedetō gozaimasu.** (Happy birthday) 2. **Itsumo iroiro arigatō gozaimasu.** (Thank you for your constant kindness.) 3. **Akemashite omedetō gozaimasu.** (Happy New Year) **Kotoshi mo dōzo yoroshiku onegaishimasu** (I hope this year will be another good one for us. [lit. "I ask for you good will this year, too."])

は IS NOT ALWAYS *HA*

1. こんにちは。
Konnichiwa.
Good afternoon.

2. 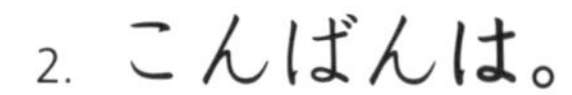
こんばんは。
Kombanwa.
Good evening.

Note that the particle *wa* is written は, not わ. When reading aloud, pause slightly after particles.

3. これは　ほんです。
Kore wa hon desu.
This is a book.

4. それは　はなです。
Sore wa hana desu.
That is a flower.

5. あれは　かさです。
Are wa kasa desu.
That over there is an umbrella.

6. あれは　ぎんこうです。
Are wa ginkō desu.
That is a bank.

7. わたしは　ささきです。
Watashi wa Sasaki desu.
I am Sasaki.

8. ささきさんは　にほんじんです。
Sasaki-san wa Nihon-jin desu.
Ms. Sasaki is a Japanese.

9. これは　ほんではありません。
Kore wa hon dewa arimasen.
This is not a book.

10. それは　きってではありません。
Sore wa kitte dewa arimasen.
That is not a stamp.

11. あれは　くるまではありません。
Are wa kuruma dewa arimasen.
That over there is not a car.

へ IS NOT ALWAYS *E*

Note that the particle *e* is written へ.

1. かいしゃへ　いきます。

Kaisha e ikimasu.
I will go to the company.

2. うちへ　かえります。

Uchi e kaerimasu.
I will return home.

3. ともだちは　にほんへ　きます。

Tomodachi wa nihon e kimasu.
My friend will come to Japan.

4. くにへ　かえります。

Kuni e kaerimasu.
I will return to my country.

WHAT IS THE DIFFERENCE BETWEEN お AND を ?

The particle *o* is written を, not お. Keep in mind that を is never used to write any word in modern Japanese other than the particle を.

1. おちゃを　ください。

O-cha o kudasai.
I'll have green tea.

2. きってを　ください。

Kitte o kudasai.
Give me a stamp.

3. それを　みせてください。

Sore o misete kudasai.
Please show me that.

4. すしを　たべます。

Sushi o tabemasu.
I will eat sushi.

5. おさけを　のみます。

O-sake o nomimasu.
I will drink sake.

6. しんぶんを　よみます。

Shimbun o yomimasu.
I will read the newspaper.

7. べんきょうを　します。

Benkyō o shimasu.
I will study.

Mi hermana, que/quien vive en Chicago, dice que hay unos restaurantes muy buenos en el centro. — *My sister, who lives in Chicago, says that there are a number of very good restaurants downtown.*

Remember that if there is a comma between the named person and *who*, you can use *quien*, but not otherwise. It's always safest to use *que*.

¿Desde cuándo... ?

To find out how long something has been going on, instead of using the present perfect tense, as in English, use the following expressions with the present or present progressive tense in Spanish.

¿**Desde cuándo** estudias/estás estudiando español? — *How long have you been studying Spanish?*

¿**Hace cuánto tiempo que** estudias/estás estudiando español? — *How long have you been studying Spanish?*

Or use the present tense of **llevar** + the gerund of the following verb.

¿Cuánto tiempo **llevas estudiando** español? — *How long have you been studying Spanish?*

Vivo/Estoy viviendo aquí desde febrero. — *I've been living here since February.*

Vivo/Estoy viviendo aquí desde hace dos meses.
Hace dos meses que vivo/estoy viviendo aquí.
Llevo dos meses viviendo aquí.
— *I've been living here for two months.*

Similar expressions indicate the length of time that something has not occurred.

Hace mucho tiempo que no hablo español.
Llevo mucho tiempo sin hablar español.
— *I haven't spoken Spanish in a long time.*

Ya

Ya can mean *now* or *already*, but its meaning is usually expressed in English by rising intonation.

Llevo **ya** tres horas esperándote. — *I've been waiting for you* ***for three hours!***

Hace **ya** veinte años que vivimos en este país. — *We've been living here* ***for twenty years!***

A ver

This is used to indicate that you are making a calculation and implies "Let's see/Let me see/Let me think."

¿Hace cuánto tiempo que conoces a mi hermano? — *How long have you known my brother?*

A ver, nos conocimos en la escuela secundaria, así que lo conozco desde hace seis años. — *Let's see, we met in high school, so I've known him for six years.*

Así que

This indicates a logical conclusion, and can be translated as *so,* with the meaning of *therefore.*

Tus padres son mis tíos, **así que** tú eres mi primo hermano.	*Your parents are my aunt and uncle, so you're my first cousin.*

Bueno

This is often used as a lead-in to a response that requires a little explanation. In this case it does not mean *good*, but more like *Well* . . . or *Actually* . . .

No estás casada, ¿verdad?	*You're not married, are you?*
Bueno, no, pero sí estoy comprometida.	*Well, no, but I am engaged.*

Parece mentira

This expression—literally, *It seems a lie*—is better translated as *It doesn't seem possible.* If you go on to say what doesn't seem possible, add **que** + a verb in the subjunctive. (See the Appendix.)

Following are examples of the subjunctive used with **parece mentira**:

Hace mucho calor. **Parece mentira** que estemos en pleno otoño.	*It's so hot. It doesn't seem possible that we're in the middle of fall.*
El tiempo pasa rápido. **Parece mentira** que ya tengas doce años.	*Time goes by so fast. It doesn't seem possible that you are already twelve years old.*

Norteamericano, -a

While people from the United States often refer to themselves as *Americans,* **americano** in Spanish refers to someone from any part of the Western Hemisphere. In fact, in Spain, **americano** usually refers to someone from Latin America. **Norteamericano** is someone from Canada or the United States (Mexicans are **mexicanos**), while **estadounidense** literally means *United States citizen.* It is common for people to use nicknames for certain nationalities or groups of people. For example:

porteño, -a	someone who lives in Buenos Aires, Argentina
nuyorican	someone of Puerto Rican descent who lives in New York
chicano, -a	someone of Mexican descent who lives in the southwestern United States
hispano, -a	someone from a Spanish-speaking country
latino, -a	someone from a Spanish- or Portuguese-speaking country
gringo, -a	someone from the United States, especially in Mexico; it's not exactly a compliment, but isn't necessarily offensive.

Tú/Usted/Ustedes/Vosotros

All of these mean *you*—so easy in English! The choice of **tú** or **usted** can be tricky, as different regions, even within the same country, often have different customs regarding this. **Tú** is used more freely in Spain than in Latin America, where it is generally reserved to address children or people whom you consider your social peers. There are exceptions, however, as in the case of parts of Colombia where **usted** can be used for your closest friends and family members!

A rule of thumb is to use **usted** until you are asked to please **"¡Tutéame, que no soy tan viejo!"** (*Use "tu" with me, I'm not that old!*) Also, pay attention to what the natives say, or even ask for advice if you're not sure.

The choice between **vosotros** and **ustedes** is simpler, especially in Latin America, where **vosotros** is not used, so **ustedes** is the plural of both **tú** and **usted**. In Spain, **vosotros** is the plural form of **tú**, and **ustedes** is the plural form of **usted**.

EJERCICIO
1·1

Fill in the blanks with the appropriate forms of the verb **ser**.

1. María ______ preciosa.
2. Yo ______ tu mejor amigo.
3. Tú y yo ya ______ viejos.
4. Tú no ______ de aquí.
5. Juan y José no ______ ingenieros.
6. Tú y Luisa ______ muy listas. [form used in Spain]
7. Tú y Luisa ______ muy listas. [form used in Latin America]
8. Víctor ______ un actor muy bueno.

EJERCICIO
1·2

Choose the most appropriate word or expression to fill in each blank.

1. Conozco a Roberto, pero no ____________ el nombre de su hermano.
   conozco   encuentra   sé   se
2. ¿____________ usted a qué hora se van a reunir?
   Sabe   Conoce   Se   Encuentra
3. ¿____________ Bolivia?
   Reune   Conoces   Sabes   Sabe
4. Nos ____________ en el Bistro a las seis y media.
   conocemos   sabemos   encontramos   conozco
5. Mi familia siempre ____________ los domingos.
   se reúne   se encuentra   se conoce   sabe

EJERCICIO
1·3

Answer each question with the appropriate form of **llamarse.**

1. ¿Cómo te llamas? ______________ Carolina.
2. ¿Cómo se llama tu hermano? ______________ Claudio.
3. ¿Cómo os llamáis? ______________ Margarita y Eva.
4. ¿Cómo se llaman ustedes? ______________ Sonia y Marta.
5. ¿Cómo se llama ella? ______________ Susana.

Choose **qué, quién, quiénes, que,** *or* **quien** *to complete the following sentences.*

1. Quiero invitar a la chica ______________ vive en la esquina.
2. ¿______________ es el profesor ______________ viene de España?
3. El profesor, ______________ acaba de mudarse a nuestra vecindad, se llama Juan Díaz.
4. ¿______________ son los actores que te gustan más?
5. ¿______________ es esto?

Answer each question in a complete sentence.

1. ¿Hace cuánto tiempo que viven ustedes en este país? (cuatro años)

   ____

2. ¿Desde cuándo trabajan ustedes juntos? (el once de febrero)

   ____

3. ¿Cuánto tiempo llevas nadando? (treinta minutos)

   ____

4. ¿Hace cuánto tiempo que no ve a su familia? (tres meses)

   ____

5. ¿Cuánto tiempo llevas sin fumar? (dos semanas)

   ____

EJERCICIO

1·6

Match the questions or statements in the left column with the most appropriate responses in the right column.

1. ______ ¿De dónde son ustedes?
2. ______ ¿Por qué no te gusta esta película?
3. ______ Tu hermano trabaja aquí también, ¿verdad?
4. ______ Hace ya veinte años que estamos casados.
5. ______ ¿Cómo te llamas?
6. ______ Soy Marcos Jiménez.
7. ______ ¿Qué te parece este vestido?
8. ______ ¿Desde cuándo vives aquí?
9. ______ ¿De dónde es su esposo?
10. ______ Tu hermana vive aquí, ¿no es así?

a. Sí, vive aquí.
b. Es de Bolivia.
c. No, no trabaja, sino que estudia.
d. Es muy feo.
e. Somos estadounidenses.
f. A ver. Ya llevo seis meses viviendo aquí.
g. Parece mentira.
h. Soy Marcos Jiménez.
i. Es un placer.
j. Bueno, me parece un poco violenta.

EJERCICIO

1·7

Circle the most appropriate word or expression for the blank space.

1. ¿Quién es esa chica? —______________ mi amiga.

   Ella es | Ellas son | Es | Eres

2. ¿Cómo se llaman tus hermanos? —______________ Germán y Javier.

   Te llaman | Se llaman | Su nombre es | Lo llamo

3. ¿Cómo te llamas? —______________ Pepe.

   Mi nombre es | Me llama | Se llama

4. Amiga, te presento a mi primo, Juan. —______________.

   Encantada | Me gustas mucho | Encantado | El gusto es mío

5. ¿______________? —Somos de la Argentina.

   Dónde estás | De dónde es | De dónde son | Dónde es

6. Tú eres de aquí, ¿______________?

   desde cuándo | así que | no es así | ya

7. No soy de aquí ______________ México.

   pero | pero de | sino | sino de

8. Es tu novio, ¿verdad? —No, no es mi novio _____________ mi esposo.

   pero pero es sino que sino

9. ¿Hace cuánto tiempo que estudias español? —_____________ cuatro años _____________ español.

   Hace... estudio Estudio... el Llevo... estudiando Desde... estudiando

10. Vivimos aquí desde hace veinte años. —Sí, _____________.

   parece mentira a ver ya mucho gusto

EJERCICIO

1·8

Fill in each blank with the present subjunctive form of the verb indicated.

1. Parece mentira que (ser, nosotros) _____________ vecinos.
2. Parece mentira que (estar, tú) _____________ aquí.
3. Parece mentira que (tener, él) _____________ dieciséis años.
4. Parece mentira que (hacer, el tiempo) _____________ 80 grados.
5. Parece mentira que (trabajar, tú y yo) _____________ juntos.
6. Parece mentira que (correr, nuestros esposos) _____________ el maratón.
7. Parece mentira que (escribir, ella) _____________ una carta tan larga.
8. Parece mentira que (pensar, ustedes) _____________ así.
9. Parece mentira que (conocer, vosotras) _____________ a mi papá.
10. Parece mentira que (dormir, ellos) _____________ durante todo el día.

EJERCICIO

1·9

Choose the most appropriate expression for each blank space.

1. No tenemos dinero, _____________ no podemos comprar flores.

   sino a ver así que sino que

2. Francisco no es mi primo, _____________ mi novio.

   sino sino que no es así así que

3. ¿Por qué te vas? _____________, tengo que irme porque mis padres me están esperando.

   A ver Parece mentira Bueno Ya

4. Parece mentira que _____________ aquí.

   estás eres son estén

EJERCICIO
1·10

¿Cómo se dice en español? *Translate each sentence into Spanish.*

1. What are your names?
2. You're from Ecuador, right?
3. No, we're not from Ecuador, we're from El Salvador.
4. How long have you been here?
5. We've been living here for two years.
6. You know our sister, right?
7. It doesn't seem possible that I don't know her.

EJERCICIO
1·11

Write a dialogue in which you introduce yourself and some friends to a new neighbor. Be sure to include as many of the new expressions as possible. Ask a Spanish speaker if your dialogue needs any corrections.

Expressing opinions, likes, and dislikes

·2·

Conversation: Getting acquainted

LAURA: Hola, ¿eres Sara? Soy Laura.¡Por fin nos conocemos! **Como** vamos a compartir el apartamento este semestre, **espero que** seamos compatibles.

Hi, are you Sara? I'm Laura. Finally we meet! Since we're going to share the room this semester, I hope we'll get along OK.

SARA: Yo también lo espero. Veo por tu camiseta que eres aficionada de béisbol, pues ¡yo también!

I hope so, too. I see from your tee shirt that you're a baseball fan—I am too!

LAURA: Bueno, la camiseta me la regaló mi hermano, que es beisbolista. Mira que en la parte de atrás, tiene la foto de todos los jugadores de su equipo. Imagínate que ganaron el campeonato de nuestra ciudad este verano.

Well, the tee shirt was a present from my brother, who's a baseball player. Look on the back—it has a photo of all the players on his team. They actually won the city championship this summer.

SARA: ¡Fantástico! Te digo que aunque no soy muy atlética, **me encanta** ver béisbol, **ya sea** un partido entre dos escuelas o uno profesional. Pero yo sólo veo, no juego. Y tú, ¿juegas algún deporte?

Fantastic! I tell you, although I'm not very athletic, I love to watch baseball, whether it's a game between two schools or a professional one. But I just watch; I don't play. And you, do you play a sport?

LAURA: Sí, juego al tenis. **De hecho** tengo una beca y voy a jugar para la universidad. Ahora dime tú, ¿qué más **te gusta** hacer?

Yes, I play tennis. As a matter of fact, I have a scholarship and I'm going to play for the university. Now, tell me, what else do you like to do?

SARA: Lo que más **me gusta** es bailar. Soy estudiante de baile clásico, pero también **me gustan** la salsa y el merengue y claro, todo lo que se baila en las discotecas.

What I like to do best is dance. I'm studying classical ballet, but I also like salsa, merengue, and of course, everything you dance at the discos.

LAURA: Entonces, tendremos que salir este mismo fin de semana para explorar los clubs de la ciudad.

Then we have to go out this weekend to check out the clubs in this city.

SARA: ¡Y los restaurantes! **A propósito** de eso, ¿tienes hambre? Dicen que hay una excelente cocina internacional aquí. ¿**Qué te parece** si vamos ahora mismo al restaurante mexicano en la esquina para probar los tacos y charlar más?

And the restaurants! Speaking of which, are you hungry? They say there's wonderful international cuisine here. How about going right now to the Mexican restaurant on the corner to try their tacos and talk some more?

LAURA: Ah, me encantaría. A mí **me gusta** mucho la cocina mexicana, sobre todo la picante. En realidad, me fascinan todas las comidas de otros países.	*Oh, I'd love to. I like Mexican food a lot, especially the hot stuff. Actually, I love all ethnic food.*
SARA: Parece que nos vamos a llevar muy bien. ¡No te imaginas lo contenta que estoy!	*It looks like we're going to get along really well. You can't imagine how happy I am!*

Más tarde:

SARA: Laura, **¿qué te parece** la decoración de nuestro cuarto?	*Laura, what do you think of the décor of our room?*
LAURA: **Para serte sincera**, realmente no **soporto** ese color oscuro de las paredes. Prefiero los tonos claros. **Por otra parte**, **quisiera** cambiar la alfombra y las cubrecamas. ¿A ti **te gustan**?	*To be honest, I really can't stand that dark color on the walls. I prefer light colors. Plus, I'd like to change the rug and the bedspreads. Do you like them?*
SARA: No, estoy de acuerdo contigo. Con una buena pintura y unos pequeños cambios, este cuarto estará mucho más cómodo y acogedor.	*No, I agree with you. With a good paint job and a few changes, this room will be much more comfortable and cozy.*

Improving your conversation

Esperar que

Esperar que followed by the subjunctive means *to hope that something happens* or *somebody else does something.*

Esperamos que nuestro equipo gane el partido.	*We hope our team wins the game.*
Ella **espera que** vayas a la reunión.	*She hopes you go to the meeting.*

When someone hopes to do something himself or herself, use an infinitive after **esperar** instead of the subjunctive.

Esperamos ganar el partido.	*We hope we win the game.*
Espero ir a la reunión.	*I hope to go to the meeting.*

Other verbs used like this include **querer**, **preferir**, **necesitar**, **gustar**, **molestar**, and others.

Quiero que me acompañes.	*I want you to go with me.*
No **quiero** ir sola.	*I don't want to go alone.*
Prefieren que no hablemos.	*They would rather that we didn't talk.*
Prefieren hablar ellos.	*They prefer to talk./They would rather do all the talking.*
Me gusta que siempre llegues a clase a tiempo.	*I like it that you always come to class on time.*
Me gusta ir a tu casa.	*I like to go to your house.*
Necesitamos que nos ayudes.	*We need you to help us.*
Le molesta que hagan ruido.	*It bothers him that they make noise.*

Esperar can also mean *to wait/wait for.*

Espérame aquí.	*Wait for me here.*
Estoy **esperando** a mi hermano.	*I'm waiting for my brother.*

Como

Como means *since* in the sense of *because.*

Como eres muy joven, no puedes ir con nosotros.	*Since you're so young, you can't come with us.*

Como has a number of other meanings.

- It is translated as *how* when used with **estar** and action verbs.

¿**Cómo** estás?	*How are you?*
No sé **cómo** haces eso.	*I don't know how you do that.*

- It is translated as *what . . . like* when used with **ser**.

¿**Cómo** eres?	*What are you like?*

- It can mean *like* in the sense of *approximately/about/more or less.*

Ella tiene **como** treinta años.	*She's like thirty years old./She's about thirty years old.*

- And it can mean *just like.*

Eres **como** una hermana para mí.	*You're just like a sister to me.*

Desde

Desde means *since* in the sense of time.

Te estoy esperando **desde** las siete.	*I've been waiting for you since seven o'clock.*

Ya sea

Sea is the present subjunctive form of **ser**. With **ya,** it can be translated as *whether,* in the sense of *whatever, whenever, whoever, however.*

Me puedes visitar cuando quieras, **ya sea** por la mañana, por la tarde o por la noche.	*You can visit me when(ever) you want, whether it's in the morning, in the afternoon, or at night.*
Invita a quien quieras, **ya sea** un chico o una chica.	*Invite whomever you wish, whether it's a boy or a girl.*

O sea

This is a common expression—so common that it is often used as a "crutch," like *you know* or *I mean.* But it has a real function as well—to put something in different words to make it clearer.

Vengan temprano, **o sea,** a las ocho o las nueve.	*Come early, in other words, at eight or nine.*

De hecho

De hecho is one of a number of conversational markers that can be translated as *actually* or *as a matter of fact*. However, its function is limited to introducing a fact that serves as an example of what was just said. It's easy to translate this into English, but much trickier use it correctly in Spanish. Think of **de hecho** as meaning *as proven by the fact that . . . .*

Mi papá es muy generoso conmigo. **De hecho,** puedo comprar toda la ropa que quiera.	*My dad is very generous with me. As a matter of fact, I can buy all the clothes I want.*
Ella es como parte de la familia. **De hecho**, celebra todos los festivos con nosotros.	*She is like family. As a matter of fact, she celebrates all the holidays with us.*

A propósito

This expression is used to add information to a conversation that relates to something said, but in a different context. It can be translated as *speaking of which . . . .*

Tenemos que ir de compras para buscar un regalo para Carlos. Su fiesta de cumpleaños es mañana.	*We have to go shopping to get a present for Carlos. His birthday party is tomorrow.*
A propósito, ¿sabes si los niños están invitados?	*Speaking of which, do you know if the kids are invited?*

¿Qué te parece?

This is a way of asking someone's impression, feeling, or opinion about something. Literally it's *How does this seem to you?*

¿**Qué te/le parece** este cuadro?	*What do you think of this painting?*
(A mí) me gusta mucho/no me gusta/me encanta/me parece muy feo.	*I like it/I don't like it/I love it/I think it's really ugly.*

¿Qué te parece si... ? can be translated as *How about if we . . ./Do you think it would be a good idea to . . . ?*

¿**Qué te parece** si llamamos a Carolina?	*How about if we call Carolina?*
¿**Qué te parece** si le compramos un osito de peluche?	*Do you think it would be a good idea to buy her a Teddy bear?*

Gustar and similar verbs

A number of verbs are used in Spanish with indirect object pronouns to indicate the effect of something or someone on somebody else. To use these verbs correctly, think about their literal translations into English, rather than their more natural translations. Remember that the subject of the sentence is the person or thing that *causes* the opinion or feeling, and the verb conjugation agrees with this subject. The person affected is indicated by the indirect object pronoun.

Me gusta la casa.	*The house appeals to me. (I like the house.)*
Me gusta Fernando.	*Fernando appeals to me. (I like Fernando.)*
A Ana le importan sus estudios.	*Her studies are important to Ana. (Ana cares about her studies.)*
A Ana le importas tú.	*You are important to Ana. (Ana cares about you.)*

Le fascinan las comedias. — *Comedies fascinate him. (He loves comedies.)*
Me fascinan Fernando y Tomás. — *Fernando and Tomás fascinate me. (I'm fascinated by Fernando and Tomás.)*

When the subject is a *thing* (rather than a *person*), it requires an article, whether it is singular or plural.

Me gusta **el** chocolate. — *I like chocolate.*
Me gustan **los** chocolates. — *I like chocolates.*

When using these verbs, a subject pronoun (**yo, tú, él, ella, nosotros, ustedes, ellos**) can replace the subject if it is a person or people, but it is omitted when the subject is a *thing*. Never use direct object pronouns with these verbs. (**Lo** and **la** can mean *it* in other places, but not here!)

Te gusta **el chocolate**? — *Does chocolate appeal to you?*
Sí, me gusta. — *Yes, it appeals to me. (Yes, I like it.)*

¿Te gusta **Fernando**? — *Does Fernando appeal to you?*
Sí me gusta **él.** — *Yes, he appeals to me. (Yes, I like him.)*

You can use the third person singular of this type of verb plus an infinitive to indicate that you *like to*, *love to*, or *don't like to* do something.

Me gusta esquiar. — *I like to ski. (Skiing appeals to me.)*
Me encanta tocar la guitarra. — *I love to play the guitar. (Playing the guitar enchants me.)*
No me gusta levantarme temprano. — *I don't like to get up early. (Getting up early doesn't appeal to me.)*

Other verbs used like this include:

molestar	*bother*	doler	*hurt*
fastidiar	*annoy*	entristecer	*sadden*
impresionar	*impress*	aburrir	*bore*
importar	*be important to*		

Compare the following:

¿Qué más te gusta? — *What else do you like?*
¿Qué te gusta más? — *What do you like best?*

Para serte sincero, -a

This expression is used to preface a statement that may seem a little uncomfortable, exactly like *to be honest with you.*

Tengo dos entradas para el concierto esta noche. ¿Quieres ir? — *I have two tickets to the concert tonight. Do you want to go?*
Para serte sincero, no soy aficionado de ese grupo. No me gusta su música. — *To be honest, I'm not a fan of that group. I don't like their music.*

Soportar

This is a real **falso amigo**—it does not mean *to support*, but rather *to tolerate.*

No quiero ir a la reunión. **No soporto** la actitud de ciertos colegas nuestros. — *I don't want to go to the meeting. I can't stand the attitude of some of our coworkers.*

To support can be expressed by several different verbs, each with a different function: **mantener, apoyar,** and **sostener.**

Mantener

Mantener means *to provide a living for someone.*

No sé cómo esa mujer **mantiene** a su familia con tan poco dinero.	*I don't know how that woman supports her family on so little money.*

Apoyar

Apoyar means *to provide moral or physical support.*

Mis padres **apoyan** mi decisión.	*My parents support my decision.*
Apóyame, por favor. Me torcí el tobillo.	*Hold me up, please. I've twisted my ankle.*

Sostener

Sostener can mean *to give physical support,* and also *to maintain a position on something.*

Esta silla antigua **no sostiene** tanto peso.	*This old chair won't support that much weight.*
El alcalde **sostiene** que los profesores merecen un incremento de sueldo.	*The mayor maintains that teachers deserve a salary increase.*

Por otra parte

Por otra parte is used to give additional back-up to an argument. It can be translated as *in addition, plus, furthermore,* or *besides.*

Esta casa es perfecta para nosotros. Tiene mucho espacio, un jardín lindo y está cerca del centro. **Por otra parte,** está en un buen distrito escolar.	*This house is perfect for us. It has a lot of space, a nice yard, and it's close to town. Plus, it's in a good school district.*
No me gusta esta casa. Es muy pequeña y no tiene jardín. **Por otra parte**, está muy lejos de mi trabajo.	*I don't like this house. It's very small, and it doesn't have a yard. Besides, it's too far from where I work.*

If you want to give the meaning of *on the other hand*—indicating a contrasting argument—you need to precede it with **pero**.

Me gusta la casa y estoy de acuerdo en que tiene muchas ventajas. **Pero por otra parte**, está muy lejos de mi trabajo.	*I like the house and I agree that it has a lot of advantages. On the other hand, it's a long way from where I work.*

Quisiera

Quisiera is an imperfect subjunctive form (see the Appendix) that can be used instead of **quiero** for the sake of politeness or to indicate a wish that may seem impossible.

Quisiera una reservación para el 12 de marzo.	*I would like a reservation for the 12th of March.*
Quisiéramos ir en un crucero al Caribe.	*We would like to go on a Caribbean cruise.*

Another way to express this is by using the conditional form (see the Appendix) of **gustar**, **encantar**, or **fascinar**.

Nos gustaría/encantaría ir en un crucero al Caribe.	*We would like/love to go on a Caribbean cruise.*
Cómo **me encantaría** volver a mi país para los festejos.	*Oh, how I'd love to go back to my country for the holidays.*
A mi mamá **le fascinaría** esta película.	*My mother would love this movie.*

This form is a polite way of making an invitation—or accepting one.

¿**Le gustaría** bailar?	*Would you like to dance?*
Sí, **me encantaría.**	*Yes, I'd love to.*

Fill in each blank with the present subjunctive form of the verb indicated.

1. Esperamos que (volver, ustedes) ______________ pronto.
2. No quiero que (irse, tú) ______________.
3. Mi papá quiere que (estudiar, yo) ______________ más.
4. Ellos prefieren que (comer, nosotros) ______________ más tarde.
5. ¿Qué quieres que (hacer, yo) ______________?
6. ¿Necesita usted que la (ayudar, yo) ______________?

Choose between the infinitive form and **que** + *the present subjunctive to complete the following sentences.*

1. No quiero (ir, yo) ______________.
2. Mi mamá prefiere (ir, yo) ______________ con ella.
3. Hoy no necesitan (trabajar, nosotros) ______________.
4. Pero nosotros necesitamos (trabajar, nosotros) ______________.
5. Espero (bailar, yo) ______________ con él.
6. Espero (bailar, él) ______________ conmigo.
7. El chico quiere (descansar, él) ______________.
8. Sus papás también quieren (descansar, ellos) ______________.

EJERCICIO
2·3

Choose between **como** *and* **desde** *to complete the following.*

1. Estudio español ______________ hace cinco años.
2. ______________ hablas tan bien español, ¡vamos a México!
3. Tenemos ______________ una hora para hacer las compras.
4. ¿______________ es tu amiga?
5. ¿______________ cuándo trabajas en esta empresa?
6. ¿Sabe usted ______________ se dice eso en inglés?
7. Ella baila ______________ una caribeña.
8. ______________ que vivo aquí, tengo trabajo.
9. ______________ vivo aquí, voy a buscar trabajo.
10. Estaré aquí ______________ a las ocho.

EJERCICIO
2·4

Choose from the following combinations of words to complete each sentence.

para ti o para tu amiga

aquí o en tu país

con un hombre o con una mujer

hoy o mañana

1. Llámame cuando quieras, ya sea ____.
2. Quiero vivir donde tú estés, ya sea ______________________________________.
3. Ven a la boda con quien quieras, ya sea ___________________________________.
4. Compra lo que te guste, ya sea ____.

EJERCICIO
2·5

Circle the most appropriate word or expression to complete each sentence.

1. Sus padres apoyan su plan de estudiar medicina, ______________ van a mantenerlo mientras estudia.

   por otra parte a propósito de hecho para serte sincero

2. Pepe, estoy muy emocionada con la idea de comprar la casa que vimos hoy.

   Cariño, ______________, no me gusta esa casa.

   o sea para serte sincero de hecho por otra parte

3. Lo que no me gusta de esa casa es que me parece pequeña, necesita muchas reparaciones y ______________, está muy lejos de la ciudad.

   por otra parte de hecho para serte sincero o sea

4. A mí me encanta el grupo Los Cuates. ______________ de eso, ¿te gustaría ir a verlos?

   Por otra parte A propósito O sea Para serte sincero

5. Somos muy buenas amigas, ______________, ella es como una hermana para mí.

   para serte sincera a propósito o sea por otra parte

EJERCICIO
2·6

Fill in each blank with the correct pronoun.

1. A mí ______ encantan estos guantes.
2. ¿A ti ______ gusta mi nuevo vestido?
3. A mis padres no ______ molesta el ruido.
4. A mi prima y a mí ______ fascina el cine.
5. ¿A ustedes ______ parece una buena idea ir al cine?
6. ¿A vosotros ______ parece una buena idea ir al cine?
7. A tus hermanos ______ gustan estas galletas.
8. A Carlos no ______ gustan las clases de baile.

EJERCICIO
2·7

Fill in each blank with the correct form of the verb indicated.

1. A Carmen le (encantar) ______________ los bailes.
2. No nos (parecer) ______________ justo.
3. A mí no me (gustar) ______________ las ensaladas que sirven aquí.
4. ¿Qué les (parecer) ______________ estas fotos?
5. ¿Te (gustar) ______________ los dulces?
6. Creo que a Jorge le (gustar) ______________ tú.
7. Tú me (importar) ______________ mucho.
8. ¿Te (importar) ______________ yo?

EJERCICIO
2·8

Match all the possible items from the right column that can complete the expressions in the left column.

1. ______ Me gusta ______________.
2. ______ Le fascinan ______________.
3. ______ Nos encantan ______________.
4. ______ Les molesta ______________.
5. ______ Me importas ______________.
6. ______ ¿Te gustan ______________?
7. ______ ¿Les gusta ______________?
8. ______ ¿Te importo ______________?
9. ______ Me parece ______________.

a. bailar
b. el ruido
c. la música
d. las fiestas
e. la clase
f. muy bonito
g. tú
h. mi hermano
i. las flores
j. él
k. yo
l. viajar

EJERCICIO 2·9

¿Cómo se dice en inglés? *Translate each sentence into English.*

1. Su actitud me molesta.

2. Les encanta jugar básquetbol.

3. ¿Qué les parece?

4. ¿Te gusta ir al cine?

5. Le fastidian los niños.

6. Me entristece la noticia.

7. Nos aburre la clase.

8. Tú me importas mucho.

¿Cómo se dice en español? *Translate each sentence into Spanish.*

1. I love to go to the beach.

2. His ideas fascinate her.

3. She doesn't like the noise.

4. She likes you.

5. His classes bore him.

____

6. I love guitar music.

____

7. We like horror movies.

____

8. They love to go shopping.

____

9. I think it's ugly. (It seems ugly to me.)

____

10. We like it.

____

EJERCICIO
2·11

Circle the most appropriate word to complete each sentence.

1. No estoy trabajando ahora, así que mis padres me ______________.

   soportan mantienen apoyan sostienen

2. Ella tiene muchos datos que ______________ su tesis.

   sostienen soportan mantienen apoyan

3. Mis padres ______________ mi decisión de hacer un semestre en el extranjero.

   mantienen soportan apoyan sostienen

4. No me gusta esa película porque yo no ______________ la violencia.

   mantengo soporto apoyo sostengo

EJERCICIO
2·12

¿Cómo se dice en español? *Translate each sentence into Spanish.*

1. Do you like to dance?

____

2. Would you like to dance?

____

3. I'd love to dance with you.

4. We'd like to rest now.

5. They like to listen to music.

6. They would love to go to a concert.

7. Does he like to play football?

8. No, he doesn't like to play football.

9. Would you all like to go to the circus?

10. Yes, we'd love to.

EJERCICIO
2·13

Write a paragraph in which you tell what you like to do and don't like to do, what things you like and don't like, and finally, what you would like to do this weekend.

Striking up a conversation

·3·

Conversation: Running into a friend

ALEJANDRA: Hola, amiga, **¿qué tal? (besos)**	*Hi, how are you? (kisses)*
GABRIELA: Todo bien, gracias. Y tú, ¿cómo va todo?	*Everything's fine, thanks. How's everything with you?*
ALEJANDRA: Bien. Estoy ocupada, como siempre. Pero, ¿qué te parece un **cafecito**?	*Good. I'm busy, as usual. But how about a cup of coffee?*
GABRIELA: Encantada. Hace tiempo que no hablamos. Ahora, **cuéntame, ¿qué hay de nuevo?**	*I'd love that. It's been a while since we've talked. Now, tell me, what's new?*
ALEJANDRA: Bueno, hay mucho que contar. Primero, he aceptado un nuevo trabajo.	*Well, there's a lot to tell. First, I've just accepted a new job.*
GABRIELA: **¿En serio?** ¿Dónde? ¿Qué vas a hacer?	*Really? Where? What are you going to do?*
ALEJANDRA: Es fantástico. Voy a ser profesora de matemáticas en una escuela de arte cerca de aquí, que **se dedica** a preparar sus alumnos para una carrera en diseño interior, diseño de ropa, dibujo—cualquier tipo de arte comercial.	*It's wonderful. I'm going to be a math teacher at an art school near here that prepares students for a career in interior design, fashion design, drawing—any kind of commercial art.*
GABRIELA: ¿Matemáticas? ¿En una escuela de arte?	*Math? At an art school?*
ALEJANDRA: Así es, **aunque** suene raro. Los alumnos, **aunque** son muy inteligentes y han enfocado bien sus estudios, necesitan tener una base en matemáticas, **pues** casi todos algún día tendrán su propio negocio.	*That's right, even though it sounds odd. The students, even though they're smart and focused on their studies, need basic math—almost all of them will have their own business one day.*
GABRIELA: Claro, ya entiendo. **¡Qué bueno!** Me parece perfecto para ti—y para tus futuros alumnos. **Fíjate** que yo también tengo una noticia emocionante.	*Of course, now I get it. That's great! I think it's perfect for you—and for your future students. Actually, I have exciting news, too.*
ALEJANDRA: Ah, ¿sí? Pero, **¡cuéntame!**	*Yeah? Tell me about it!*

GABRIELA: **Acabo de** comprarme un condominio en la ciudad. **Me mudo** el próximo lunes.	*I just bought a condo in the city. I'm moving next Monday.*
ALEJANDRA: **¡Qué bueno!** ¿Dónde está? ¿Cómo es?	*That's great! Where is it? What's it like?*
GABRIELA: Está en el centro, cerca de todo. Podré ir andando de compras, a los restaurantes, **incluso** al trabajo. El apartamento no es muy grande, pero está en un edificio antiguo que han convertido en modernos apartamentos. Está muy bien planeado. ¡Estoy contentísima!	*It's downtown, near everything. I'll be able to walk to the shops, restaurants, even to work. The apartment isn't very big, but it's in an old building that they've converted to modern units. It's very well designed. I'm just thrilled.*
ALEJANDRA: ¡Qué suerte tenemos las dos! Mira, tendremos que vernos con más frecuencia, para hablar de nuestra nueva vida. (besos) ¡**Chao**, amiga! Nos vemos pronto.	*We're both lucky. Look, we have to see each other more often, to talk about our new lives. Bye, I'll see you soon. (kisses)*

Improving your conversation

Besos

When women greet or say good-bye to a friend, male or female, they usually touch right cheeks and "kiss the air"; in Spain, this is done with both cheeks, right first, then left. Men greet each other with a handshake or an **abrazo**: with right cheeks facing, but not touching, they give each other a pat on the back.

¿Qué tal?

This is another way of saying **¿Cómo está?**, *How are you?* You may also hear **¿Quiúbole?/¿Qué hubo?/¿Quiú?**, which are more informal, like *What's up?* The answer is usually **Bien, gracias, ¿y usted?/¿y tú?**

¿Qué hay de nuevo?

This is a way to ask *What's new?* Other expressions for the same purpose are:

¿Qué noticias tienes?	*What's new?*
¿Qué hay de tu vida?	*What's new?*

Cafecito

It is common, more in some areas than others, and sometimes as a characteristic of an individual's speech, to add **-it** before the final **o** or **a** to nouns or adjectives. This **-ito** or **-ita** indicates that the objects or people described are small, unimportant, cute, ridiculous, dear, slightly naughty or illegal, just informal, or something else! Obviously, the meaning denoted can be tricky, so it's best to learn the ropes while listening to others.

casa	casita	*a small house/cabin/cottage*
perro, -a	perrito, -a	*small dog/puppy*
ojos	ojitos	*beautiful eyes*

pequeño, -a	pequeñito, -a	*tiny*
bajo, -a	bajito, -a	*very short*

When the noun or adjective ends in an **e**, an **n**, or an **r**, **-cito** is added instead.

café	cafecito	*a quick cup of coffee*
valle	vallecito	*a little valley*
rincón	rinconcito	*an intimate corner*
mujer	mujercita	*a small woman/an adolescent girl*

The ending **-ecito** is used with one-syllable words and with words with two vowels in the stem.

red	redecita	*a small net*
pez	pececito	*a little fish*
pueblo	pueblecito	*a small town*

Also, there are automatic spelling changes if the original word ends with the following letters.

co/ca	quito/quita	chico → chiquito	chica → chiquita
go/ga	guito/guita	luego → lueguito	
guo/gua	güito/güita		agua → agüita
zo/za	cito/cita		plaza → placita

There are some exceptions to these guidelines, for example:

mamacita/mamita	*mommy*
papacito/papito	*daddy*
Carlitos	*little Carlos*

Cuéntame

This is the **tú** command form of the verb **contar**, and it means *Tell me all about it.* You could also use **dime** from **decir**.

¿En serio?

This is a way to react to something surprising, equivalent to *Seriously?* Other ways to express this include:

¿De verdad?	*Really?*
¿De veras?	*Is that so?*
¿Sí?	*Are you sure?*
¡No!	*No way!*
¡No me lo puedo creer!	*I can't believe it!*
¡Increíble!	*Unbelievable!*

Dedicarse

This verb, used with reflexive pronouns, indicates the purpose of an institution or organization.

La organización **se dedica** a enseñar a leer a los adultos analfabetos.	*The organization teaches illiterate adults to read.*

It is also used to tell what someone devotes a lot of time to.

Esa mujer **se dedica** a mantener limpia su casa.	*That woman spends her life cleaning her house.*

And it is the verb used to ask what someone does for a living.

¿A qué **se dedica** su esposo?	*What does her husband do?*
¿A qué **te dedicas**?	*What do you do?*

But instead of using **dedicarse** in the answer, use the verb **ser**. Note that in telling what somebody does for a living, you do not use an article.

Es ingeniero.	*He's an engineer.*
Soy estudiante.	*I'm a student.*

However, if you want to tell *how* someone does his job by adding an adjective, you do need the article.

Es un ingeniero bueno.	*He's a good engineer.*
Soy una estudiante seria.	*I'm a serious student.*

Aunque

Aunque means *even though/although.* It is followed by a verb in the indicative if the information that it introduces is new to the listener.

Voy a prepararte algo de comer, **aunque** no soy experto en la cocina.	*I'm going to make you something to eat, although I'm no expert in the kitchen.*

Aunque is followed by a verb in the subjunctive when the information it introduces is already known by the listener.

Aunque no seas experto en la cocina, el sándwich que me preparaste estuvo muy rico.	*Although you're not an expert in the kitchen, the sandwich you made for me was delicious.*

Pues

Pues has a number of different meanings. One of them is to indicate a reasoning for what was previously said. You could use **porque** instead here.

Lleva el paraguas—**pues** parece que va a llover.	*Take your umbrella—it looks like it's going to rain.*
Voy a salir temprano—**pues** no me siento bien.	*I'm leaving early—I feel a little sick.*

Claro

This indicates that you agree with something, or that it goes without saying, like *of course.*

¿Me ayudas con estos paquetes?	*Will you help me with these packages?*
¡**Claro** (que sí)! Con mucho gusto.	*Of course! I'll be glad to.*
¿Vas a comprar esta casa?	*Are you going to buy this house?*
¡**Claro**! Es perfecta para mí.	*Of course! It's perfect for me.*

¡Qué bueno!

This indicates that you are happy with the news, either for yourself or for somebody else.

Me acaban de aceptar en la Facultad de Leyes.	*I just got accepted to law school.*
¡Qué bueno!	*That's great!*

You could also use:

¡Fantástico!	*Fantastic!*
¡Super!	*Great!*
¡Fenomenal!	*Wonderful!*
¡Qué bien!	*That's terrific!*

Fíjate que

This expression is used to introduce information that you think may slightly surprise your listeners, or at least get their attention. You could alternatively use **Imagínate que**.

¡Vamos a comer!	*Let's go eat!*
Fíjate que no tengo hambre.	*Actually I'm not hungry.*
Ese chico es guapo pero, ¿es simpático?	*That boy is cute, but is he nice?*
Imagínate que sí!	*He actually is!*
¡**Fíjate/Imagínate** que me caso en septiembre!	*Just imagine—I'm getting married in September!*

Acabar de

When this verb is conjugated, it indicates that the subject has recently done something. This is expressed in English as *to have just.*

Acabo de hablar con mi mamá.	*I (have) just talked to my mom.*
Acabamos de ver esa película.	*We just saw that movie./We have just seen that movie.*

No acabar de indicates that something *just seems impossible.*

No acabo de entender lo que escribe este autor.	*I just don't understand what this author writes.*

Mudarse

This verb, used with reflexive pronouns, means *to move* (to a new residence). (In Spain, it is more common to use **trasladarse** for this purpose.)

El próximo mes **nos mudamos** a otro estado.	*Next month we're moving to another state.*

Moverse, used with a reflexive pronoun, means *to move your body.*

No me gusta bailar porque no sé **moverme.**	*I don't like to dance because I don't know how to do the movements.*
Cada vez que intento sacar una foto, **¡te mueves!**	*Every time I try to take a photograph, you move!*

Mover, without a reflexive pronoun, means *to move a part of your body.*

Trata de **mover** los dedos.	*Try to move your fingers.*

To express moving something from one place to another, use **poner**.

Vamos a **poner** el sofá allí.	*We're going to move the sofa over there.*

Incluso

Incluso indicates that you are including something or someone in a category that seems surprising.

Todos, **incluso** mi papá, bailamos en la fiesta.	*Everybody, including/even my dad, danced at the party.*

Chao

This is a common way of saying good-bye. It can also be spelled the Italian way, **ciao**. Or you could say any of the following:

Hasta luego.	*See you later.*
Hasta pronto/prontito.	*See you soon/very soon.*
Nos vemos.	*See you.*
Cuídate.	*Take care.*

And in Mexico, *Bye* is very common.

EJERCICIO
3·1

Fill in the blanks with appropriate words or phrases.

1. ¿Cómo estás? ______________ bien.
2. ¿Cómo está tu mamá? ______________ mejor, gracias.
3. Y tus hermanos, ¿cómo ______________?
4. ¿Cómo están ustedes? ______________ muy cansados.
5. Mi amiga tiene que ir al hospital, pues ______________ ______________.
6. Los muchachos quieren descansar, pues ______________ ______________.
7. Hoy tengo una fiesta y ______________ ______________.
8. Tenemos un examen mañana, así que ______________ ______________.

EJERCICIO
3·2

Fill in the blanks with the correct words or phrases.

1. Su mamá ______ dedica a preparar comida sana.
2. ¿A qué ______ dedicas?
3. ¿A qué ______ dedican ustedes?
4. Las maestras se ______________ a enseñar a los niños.
5. ______ mudamos en junio.
6. ¿Por qué te mud______?
7. Me mud______ porque no estoy contenta aquí.
8. ¿Cuándo ______ mud______ tu compañero de cuarto?

EJERCICIO
3·3

Give the following commands.

To a good friend:

1. Tell me ______________
2. Don't tell me ______________
3. Listen! ______________
4. Don't move! ______________

To your boss:

5. Tell him . . . ______________
6. Write a letter ______________

To three friends:

7. Wait for me. ______________
8. Don't forget! ______________

EJERCICIO
3·4

Rewrite each word, adding **-ito**, **-ita**, **-cito**, *or* **-cita**, *as appropriate. Make spelling changes as necessary.*

1. suave ______________ *very soft*
2. chica ______________ *very small*
3. loco ______________ *a little crazy*
4. boca ______________ *a small mouth*
5. animal ______________ *a small animal*
6. casa ______________ *a small house*
7. pájaro ______________ *a small bird*
8. flor ______________ *a small flower*
9. Diego ______________ *little Diego*
10. Carmen ______________ *little Carmen*

EJERCICIO
3·5

Choose the most appropriate responses.

1. ¿Qué tal? ______________

   ¡Claro! Bien. ¿En serio? ¡Qué bien!

2. ¿Qué hay de nuevo? ______________

   Pues. ¡Qué bueno! Acabo de comprar un carro. Cuéntame.

3. Mañana me mudo. ______________

   ¿En serio? Claro. Somos amigos. Está peor.

4. Acabo de comprar un carro. ______________

   ¡Qué bueno! Pues. Bueno. ¡Claro!

5. ¿Te gusta mi nuevo carro? ______________

   ¡Bueno! ¡Claro! ¡Fíjate! Nos vemos.

EJERCICIO
3·6

Match the situation in the column on the left with an expression in the column on the right.

1. ______	You run into a girlfriend at the mall.	a. pues
2. ______	You ask your friend how she is.	b. incluso
3. ______	You tell what you have just done.	c. ¿Qué tal?
4. ______	You are about to tell your friend something surprising.	d. ¿Qué hay de nuevo?
5. ______	You indicate that something is true in spite of another fact.	e. ¡Fantástico!
6. ______	You include someone in an unusual category.	f. ¡Cuéntame!
7. ______	You explain why a situation exists.	g. Fíjate que...
8. ______	You ask about your friend's news.	h. (Besos)
9. ______	Your friend has told you something unbelievable.	i. Acabo de...
10. ______	You want to know the whole story.	j. aunque...
11. ______	You indicate that you are happy about your friend's news.	k. ¿De verdad?
12. ______	You indicate that there's no question about it.	l. ¡Claro!

EJERCICIO
3·7

¿Cómo se dice en español? *Translate each sentence into Spanish.*

1. What does your boyfriend do?

____

2. He's a teacher.

____

3. He's an excellent teacher.

____

4. Elena spends all her time cleaning the house.

____

5. Please don't move away.

____

6. Don't move! I want to take a picture of you.

____

7. We (have) just finished the exam.

8. What did you just say?

9. Just imagine! I'm moving next week.

Complete each of the following sentences with the verb in the present indicative, indicating that what you write is new information to your reader.

1. Quiero invitar a ese chico a la fiesta aunque *he doesn't know my other friends.*

2. No voy a estudiar informática este semestre aunque *the teacher is very good.*

3. Carlos va a ver esa película aunque *he's already seen it twice.*

4. Nos mudamos a Springfield aunque *we love this city.*

5. Vivo en una ciudad grande aunque *I prefer small towns.*

Complete each of the following sentences with the verb in the present subjunctive, indicating that what you write is information already known by your reader.

1. Quiero invitar a ese chico a la fiesta aunque *he doesn't attend our school.*

2. No voy a estudiar informática este semestre aunque *the teacher is excellent.*

3. Carlos va a ver esa película aunque *nobody wants to go with him.*

4. Nos mudamos a Springfield aunque *it's a long way from here.*

5. Vivo en una ciudad grande aunque *there's more traffic here than in a small town.*

EJERCICIO

3·10

Write a conversation between yourself and a friend when you run into each other unexpectedly. Use as many as possible of the expressions that are new to you. Ask a Spanish-speaking friend to read and correct it for you.

Making dates and appointments

Conversation: Making an informal date

Suena el teléfono.

INÉS: **¿Bueno?** — *Hello?*

SERGIO: Hola, Inés, **soy Sergio. Te llamo** para ver si quieres acompañarme al cine **el viernes por la noche**. Están dando una nueva película **mexicana** en el cine de Shirlington. — *Hi, Inés, this is Sergio. I'm calling to see if you'd like to go to the movies with me on Friday night. They're showing a new Mexican film at the Shirlington theater.*

INÉS: Uuy, sí, **me encantaría** ir contigo. Es la película basada en la novela de Ángeles Mastretta, ¿verdad? — *Ooh, yes, I'd love to go with you. It's the movie based on Ángeles Mastrettas's novel, right?*

SERGIO: **Efectivamente**. Yo también **tengo ganas** de verla. — *Yes, exactly. I really want to see it, too.*

INÉS: Sí, dicen que es muy buena. ¿A qué hora empieza? — *Yeah, they say it's very good. What time does it start?*

SERGIO: Bueno, la película empieza a las ocho, pero estaba pensando que podríamos **cenar** algo antes, en uno de los restaurantes del mismo barrio. **¿Estás de acuerdo?** — *Well, the movie starts at eight o'clock, but I was thinking that we could eat dinner beforehand, in one of those restaurants in the same neighborhood. Is that OK with you?*

INÉS: Ay, qué pena, es que el viernes no salgo del trabajo hasta las seis, y con el tráfico no llegaré a casa hasta las siete. Creo que sería mejor que nos encontráramos en el cine a eso de las ocho menos cuarto. ¿Qué te parece? — *Oh, what a shame—on Friday I don't leave work until six o'clock, and with the traffic I won't get home until seven o'clock. I think it would be better if we met at the theater at around a quarter to eight. Does that sound OK?*

SERGIO: **Está bien. Entonces**, nos vemos en la entrada del cine el viernes un poco antes de las ocho. Y **después**, si quieres, podemos ir a un café por ahí para charlar de la película. — *Good. I'll see you at the theater entrance on Friday, then, a little before eight o'clock. Then, if you like, we can go to a nearby café to discuss the movie.*

INÉS: **Bien**, Sergio. Me dará mucho gusto verte el viernes. Hasta **entonces**. — *OK, Sergio. I'll look forward to seeing you on Friday. Bye.*

SERGIO: Chao, hasta el viernes. — *Bye, see you Friday.*

Improving your conversation

Bueno

This is what you say in Mexico when you answer the phone, but only in Mexico. In other countries the typical answers when the phone rings are as follows:

Diga/Dígame	Spain
Hola	Argentina
Aló	Other countries

Soy [Sergio]

The most common way to identify yourself on the telephone is **Soy** ______________. Another common way to say this is **Habla Sergio**, or **Te habla Sergio**. *(Sergio calling/Sergio calling you.)*

Te llamo

Either **Te llamo** or **Te estoy llamando** can be used here. The present tense is often used in Spanish where only the present progressive (*be* + *-ing* form of verb) is used in English.

Be careful with the pronunciation of **Te llamo**. The *ll* (and also *y* at the beginning of a word or syllable) is a strong consonant, not as relaxed as the English *y* but more like the double *y* of *Say yes!* Some effort is required to lengthen this *y*, and many Spanish speakers often let their tongues touch the palate, making a sound exactly like English *j*. In Argentina and Uruguay, this sound is more like a *sh* (as in *sugar*) or a *zh* (as in *pleasure*). It's better to make the *j* sound than to make the *y* too weak: this would produce **Te amo** (*I love you*)—probably not what Inés was expecting when she answered the phone.

El viernes

When used with a present or future tense verb, **el viernes** means *on Friday*, or *this coming Friday*. You could also use **el próximo viernes** or **el viernes que viene**. If you use a past tense verb, **el viernes** would mean *this past Friday/last Friday*. You could also use **el viernes pasado**.

Mañana es **viernes**.	*Tomorrow is Friday.*
Te veo **el viernes**.	*I'll see you (on) Friday.*
Lo vi **el viernes**.	*I saw him last Friday.*

Por la noche

Por la noche or **en la noche**, following the name of a day, indicate *night* or *at night. On Saturday night*, then, would be **el sábado por la noche/el sábado en la noche**. Use the same pattern for morning and afternoon.

el lunes por la mañana	*on Monday morning*
el martes en la tarde	*on Tuesday afternoon*

Note that the days of the week are not capitalized (in case you're texting your conversation).

Tonight can be **esta noche** or **hoy en la noche**. Also:

esta tarde/hoy en la tarde	*this afternoon*
mañana por la mañana	*tomorrow morning*

So, when do you use **de la noche, de la mañana,** and **de la tarde**? Only after a specific time, for example, **las diez de la noche** (10:00 P.M.). Think of **de la mañana** as A.M. and **de la tarde** and **de la noche** as P.M.

Estudio **por la noche/en la noche**.	*I study at night.*
Tengo una clase a las ocho **de la noche**.	*I have a class at eight* P.M.

Also remember to use **son las tres**, **son las cuatro**, and so on, only when telling the current time. Use **a las tres, a las cuatro,** and so on, when giving the time of an event.

Son las nueve.	*It's nine o'clock.*
La fiesta es a las nueve.	*The party is at nine o'clock.*

When giving the *place* of an event, you also use the verb **ser**.

¿Dónde **es** la fiesta?	*Where's the party?*
Es en la casa de Marta.	*It's at Marta's house.*
¿Dónde **es** el concierto?	*Where is the concert?*
Es en el Centro Cultural.	*It's at the Cultural Center.*

Note that this is different from all the other ways of telling where something is, which use **estar**.

¿Dónde **estás**?	*Where are you?*
Estoy en casa.	*I'm at home.*
¿Dónde **está** tu país?	*Where is your country?*
Está en Centroamérica.	*It's in Central America.*
¿Dónde **están** mis gafas?	*Where are my glasses?*
Están en la mesa.	*They're on the table.*

Mexicana

Again, for the texters—be sure to write nationalities (and religious affiliations) in lowercase letters.

una mujer **española**/una **española**	*a Spanish woman*
dos muchachos **católicos**	*two Catholic boys*

Pay attention to the gender and number of the nouns you are describing, and reflect them in the adjective.

las costumbres **peruanas**	*Peruvian customs*
el vino **chileno**	*Chilean wine*

Both singular and plural nouns need an article when used as the subject of a sentence.

El vino chileno es barato aquí.	*Chilean wine is cheap here.*
Las verduras son un componente importante en una dieta sana.	*Vegetables are an important part of a healthy diet.*
Me gustan **las verduras**.	*I like vegetables. (Vegetables appeal to me.)*

Singular and plural nouns used as direct objects require an article when they refer to something specific.

Compra **el vino chileno.**	*Buy the Chilean wine (rather than the Argentinean).*
No compres **las verduras** aquí.	*Don't buy the vegetables here (the ones we need for tonight).*

Singular and plural nouns used as direct objects do not need an article when they refer to the whole category in general.

Siempre trae **vino chileno.**	*He always brings Chilean wine.*
Ella no come **verduras.**	*She doesn't eat vegetables.*

En el cine

En el cine means *at the movies.* **En** in Spanish indicates *in, on,* or *at.* **Al cine**, on the other hand, indicates where you are going: *to the movies.*

Sara está **en el aeropuerto.**	*Sara is at the airport.*
Vamos **al aeropuerto** a buscar a Sara.	*Let's go to the airport to get Sara.*
Vamos a comer **al restaurante.**	*Let's go to the restaurant to eat.*

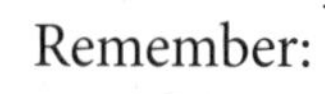

Remember:

- To use **en** to indicate a location, and **a** to indicate a destination.
- That **a** followed by **el** is always contracted to **al**.

Me encantaría

Me encantaría (ir al cine) means *I would love to (go to the movies).* Literally, *It would enchant me (to go to the movies)* or *Going to the movies would enchant me.* The subject of this sentence is **ir al cine**, and when an infinitive such as **ir** is used as a subject, it is considered singular; this is why the main verb, **encantaría,** has a singular conjugation. Note the difference between *Me encanta* and *me encantaría.*

Me encanta ver películas.	*I love watching movies./I love to watch movies.*
Me encantaría ver una película.	*I would love to watch a movie.*

Remember that both people and objects can **encantar,** but you can **amar** only people you know.

Me encantan las telenovelas.	*I love soap operas.*
Me encanta el actor principal.	*I love the main actor.*
Amo a mi esposo.	*I love my husband.*

Querer can also mean *to love*—in the sense of "to care about"—as you would say this to a member of your family or a good friend as well as to a boyfriend, girlfriend, or spouse. **Te quiero** does not mean *I want you.* Physical attraction is better expressed by the verb **gustar.**

Me gustas mucho.	*I'm really attracted to you./I like you.* (Literally: *You please me a lot.*)
Le gusta Sonia.	*He has a crush on Sonia./He likes Sonia.*
Es mi mejor amiga y **la quiero** mucho.	*She's my best friend and I like her a lot.*

Efectivamente/en efecto

These are real **falsos amigos**, as they do not mean *effectively* or *in effect*. **Efectivamente** and **en efecto** are interchangeable, and are used to comment that what was just said is correct, kind of like *exactly* or *that's true*.

Dicen que ustedes han invitado a más de 200 personas a la boda.	*I hear that you invited more than 200 people to the wedding.*
En efecto. Es que los dos tenemos muchos familiares y muchos amigos y además, casi todos viven aquí en la ciudad.	*Yeah, that's right. We both have a lot of relatives and friends, plus almost all of them live here in the city.*

When **en efecto** or **efectivamente** occur in the middle of a sentence, they are better translated as *indeed* or *as was just pointed out*.

El próximo semestre vamos a tener clases más grandes, pues más de 300 estudiantes nuevos ya se han matriculado.	*Next semester we're going to have bigger classes, as more than 300 new students have already registered.*
El número de estudiantes matriculados, **efectivamente,** es mucho mayor de lo que hemos experimentado en los últimos años.	*The number of new students already registered, indeed, is much larger than what we've seen in recent years.*

Remember that **en efecto** and **efectivamente** are used to answer a yes-or-no question affirmatively or to confirm a previous statement. *Effectively,* and *in effect,* on the other hand, mean *essentially.*

efectivamente/en efecto	*exactly/yes, that's correct/indeed*
esencialmente/casi como si fuera	*effectively/in effect*

Ella lleva seis años dirigiendo la compañía y es ahora **esencialmente/casi como si fuera** su presidente.	*She's been in charge of the company for six years, and is now effectively its president.*

Tener ganas de (+ infinitive)

Literally, *to have desires to (do something)*, this expression is better translated as *to feel like (doing something)* or *to really want to (do something)*.

Tengo ganas de ir de compras.	*I feel like going shopping.*
Mi esposo **no tiene ganas de acompañarme**.	*My husband doesn't want to go with me.*
Mi esposo **tiene muy pocas ganas de ir** de compras.	*My husband really doesn't feel like going shopping.*

Cenar

Cenar means literally—and elegantly in English—*to dine*. But in Spanish, it's just eating dinner, even a plain, boring one. The point here is that you don't *eat* **la cena**; you can **planear la cena, prepararla**, or **servirla**—but to eat it is **cenar**. And it's the same with breakfast—**desayunar**—and lunch—**almorzar**.

¿A qué hora **cenan** ustedes?	*What time do you (all) eat dinner?*
Hoy no **almorcé.**	*I didn't eat lunch today.*
Vamos a desayunar en casa.	*We're going to eat breakfast at home.*

In Spain, **comer** can mean to have **la comida**, the main meal of the day, some time after two P.M. So if someone tells you **Hoy no he comido**, it doesn't mean that he didn't **desayunar**, or even have a snack, but that he missed his main meal—and may therefore be in a very bad mood!

Bien

Bien (*Fine*) is the perfect answer to **¿Cómo está?** (*How are you?*). You can also use it to agree to a suggestion—one translation of *OK* or *Good.* An alternative to this **Bien** is **De acuerdo.** In Spain, **Vale** is commonly used for this purpose.

Te llamo mañana a las 5.	*I'll call you tomorrow at 5.*
Bien./Está bien./De acuerdo./Vale. Esperaré tu llamada.	*OK/Good. I'll wait for your call.*

Always think of the function of the word rather than the translation. While **bueno** often translates as *good,* in this case it doesn't work. **Bien** is the best answer here.

Estar de acuerdo means *to agree with someone.*

No me gusta este restaurante. No quiero volver.	*I don't like this restaurant. I don't want to come back.*
Estoy de acuerdo contigo. La próxima vez iremos a otro lugar.	*I agree with you. The next time we'll go someplace else.*

Entonces

One function of **entonces** translates as *then* in the sense of *so* or *therefore.*

No voy a poder salir contigo de ahora en adelante.	*I'm not going to be able to go out with you anymore.*
Entonces, ¿es cierto? ¿ Te vas a casar con Julio?	*Then/So it's true? You're going to marry Julio?*

Alternatively, **entonces** can also mean *then* as in *at that time. So* cannot be used here.

Me dijiste hace dos meses que te ibas a casar con Julio.	*You told me two months ago that you were going to marry Julio.*
Sí, pero **entonces** pensé que estaba enamorada de él.	*Yes, but back then I thought I was in love with him.*

In the following example, **entonces** is translated by *so* but not by *then.*

Entonces, ¿vienes o no vienes?	*So, are you coming or not?*

Después/Luego

Después and **luego** are the best translations of *then* when it means *after that.*

Estuvieron dos semanas en Chile y **después/luego** fueron a Argentina.	*They were in Chile for two weeks and then they went to Argentina.*

Hasta luego

This is a very common way of saying *See you later* in Spanish—easy—but watch the pronunciation! Just as **hasta** has two syllables, so does **luego**. That is, the combination of *u* and *e* (when there's no written accent mark) is pronounced as one syllable: *ue* = weh. Granted, it's a little hard to say when it follows the letter *l*. Try putting the *l* on the end of **hasta:** "ah stahl WEH goh." And in Spain, you often hear just "staluego" (stahl WEH goh).

Adiós

Adiós can indicate a long time before you expect to see someone again. Literally, it means, *(I leave you) to God*. And, especially in Mexico and Central America, it's followed by **Que te/le/les vaya bien**—*May all go well for you*. In English, people say *Hi* when passing in a car (or bus full of kids) going in the other direction, but in Spanish you would call out, "**¡Adiós!**"

Adiós, like **luego**, is pronounced in two syllables: "ah dyos." The combination of *i* and *o* in Spanish (when there's no written accent) is pronounced as one syllable. Again, you might find it easier to say if you put the *d* at the end of the first syllable: "ad YOHS." But be careful here, too, as the *d* (between two vowels) is pronounced like English *th* (as in *brother*). So you have "ath YOHS."

But **adiós** has a written accent! This is because of another convention: when a word ends in *s* (or *n, a, e, i, o, u*), it is pronounced with emphasis on the next-to-last syllable. Any exception to this rule requires a written accent. Compare *Dios* (one syllable) with *Adiós* (two syllables). If there were no accent mark, it would be mispronounced as "AH thyohs," which would probably be worse than the *gringo* "ah dee OHS."

EJERCICIO
4·1

Fill in the blanks with the most appropriate words.

1. ¿Quieres ir a una fiesta ______________?

   los sábados — el sábado — en el sábado — en sábado

2. La fiesta es ______________.

   por la noche — a la noche — a noche — anoche

3. Voy a tu casa ______________.

   a ocho — en las ocho — son las ocho — a las ocho

4. Fíjate que ya son las diez ______________.

   a la noche — por la noche — de la noche — a noche

5. Me gusta salir a bailar ______________.

   los jueves — el jueves — a la mañana — anoche

6. Me gustaría salir a bailar ______________.

   el jueves — anoche — en domingo — son las once

EJERCICIO
4·2

¿Cómo se dice en español? *Translate each sentence into Spanish.*

1. This is Margarita (calling). ____________________
2. I'm calling you . . . ____________________
3. The party is on Sunday night. ____________________
4. It's at eight P.M. ____________________
5. Where's the party? ____________________
6. It's at my house. ____________________

EJERCICIO
4·3

Fill in the blanks with the most appropriate words.

1. Voy a tomar agua porque no me gusta ______________.
   cerveza   vino   la cerveza   las cervezas
2. Queremos ver esa película porque ______________ el actor principal.
   no me gusta   amo   amamos   nos encanta
3. Por favor, espérame ______________.
   al cine   a la película   por mi casa   en el cine
4. ______________ mucho a todos mis amigos.
   Me gusta   Me encanta   Quiero   Amo
5. ¿Me acabas de llamar? ______________.
   En efecto   Bueno   Bien   Adiós
6. No tengo ganas de ______________.
   estudiando   estudiar   estudio   estudiamos
7. Quiero ______________ mañana a las seis.
   comer el desayuno   comer desayuno   desayunar   desayuno

EJERCICIO 4·4

Match each situation with the most appropriate remark in Spanish. Note: there may be more than one answer for certain situations.

1. ______ Introducing a friend
2. ______ Saying who is calling
3. ______ Saying you'll meet the day after Wednesday
4. ______ Naming the day after Wednesday
5. ______ Giving the actual time
6. ______ Telling the time of an event
7. ______ Saying which dress you like
8. ______ Saying what kind of dress you are looking for
9. ______ Saying where you are going
10. ______ Saying where you are
11. ______ Saying you love chocolate
12. ______ Saying you love your sister
13. ______ Saying you love your wife
14. ______ Saying you have a crush on someone
15. ______ Acknowledging that something is correct
16. ______ Saying you're not in the mood
17. ______ Prefacing an answer that requires a little explanation
18. ______ Agreeing to a suggestion
19. ______ Prefacing a conclusion
20. ______ Saying you'll see someone later
21. ______ Saying you'll see someone at an appointed time
22. ______ Greeting someone on the phone
23. ______ Waving to a bunch of kids on a bus

a. a las ocho
b. Adiós
c. al aeropuerto
d. Bien
e. Bueno
f. el jueves
g. el vestido rojo
h. Ella es
i. En efecto
j. en el aeropuerto
k. Entonces
l. hasta entonces
m. Hola
n. jueves
o. La amo
p. La quiero
q. hasta luego
r. Me encanta
s. Me gusta
t. No tengo ganas
u. Son las ocho
v. Soy
w. un vestido rojo

EJERCICIO

4·5

¿Cómo se dice en español? *Translate each sentence into Spanish.*

1. I love Peruvian food.
____
2. Do you love me?
____
3. You have a crush on my sister, don't you?
____
4. Exactly.
____
5. Would you like to talk to her?
____
6. Yes, I'd love to.
____
7. Do you feel like going to the movies?
____
8. No, I don't feel like going.
____

EJERCICIO

4·6

Write questions that ask where the following are.

1. la biblioteca ______________________________
2. José y Carlos ______________________________
3. Uruguay ______________________________
4. los conciertos ______________________________
5. nosotros ______________________________
6. la reunión ______________________________
7. yo ______________________________
8. la fiesta ______________________________

EJERCICIO
4·7

¿Cómo se dice en español? *Translate each sentence into Spanish.*

1. It's me.
2. Do you feel like eating lunch?
3. Um, I'm busy now.
4. Fine. I'll call you on Saturday.
5. Then you're not mad?
6. No. I'll see you later.

EJERCICIO
4·8

¿Cómo se dice en español? *Translate each sentence into Spanish.*

1. What do you want?
2. I'd love to see you tonight.
3. I'm going to the movies with Sara.
4. Then you can't have dinner with me?
5. Exactly.
6. OK, bye.

EJERCICIO
4·9

¿Cómo se dice en español? *Translate each sentence into Spanish.*

1. Hi, this is Miguel.
2. I'm calling to see if you can eat dinner with me tonight.
3. OK. What time?
4. At seven?
5. Fine.

At the restaurant . . .

6. Marta doesn't love me.
7. Then why don't you go out with Patricia? She has a big crush on you!
8. Well, then—why not?

EJERCICIO
4·10

Write an original conversation in which you call someone and invite him or her to do something with you.

Describing people, places, and things

·5·

Conversation: Discussing roommates

Paco: Dime, Carlos, ¿cómo es tu nuevo compañero de cuarto?

Tell me, Carlos, what's your new roommate like?

Carlos: Bueno, si tienes todo el día libre, te lo puedo describir. Es **un tipo bastante** raro.

Well, if you have all day, I can describe him. He's a very strange character.

Paco: **Mira**, todo el día no tengo, pero en general, ¿**se llevan** bien?

Look, I don't have all day, but in general, do you get along?

Carlos: Imagínate que nos llevamos muy bien porque no nos vemos casi nunca. El **tipo** duerme durante el día. A veces se levanta sólo para ir a sus clases y luego vuelve al cuarto y **se queda** dormido hasta las diez de la noche. Luego **vuelve a** levantarse y estudia toda la noche.

Actually, we get along really well because we hardly see each other. The guy sleeps during the day. Sometimes he gets up just to go to his classes, then he comes back to the room and stays asleep until ten P.M. Then he wakes up again and studies all night.

Paco: Entonces, no comen juntos.

You don't eat together, then.

Carlos: **La verdad**, no sé cuándo come él, ni dónde.

The truth is, I don't know when he eats, or where.

Paco: Entonces, al menos no ensucia la cocina.

Then at least he doesn't leave the kitchen dirty.

Carlos: ¡No! Es un tipo increíblemente pulcro. **Incluso deja** el baño limpio todos los días y parece no tener ropa sucia. Es casi un fantasma.

No! The guy is incredibly neat. He even leaves the bathroom clean every day, and he doesn't seem to have dirty clothes. He's like a ghost.

Paco: Amigo, ¡creo que tienes el compañero de cuarto perfecto!

Man, I think you have the ideal roommate!

Carlos: ¿Y el tuyo? ¿Cómo es?

And yours? What's he like?

Paco: Bueno, es **todo lo contrario** del tuyo, pues **tenemos mucho en común** y estamos juntos casi todo el día. **Es decir**, tenemos dos clases juntos y estamos en la misma asociación de estudiantes, así que somos muy buenos amigos.

Well, he's the exact opposite of yours. We have a lot in common and we're together all day. That is, we have two classes together and we're in the same fraternity, so we're really good friends.

Carlos: Entonces, también tienes el compañero ideal...

Then you have the ideal roommate too . . .

PACO: Pues, sí—y no. El mío es un desastre en la casa. En primer lugar, siempre **deja** la cocina sucia, **no** lava los platos **ni** saca la basura. Además, tira su ropa por todos lados, **ni hablar** de cómo deja el baño...

Well, yes—and no. Mine is a disaster in the house. In the first place, he always leaves the kitchen dirty, he doesn't wash the dishes or take out the trash. Plus, he throws his clothes all over the place, not to mention how he leaves the bathroom . . .

CARLOS: **Vamos**, Paco—en todo eso **se parece** mucho a ti. ¡**Con razón** se llevan tan bien!

Come on, Paco—he sounds a lot like you. No wonder you get along so well!

Improving your conversation

Mira

This is a way to get someone to understand your situation or point of view.

¿Me puedes ayudar?	*Can you help me?*
Mira, me gustaría pero hoy no tengo tiempo.	*Look, I'd like to, but today I don't have time.*

Llevarse

This verb, used with reflexive pronouns, means *to get along with each other.*

Me llevo muy bien con mi hermana.	*I get along really well with my sister.*
Mi hermana y yo **nos llevamos** muy bien.	*My sister and I get along really well.*
Él **se lleva muy mal** con sus padres.	*He doesn't get along with his parents.*
Él y sus padres **se llevan muy mal**.	*He and his parents don't get along.*

El tipo/la tipa

This is a way to refer to someone in a slightly deprecating or impersonal manner.

El amigo de Sergio me invitó a cenar, pero no quiero salir con **ese tipo.**	*Sergio's friend invited me to dinner, but I don't want to go out with that jerk.*
El tipo del garaje acaba de llamar para avisarte que tu carro está listo.	*The guy from the garage just called to tell you that your car is ready.*

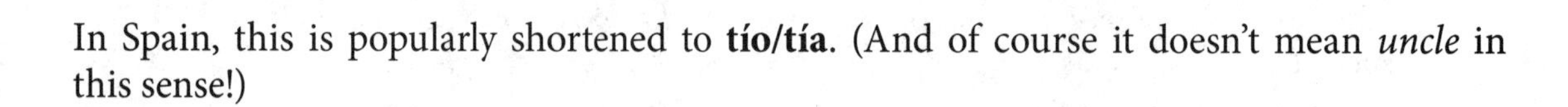

In Spain, this is popularly shortened to **tío/tía**. (And of course it doesn't mean *uncle* in this sense!)

Bastante

This is an adverb, meaning *quite/rather/pretty,* when it precedes an adjective.

Soy **bastante** alto.	*I'm pretty tall.*

Other adverbs that describe adjectives include:

poco	*not very*
muy/bien/realmente	*very*
excesivamente/demasiado	*excessively*

Note that **bien** in this context has a very different meaning from its other uses.

Esa tipa es **bien** rara.	*That girl is really strange.*

Also note that **demasiado**, which is often translated as *too*, does not necessarily have a negative meaning, as *too* does in English.

Es posible que sea rara, pero yo creo que es **demasiado bonita.**	*She may be strange, but I think she's absolutely gorgeous.*

When **bastante** modifies a verb, it is translated as *quite a bit.*

Estudiamos bastante.	*We study quite a bit.*

Quedarse

This verb, used with reflexive pronouns, means *to stay/to remain/to keep* and can be followed by an adjective.

Cuando ella está con él, **se queda tranquila.**	*When she's with him, she keeps quiet.*
Los jóvenes **se quedan dormidos** hasta después de mediodía.	*The young ones stay asleep until after noon.*

When not followed by an adjective, it means *to stay/to remain* in a place.

No voy a mi casa esta noche. Quiero **quedarme** aquí con ustedes.	*I'm not going home. I want to stay here with you all.*

Volver a + infinitive

This construction is used to mean *do something again.*

Si no contesto el teléfono, **vuelve a llamarme.**	*If I don't answer the phone, call me again.*
Quiero **volver a verte** muy pronto.	*I want to see you again soon.*

La verdad

La verdad means *the truth.* It can also be used to preface something you might feel uncomfortable saying.

¡Vamos a la casa de Cristina!	*Let's go to Cristina's house!*
La verdad, ella y yo no nos llevamos muy bien.	*The truth is/Actually, she and I don't get along very well.*

Incluso

Incluso can indicate that what follows it seems a bit out of the ordinary.

Su mamá le plancha toda la ropa, **incluso** los calcetines.	*His mother irons all his clothes for him—even/including his socks.*

Dejar

When **dejar** is followed by an adjective, it means *to leave something in that condition.*

No dejes el piso **mojado**.	*Don't leave the floor wet.*

When followed by a noun, it means *to leave something or someone.*

Ella **deja los platos** sucios en el fregadero.	*She leaves the dirty dishes in the sink.*
El papá **deja a los niños** con una niñera.	*The father leaves the children with a babysitter.*

When followed by an indirect object, it means *to allow/to let someone do something.*

Papá, **déjame** comprar el videojuego.	*Dad, let me buy the video game.*

When followed by the preposition **de**, it means *to stop doing something.*

El médico me dice que tengo que **dejar de** tomar café.	*The doctor tells me I have to stop drinking coffee.*

Verbs that mean *to leave (a place)* include:

salir (de)

Salimos (de la oficina) a las cinco.	*We leave (the office) at five.*

partir (de)

Parten (de Bogotá) mañana por la mañana.	*They leave (Bogotá) tomorrow morning.*

irse/marcharse

Me voy./Me marcho.	*I'm leaving.*
¿A qué hora **te vas?/te marchas?**	*What time are you leaving?*

Todo lo contrario

This expression means *exactly the opposite/quite the contrary.*

Dicen que te vas a casar pronto.	*They say you're getting married soon.*
Es todo lo contrario. Acabo de romper con mi novio.	*It's quite the contrary. I just broke up with my boyfriend.*

Tener en común

This means *to have in common.*

Creo que **tenemos mucho en común**.	*I think we have a lot in common.*

The opposite is **no tener nada en común/no tener nada que ver.**

Ella **no tiene nada que ver** contigo.	*She is nothing like you.*

Es decir

This is used to explain something you have just said in more detail.

Ella está bastante ocupada. **Es decir,** aparte de su trabajo, también estudia y cuida a su familia.	*She's quite busy. That is, besides her job, she also studies and takes care of her family.*

No... ni

This combination expresses *neither . . . nor.*

Él **no fuma ni toma** alcohol.	*He neither smokes nor drinks./ He doesn't smoke or drink.*

Ni hablar

¡Ni hablar! is a way of saying *Nothing compares to it!* When it is followed by **de** + an object, it is better translated as *not to mention.*

Y la cocina de mi abuela, **¡ni hablar!**	*And my grandmother's cooking—there's nothing like it!*
Hay mucho que disfrutar en México: la gente amistosa, la música, **¡ni hablar** de la cocina!	*There's a lot to enjoy in Mexico: the friendly people, the music, not to mention the food!*

Vamos

Vamos means *we're going/we go* but it can also be used like *Come on . . .* to get someone to accept or admit a situation, or at least be a little more realistic.

No voy al partido con ustedes, pues no tengo dinero.	*I'm not going to the game with you guys because I don't have any money.*
Vamos, Jorge, tú tienes más dinero que nadie.	*Come on, Jorge, you have more money than anybody.*

Parecerse

This verb, used with reflexive pronouns, means *to be like something or someone else.*

Tu apartamento **se parece** al mío.	*Your apartment is like mine.*
Carolina **se parece** a su mamá.	*Carolina looks like her mother.*

Con razón

Literally, *with reason*, this expression is better translated as *No wonder.*

¿Ya tienes novia? ¡**Con razón** no tienes dinero!	*Now you have a girlfriend? No wonder you don't have any money!*

EJERCICIO
5·1

Choose the most appropriate word to fill in each blank.

1. Mi compañera de cuarto es ______________.

simpático	bien	contentas	irresponsable

2. Nuestro equipo de básquetbol tiene muchos jugadores ______________.

altas	buenos	mal	enérgicas

3. La gente de esta ciudad es ______________.

amistosa	serio	malo	bien

4. El nuevo profesor me parece ______________.

seria	exigente	interesantes	buena

EJERCICIO
5·2

Fill in each blank with the correct form of **ser** *or* **estar**, *as appropriate.*

1. Llévame al médico, por favor. No ______ bien.
2. Mi hermana ______ enferma, también.
3. Los chicos ______ peor.
4. Los chicos ______ peores.
5. Todos mis amigos ______ simpáticos.
6. Él ______ un médico muy bueno.
7. Nuestros jugadores ______ mejores que los suyos.
8. Las chicas de esa clase ______ muy inteligentes.

EJERCICIO
5·3

Complete each of the following sentences with a logical comparison.

Diego mide 5 pies, 10 pulgadas. Arturo mide 6 pies.

1. Arturo es ____________________.
2. Diego es ____________________.
3. Diego no es ____________________.

Yo tengo 10 dólares. Mi hermano tiene 12 dólares.

4. Mi hermano tiene ____________________ 10 dólares.
5. Yo tengo ____________________ 15 dólares.
6. Mi hermano es ________________ rico ________________ yo.
7. Yo no soy ________________ rico ________________ mi hermano.

Berta tiene 10 libros. Ana tiene 7 libros.

8. Berta tiene ____________________.
9. Ana no tiene ____________________.

EJERCICIO
5·4

Use one of the following words in each blank to complete each sentence.

bastante   muy   bien   demasiado

1. María tiene 85 puntos en el examen. Ella es ______________ lista.
2. Alejandra tiene más de 100 puntos porque tiene crédito extra. Ella es ______________ lista.
3. Susana tiene 90 puntos. Ella es ______________ lista.
4. Julia tiene 95 puntos. Ella es ______________ lista.

EJERCICIO
5·5

Compare the girls in Exercise 5-4.

1. Julia es ________________ lista ________________ Susana.
2. Alejandra es ____________________.
3. María no es ____________________ Susana.
4. Julia es ____________________ María.

EJERCICIO
5·6

Use the appropriate form of one of the following verbs to fill in each blank.

dejar salir irse marcharse partir

1. Mi compañero de cuarto quiere ______________ de fumar.
2. ¿A qué hora ______________ (tú) del trabajo?
3. No quiero estar sola. ¡No me ______________ (tú)!
4. Es una buena fiesta. ¿Por qué ______________ (ustedes)?
5. El tren ______________ a las seis.
6. Su mamá no le ______________ ver televisión después de las ocho.

EJERCICIO
5·7

Fill in each blank with the most appropriate word or expression.

1. ¿Me vas a acompañar a la fiesta?

   ______________, mi mamá está enferma y la tengo que visitar.

   Es decir Vamos Con razón Mira
2. Mi profesor es bien exigente, ______________, da exámenes difíciles y asigna muchos trabajos escritos.

   todo lo contrario es decir mira la verdad
3. Tengo dos entradas para el ballet. ¿Quieres ir conmigo?

   ______________, no me gusta el ballet.

   La verdad Mira Ni hablar Vamos
4. A veces creo que nadie me quiere.

   ______________, eres la chica más popular de la escuela.

   La verdad Mira Vamos Es decir
5. Mi mamá prepara ricos tacos, frijoles, enchiladas, ¡______________ de sus tamales!

   con razón es decir ni hablar vamos
6. Tu hijo es muy exitoso. ¡______________ estás tan orgullosa!

   La verdad Con razón Ni hablar Vamos
7. Esa chica me parece muy floja.

   Es ______________, trabaja mucho.

   ni hablar la verdad todo lo contrario mira

EJERCICIO 5·8

Add your own words in the blank spaces to complete the following sentences. Have a Spanish-speaking friend check your answers.

1. Germán siempre saca muy buenas notas. ¡Con razón ________________!
2. ________________. Es todo lo contrario—es muy simpática.
3. Beatriz es una chica bastante egoísta, es decir, ________________.
4. ¿Quieres leer este libro? La verdad, ________________.
5. Amigo, todos vamos a la playa para el fin de semana. ¿Puedes ir tú? Mira, ________________ ________________.
6. La playa lo tiene todo: el sol, las olas del mar, ¡ni hablar de ________________ ________________!
7. No quiero hacer la fiesta en mi apartamento, pues es bien pequeño. Vamos, ¡________________ ________________!

EJERCICIO 5·9

Write in the imperfect form of each conjugated verb.

1. canta ________________
2. cocino ________________
3. pensamos ________________
4. como ________________
5. pierden ________________
6. debes ________________
7. hacemos ________________
8. están ________________
9. escribo ________________
10. voy ________________
11. conozco ________________
12. miran ________________
13. caminamos ________________
14. juegan ________________
15. disfruta ________________
16. corren ________________
17. puedo ________________
18. tiene ________________
19. somos ________________
20. vemos ________________
21. salgo ________________
22. dejamos ________________
23. parece ________________
24. mienten ________________

EJERCICIO
5·10

Change each sentence from the present tense to the imperfect tense.

PRESENT	IMPERFECT
1. Son pequeños.	______
2. Estamos contentos.	______
3. ¿Eres responsable?	______
4. Estoy aburrida.	______
5. Lee muy bien.	______
6. Vamos a la playa.	______
7. Se divierten mucho.	______
8. No conozco a nadie.	______
9. Me gusta el chocolate.	______
10. Te quiero.	______
11. Ellos no me dejan salir.	______
12. Se parece a su mamá.	______

EJERCICIO
5·11

Translate the sentences in Exercise 5-10 into English, as if you were describing a period of time in the past.

1. ______
2. ______
3. ______
4. ______
5. ______
6. ______
7. ______
8. ______
9. ______

10. ______________________________

11. ______________________________

12. ______________________________

EJERCICIO
5·12

¿Cómo se dice en español? *Translate the following sentences into Spanish.*

1. When she was four years old, she was very shy.
____
2. She liked to play alone.
____
3. She had two favorite dolls.
____
4. Their names were Barbie 1 and Barbie 2.
____
5. Her parents understood her.
____
6. They would talk to her a lot.
____
7. They didn't let her watch TV every day.
____
8. They used to go to the park together.
____
9. Now she's not shy.
____
10. She has lots of friends, and she doesn't play with dolls anymore.
____

EJERCICIO
5·13

¿Cómo es tu mejor amigo? *Write at least eight sentences that describe your best friend. Use the present tense. Ask a Spanish-speaking friend to check your work.*

EJERCICIO
5·14

¿Cómo eras tú cuando tenías diez años? *Write at least eight sentences that tell what you were like when you were ten years old. Include activities that you always did at that age. Use the imperfect tense. Ask a Spanish-speaking friend to check your work.*

·6· Expressing wants and needs

Conversation: Looking for a new apartment

AGENTE: Buenos días, señor. ¿En qué puedo ayudarlo?
Good morning, sir. How can I help you?

ALBERTO: Me gustaría alquilar un apartamento **que esté** aquí en la ciudad.
I'd like to rent an apartment here in the city.

AGENTE: Siéntese, por favor, y dígame qué tipo de apartamento quiere. ¿Es sólo para usted?
Have a seat, please, and tell me what kind of apartment you want. Is it just for you?

ALBERTO: Bueno, eso depende de lo que **esté** disponible. Prefiero vivir solo, pero si no veo nada que sea apropiado, podría compartir un apartamento más grande con un amigo mío.
Well, that depends on what's available. I'd rather live alone, but if I don't see anything that works, I could share a bigger apartment with a friend of mine.

AGENTE: Bien. Primero, dígame sus preferencias.
OK. First, tell me what you're looking for.

ALBERTO: **Lo más importante** es la ubicación. **Quiero que** el apartamento **esté** en la ciudad, cerca de la universidad. Por otra parte, **es importante que esté** cerca del metro—pues no tengo carro.
The most important thing is the location. I want the apartment to be in the city, near the university. Also, it's important that it be near a metro station—I don't have a car.

AGENTE: Bien, entonces, no le importa si no tiene estacionamiento.
OK, then you don't mind if there's no parking space.

ALBERTO: Efectivamente. Pero **quiero** un edificio que tenga **vigilancia**. **Necesito**, además, **que tenga** sala, comedor, un dormitorio y, claro, cocina y baño modernos. Ah, y si fuera posible, me gustaría tener balcón.
Exactly. But I want a secure building. I also need it to have a living room, dining room, one bedroom, and, of course, a modern kitchen and bathroom. Oh, and if possible, I'd like to have a balcony.

AGENTE: ¿Y cuál es su presupuesto? O sea, ¿cuánto piensa pagar mensualmente, **incluyendo** luz, calefacción y agua?
And what is your budget? I mean, what monthly rent are you thinking about, including utilities?

ALBERTO: Espero encontrar algo por unos setecientos dólares.
I'm hoping to find something for about seven hundred dollars.

AGENTE: Mire, por setecientos dólares, no va a encontrar **nada que sea** decente en el centro de la ciudad. Hay edificios modernos y seguros, que **incluso** están cerca del metro, pero quedan por lo menos seis millas del centro.

Look, for seven hundred dollars you're not going to find anything decent in the city. There are modern, secure buildings that are actually near the metro, but they're all at least six miles outside the city.

ALBERTO: ¿Será posible **encontrar algo** más céntrico **que tenga** dos dormitorios por lo doble de esa cantidad, esto es, alrededor de $1,400 al mes?

Would it be possible to find a two-bedroom place closer in for twice that amount—around $1,400 a month?

AGENTE: Déjeme averiguarlo. No le voy a decir que sea imposible, pero no le puedo prometer nada. Déme unas horas para ver qué posibilidades hay. Si encuentro algo que **valga la pena**, podemos ir a verlo hoy mismo por la tarde. Mientras tanto, **necesito que** usted **rellene** este **formulario** con sus datos e información de contacto. Por cierto, tanto usted como su amigo tendrán que rellenar una **solicitud** para que los aprueben como inquilinos. Presumo que quieren el alquiler por un año, ¿correcto? **Asegúrense** de traer los documentos relativos a sus finanzas y su crédito.

Let me have a look. I'm not going to tell you that it's impossible, but I can't promise anything. Give me a couple of hours to see what's out there. If I see anything worthwhile, we can go look at it this afternoon. In the meantime, I need you to fill out this form, so I have your contact information. As a matter of fact, both you and your friend will have to fill out an application in order to be approved as tenants. I'm assuming you are looking for a one-year lease. Is that correct? Be sure to bring your financial and credit information with you.

ALBERTO: **De acuerdo**. Sí, estamos dispuestos a firmar un contrato por un año. Ahora voy a buscar a mi amigo y reunir la documentación requerida. Regreso con él a mediodía. Muchísimas gracias. **Hasta luego**.

Fine. Yes, we're willing to sign a one-year lease. Now I'm going to look for my friend and get my papers. I'll be back with him at noon. Thank you very much. See you shortly.

AGENTE: **Hasta luego**.

See you later.

Improving your conversation

To express *wanting, needing, hoping for,* or *looking for* a person or a thing that fits a certain description—but which you are not certain exists—the subjunctive is used for that description. In other words, if you know what you want but can't take a picture of it, it's still in your imagination, so choose the subjunctive to describe it. Use the following formula:

Conjugated form of **querer/necesitar/esperar encontrar/buscar + una casa/un trabajo/un médico/una pareja/un profesor + que** + subjunctive verb

Quiero una casa **que tenga** piscina. — *I want a house that has a swimming pool.*

Necesita un trabajo **que pague** bien. — *He needs a job that pays well.*

Esperamos encontrar un médico **que sepa** curar esta enfermedad. — *We're hoping to find a doctor who can cure this disease.*

Buscan un profesor **que dé** exámenes fáciles. — *They're looking for a professor who gives easy exams.*

When what is desired is a *person*, no personal **a** is used (because, essentially, it is not yet known who that person might be). However, and not so logically, if you want to express *someone*—**alguien**—you do precede it with **a**.

Busco a alguien que me pueda ayudar.	*I'm looking for someone who can help me.*

If you want, need, or are looking for something that you know exists, or someone you already know (you can take a picture of them!), then you use the indicative and the personal **a**.

Necesito a mi hermana, que sabe solucionar este problema.	*I need my sister, who knows how to solve this problem.*

Compare the following sentences, the first using the subjunctive and the second using the indicative.

Busco una persona que **hable** español.	*I'm looking for somebody who speaks Spanish. (who might practice with me)*
Busco a una persona que **habla** español.	*I'm looking for somebody who speaks Spanish. (she's lost at the shopping mall)*

Buscar, in addition to meaning *to look for*, can also mean *to go get*.

Voy a buscar a mi hija, que me puede ayudar.	*I'm going to get my daughter, who can help me.*
Ve a buscar las llaves, están en la cocina.	*Go get the keys, they're in the kitchen.*

There are other ways to express *get*, all with different meanings. **Conseguir** and **obtener** mean *to get* in a general sense, like *obtain*.

Espero **conseguir** trabajo.	*I hope to get a job.*
Está tratando de **obtener** el dinero.	*He's trying to get the money.*

Ponerse

Ponerse followed by an adjective expresses *to get in that condition*.

La chica **se pone** roja cuando tiene vergüenza.	*The girl gets red when she's embarrassed.*
Me pongo triste cuando pienso en mis padres.	*I get sad when I think about my parents.*
Abrígate. **Te vas a poner** enfermo. (used in Spain rather than **enfermarse**)	*Put your coat on. You're going to get sick.*

A large number of verbs used with reflexive pronouns can express *to get*. For example:

aburrirse	*to get bored*	emborracharse	*to get drunk*
cansarse	*to get tired*	emocionarse	*to get excited*
casarse	*to get married*	frustrarse	*to get frustrated*
enfadarse (Spain)	*to get angry*	herirse	*to get hurt*
enfermarse	*to get sick*	mejorarse	*to get better*
enojarse (L.A.)	*to get angry*	perderse	*to get lost*
enriquecerse	*to get rich*	preocuparse	*to get worried*

No voy a pedir postre, pues no quiero **ponerme gordo**.	*I'm not going to order dessert—I don't want to get fat.*
Ella no puede caminar esa distancia. **Se cansa.**	*She can't walk that far. She gets tired.*
Siempre usamos el sistema de SPG (Sistema de Posicionamiento Global) porque no queremos **perdernos.**	*We always use the GPS because we don't want to get lost.*
Espero que no **se enojen** conmigo.	*I hope you all don't get mad at me.*

Lo importante

Lo importante means *the important thing.* When it is followed by a known fact, it is stated in the indicative.

Lo importante es que todos están bien.	*The important thing is that everybody is all right.*

When it is followed by something that is hoped for, that is stated in the subjunctive.

Lo importante es que encuentre trabajo.	*The important thing is that I find work.*
Es importante que vengas a clase mañana.	*It's important that you come to class tomorrow.*

Other impersonal expressions that actually state personal opinions are also followed by the subjunctive.

Es ridículo que él no lo trate con más respeto.	*It's ridiculous that he doesn't treat him with more respect.*
Es una lástima que estén enfermos.	*It's a shame that they are sick.*

To indicate that something *needs to be done,* use the subjunctive after an impersonal expression.

Es necesario que practiques.	*It's necessary that you practice./You need to practice.*
Es imprescindible que protejamos los recursos naturales.	*It's absolutely necessary that we protect our natural resources.*

Ir and venir

The verbs that express *coming* and *going* are a little tricky for English speakers. In English, *come* indicates where you are or where the person you are talking to is, or will be, at the time of the expected arrival; and *go* indicates a third place where neither the speaker or the hearer is expected to be. In other words, in Engish, one can *come here, come there*, or *go there.* In Spanish, it's much simpler: **venir** is used with **aquí** (Spain) and **acá** (Latin America); **ir** is used with **allí** and **allá**. It does not matter whether the person will be there or not. Consider the following examples, and you will see that while **venir** is always translated as *to come,* **ir** can be translated as *to come* or *to go.*

Ven a mi casa.	*Come to my house.*
Voy a tu casa.	*I'm coming to your house. (You will be there then.)/I'm going to your house. (You won't be there then.)*
Ve al mercado.	*Go to the market.*
(Suena el timbre)—**¡Voy!**	*(The doorbell rings)*—I'm coming!

Incluyendo

Incluyendo means *including* something that may or may not ordinarily be included:

El alquiler es sólo a quinientos dólares al mes, **incluyendo** luz y agua.	*The rent is only five hundred dollars a month, including electricity and water.*

Incluso can mean *including* or *even* when it refers to something that is not necessarily always considered to be a member of the group mentioned.

Toda la familia, **incluso** el perro, fue a la playa.	*The whole family, including/even the dog, went to the beach.*

Incluso can also be translated as *actually.*

Esta ciudad es muy agradable. Es **incluso** la ciudad que más me gusta de todas.	*This city is very pleasant. It's actually the city I like best of all.*
Esa mujer está siempre con su perro. **Incluso** quiso llevarlo a una boda.	*That woman is always with her dog. She actually tried to take it to a wedding.*

Formulario

A **formulario** is a document with blank spaces that individuals fill in with their personal information.

Es necesario que rellene **este formulario.**	*It's necessary that you fill out this form.*

Forma has several meanings. It can mean *shape.*

¿De qué forma es este objeto?	*What shape is this object?*
Es un triángulo.	*It's a triangle.*

It can mean *form*, to refer to elements of grammar.

Las formas del subjuntivo no son difíciles de aprender.	*Subjunctive forms aren't hard to learn.*
Usa **la forma** del infinitivo después de una preposición.	*Use the infinitive form after a preposition.*

To express *to form* use **formar**.

Van a **formar** un grupo de protesta.	*They're going to form a protest group.*

Forma can also refer to the *way* something is or can be done. Alternatives to this meaning of **forma** are **manera** and **modo**.

Debe de haber **alguna forma/alguna manera/algún modo** de hacer esto más rápido.	*There must be a faster way to do this.*
Yo lo hago de **esta forma/de esta manera/de este modo/así.**	*I do it like this.*

De todas formas

De todas formas/De todas maneras/De todos modos can be translated as *anyway*, in the sense that no matter what happened before, what comes next takes precedence.

Hace mucho frío, pero voy a llevar mis nuevas sandalias **de todas formas.**	*It's really cold, but I'm going to wear my new sandals anyway.*
A veces se porta muy mal, pero la quiero **de todos modos.**	*Sometimes she behaves badly, but I love her anyway.*

Solicitud

Solicitud means *application*, in the sense of an appeal for a job or entrance to a school or other organization. The verb for *to apply*, in the same sense, is **solicitar**.

La **solicitud** para la entrada a aquella universidad es muy larga y detallada.	*The application for entrance to that university is long and detailed.*
¿Vas tú a **solicitar** el puesto?	*Are you going to apply for the job?*

Aplicación and aplicar

Aplicación and **aplicar** are only sometimes **falsos amigos**, as they refer to the *application* or *applying* of some kind of liquid or paste to a surface.

Van a **aplicar** tres manos de pintura a las paredes.	*They're going to apply three coats of paint to the walls.*
Deberías **aplicar** protector del sol antes de salir.	*You should apply sunscreen before going out.*

Aplicarse, used with a reflexive pronoun, means *to apply*, in the sense of a law or rule.

La regla **se aplica** a todos los estudiantes, incluso a los que están en su último año.	*The rule applies to all students, including seniors.*

Valer la pena

This expression means *to be worthwhile, worth the time or trouble*, or *to be of great value.*

No gano casi nada. **No vale la pena** seguir trabajando aquí.	*I hardly earn anything. It's not worth the trouble to keep on working here.*
Pon atención a los detalles. **Vale la pena** llenar la solicitud con cuidado.	*Pay attention to the details. It's worthwhile to fill the application form out carefully.*
Su hijo se casa con una chica que realmente **vale la pena.**	*Her son is marrying a girl who is a real treasure.*

Before a word that begins with the letter *i* or the letters *hi*, the word **y** *(and)* changes to **e**.

Esa chica estudia medicina **e ingeniería** a la vez.	*That girl is studying medicine and engineering at the same time.*
Voy al congreso con Margarita **e Inés.**	*I'm going to the conference with Margarita and Inés.*

Asegurarse de

Asegurarse de means *to make sure that you do something.* It is followed by a verb in infinitive form.

Tenemos que **asegurarnos de** cerrar la puerta con llave.	*We have to make sure we lock the door.*
Asegúrate de repasar las formas del subjuntivo.	*Make sure you review the subjunctive forms.*

EJERCICIO
6·1

Fill in each blank with the subjunctive form of the verb indicated.

1. Necesitamos una secretaria que (ser) ______________ bilingüe.
2. Buscan una casa que (tener) ______________ una cocina grande.
3. Espero encontrar a alguien que (conocer) ______________ a mi hermano.
4. Quiero conseguir un trabajo que me (ofrecer) ______________ la oportunidad de viajar.
5. Tú necesitas un amigo que te (comprender) ______________.
6. Él busca un profesor que le (aconsejar) ______________.

EJERCICIO
6·2

Choose the infinitive, the indicative, or the subjunctive form of each verb indicated, as appropriate.

1. Queremos una persona que (sabe) ______________ contabilidad.
2. Están buscando al antiguo contador, que (saber) ______________ hacer las cuentas.
3. Mi amiga sabe (hacer) ______________ las cuentas.
4. Ella necesita un jefe que la (apreciar) ______________.
5. Ellos esperan contratar una persona que (poder) ______________ vender sus productos.
6. Mis amigos no quieren (pintar) ______________ su casa.
7. Buscan a alguien que (estar) ______________ dispuesto a pintar su casa.
8. Él necesita un profesor que (tener) ______________ paciencia.
9. Yo quiero mucho a mi profesor, que (tener) ______________ mucha paciencia.
10. Esperamos encontrar un restaurante que (servir) ______________ comida sana.

EJERCICIO
6·3

¿Cómo se dice en español? *Translate the following sentences into Spanish.*

1. We want a roommate who doesn't smoke.
____
2. I'm looking for my cousin, who works here.
____
3. She's looking for someone who works here.
____
4. They want a car that doesn't use much gas.
____
5. We need a salesman who speaks Spanish.
____
6. They have a salesman who speaks Spanish.
____

EJERCICIO
6·4

Fill in each blank with the most appropriate expression.

1. Él espera (*get*) ______________ un puesto importante.
2. La chica siempre (*turns*) ______________ roja cuando la maestra le hace una pregunta.
3. No queremos (*get fat*) ______________, de modo que no vamos a comer ni pizza ni pasta.
4. Ella siempre (*gets*) ______________ lo que quiere, de alguna manera.
5. Yo (*get*) ______________ triste cuando me despido de mis amigos.
6. Mi amiga compra y vende acciones por Internet, esperando (*get rich*) ______________.
7. Si tú (*get sick*) ______________, te llevo al médico.
8. Si tú (*get lost*) ______________, llama a mi celular.

EJERCICIO 6·5

¿Cómo se dice en español? *Express the following in Spanish.*

1. Don't get sick!

    ____

2. I hope he doesn't get mad.

    ____

3. He wants to get married.

    ____

4. Get better soon!

    ____

5. She gets frustrated easily.

    ____

6. We get bored in that class.

    ____

7. I don't want you to get worried.

    ____

8. They get excited when they think about the trip.

    ____

Fill in each blank with the subjunctive form of the indicated verb.

1. Es horrible que (haber, una persona singular) ______________ guerras.
2. Es ridículo que no (darse cuenta, ellos) ______________ del peligro.
3. Es una lástima que (enojarse, él) ______________ por tan poca cosa.
4. Es importante que (preservar, nosotros) ______________ el medio ambiente.
5. Es necesario que (portarse, tú) ______________ bien.
6. Es imprescindible que (perder, usted) ______________ peso.

EJERCICIO
6·7

¿Cómo se dice en español? *Express the following in Spanish.*

1. Can you come to my house?
   ____
2. Are you going to the market?
   ____
3. Are you coming to our wedding? It's at the Botanical Garden.
   ____
4. Is he coming to the movies with us?
   ____
5. Do you come here often?
   ____
6. Are you all going to class?
   ____
7. Are you all coming to class tomorrow?
   ____
8. What time are you coming?
   ____

EJERCICIO
6·8

Answer each of the questions in Exercise 6-7 using a form of **ir** *or* **venir**, *as appropriate.*

1. ______________________________
2. ______________________________
3. ______________________________
4. ______________________________
5. ______________________________
6. ______________________________
7. ______________________________
8. ______________________________

Choose the most appropriate word to fill in each blank.

1. Todo esto nos va a costar $869.32, ______________ los impuestos.

   incluyendo   incluso

2. La niña quiere invitar a toda la clase, ______________ a la maestra, a su fiesta de cumpleaños.

   incluyendo   incluso

3. Ese actor es muy guapo. Puede ser ______________ el actor más guapo de Hollywood.

   incluyendo   incluso

4. Para poder estudiar en la universidad, el primer paso es llenar esta ______________.

   forma   aplicación   solicitud   papel

5. ¿Hay algún ______________ que tengo que llenar?

   formulario   forma   aplicación   papel

6. La película tiene violencia, pero voy a verla de todas ______________.

   aplicaciones   solicitudes   formas   formulario

7. Necesitan meseros en el nuevo restaurante. ¿Quiénes van a ______________?

   solicitar   aplicar   venir   cocinar

8. Esta ley no puede ______________ a los niños.

   pertenecer   asegurarse   aplicarse   ponerse

9. Tenemos que ______________ de llevar el paraguas, por si llueve.

   aplicarnos   asegurarnos   valer la pena   ponernos

10. En serio, ______________ asistir a todas las clases.

    asegura   vale la pena   ponte   solicita

EJERCICIO
6·10

Write a paragraph of six to eight sentences in which you describe the kind of job, place to live, or lifetime partner you would like to have one day. Use as many as possible of the constructions outlined in this chapter.

Making requests and offers

·7·

Conversation: Helping a classmate

Federico: **Oye**, amigo, ¿te puedo **pedir** un favor?	*Hey, buddy, can I ask you a favor?*
David: **Por supuesto, ¿de qué se trata?**	*Of course—what can I do for you?*
Federico: ¿**Me prestas** tus **apuntes** de la clase de biología? **Es que** estuve enfermo y **falté a** unos días de clase y ahora estoy algo perdido.	*Will you lend me your biology notes? When I was sick I missed a couple of classes, and now I'm totally lost.*
David: Bueno. Acompáñame a la biblioteca y haremos una fotocopia de mi cuaderno. Luego vamos a tu casa para repasar las lecciones que **te perdiste**. Yo **te las explico** con mucho gusto.	*OK. Come to the library with me and we'll copy my notebook. Then we can go to your house and review the lessons you missed. I'll be glad to explain them to you.*
Federico: Pues, muchas gracias. No sé qué haría sin ti.	*Man, thanks a lot. I don't know what I'd do without you.*
David: No es nada. **Por cierto**, yo también quiero pedirte un gran favor.	*It's nothing. As a matter of fact, I have a favor to ask of you.*
Federico: ¿Ah, sí? ¡No me digas que quieres otro consejo sobre tu novia!	*Oh yeah? Don't tell me that you want more advice about your girlfriend!*
David: No, no es exactamente eso. Lo que pasa es que este fin de semana viene su hermana a verla. ¿Estarías dispuesto a salir con ella el sábado por la noche? Iríamos los cuatro al teatro y luego a comer. ¿Qué te parece?	*Well, not exactly. It's that her sister is coming to visit this weekend. Would you be willing to go out with her on Saturday night? We'd all four go to the theater and then out to eat. How does that sound?*
Federico: Mira, ya **he quedado con** José para ir al cine. Pero, ¿qué te parece si la invito a ir al cine conmigo y con José? Y claro, luego iríamos a comer algo, aunque no sea a un lugar muy elegante.	*Look, I already agreed to go to the movies with José. But how about if I invite her to go to the movies with me and José? Of course, afterwards we'd get something to eat, although it won't be a very fancy place.*
David: Me parece una buena solución, pero primero la tendré que hablar con mi novia. Mira, **te llamo en cuanto tenga** su respuesta.	*That sounds like a good solution, but first I'll have to discuss it with my girlfriend. Look, I'll call you as soon as I have her answer.*

FEDERICO: De acuerdo. Y **por cierto**, mil gracias por la ayuda con la biología. — *Good. And by the way, thanks a lot for the help with biology.*

DAVID: No es nada. **No dudes en llamarme** si tienes alguna pregunta. — *No problem. Don't hesitate to call me if you have any questions.*

Improving your conversation

Oye

This is the **tú** command form of **oír**, and it is used to get someone's attention, kind of like *Hey.* The **usted** form is **Oiga.**

Oye, Luis, ¿estás ocupado? — *Hey, Luis, are you busy?*
Oiga, señor—¿se le cayó este cuaderno? — *Excuse me, sir—did you drop this notebook?*

Pedir

Pedir is used to make a request or ask someone to do something. To use it in a sentence, follow this pattern:

indirect object pronoun + conjugation of **pedir** + **que** + verb in subjunctive

Te pido que vengas a la oficina ahora mismo. — *I'm asking you to come to the office right now.*
Él siempre **me pide que hable** más despacio. — *He always asks me to speak more slowly.*

Other verbs used to make requests—in a more urgent manner—include:

rogar — *beg*
suplicar — *beg (on one knee)*
implorar — *implore/beseech/beg (on both knees!)*

These verbs follow the same pattern as **pedir**.

Le ruego que me ayude. — *I beg you to help me.*
Le suplican que les dé dinero. — *They beg him to give them money.*
Les imploramos que no vayan a la calle. — *We beseech you not to go out into the street.*

Another way to ask a favor is to simply make a question in the present tense, beginning with the indirect object pronoun that indicates the person who is the recipient of the favor. This translates to English as *will you . . . for me/us?*

¿Me ayudas? — *Will you help me?*
¿Me haces un favor? — *Will you do me a favor?*
¿Nos escribe una carta? — *Will you write us a letter?*
¿Nos das las instrucciones? — *Will you give us the directions?*

The most direct way to ask for something is to give a command. (See the Appendix.)

¡Ayúdame! — *Help me!*
Mándame un email. — *Send me an e-mail.*

Escríbanos una carta.	*Write us a letter.*
Danos las instrucciones.	*Give us the directions.*

You could also use the expression **Hazme/Hágame el favor de + infinitive**, which can be a little sarcastic.

Hazme el favor de llamarme esta noche.	*Do me a favor and call me tonight.*

Of course, with any method of asking for something, it's always better to use **Por favor**!

Tratar de

Tratar de means *try to* when it is followed by a verb in infinitive form.

Siempre **trato de** terminar mi trabajo antes de volver a casa.	*I always try to finish my work before I go home.*

It can be used with the impersonal pronoun **se**, giving it the meaning *to be about (something).*

¿**De** qué **se trata**?	*What's it about?*
Se trata de un asunto personal.	*It's about a personal matter.*

Ofrecer

When used with reflexive pronouns, this verb indicates an offer to do something for someone else.

La profesora siempre **se ofrece** para ayudarnos.	*The teacher always offers to help us.*

The expression, **¿Qué se te/le/les ofrece?** means *What can I do for you?* Another way to offer a favor to someone is to use the present tense in question form.

¿Te ayudo?	*Can I help you?*
¿Les presto el dinero?	*Can I lend you (plural) the money?*

You could also use **querer que + subjunctive**.

¿Quieres que te ayude?	*Do you want me to help you?*
¿Quieren ustedes que les preste el dinero?	*Do you all want me to lend you the money?*

Por supuesto

Por supuesto indicates *of course/naturally/that goes without saying.*

Por supuesto te acompaño.	*Of course I'll go with you.*
¿Siempre vamos a Cancún para el descanso de primavera?	*Are we still going to Cancún for spring break?*
¡Por supuesto!	*Of course!*

Prestar

Prestar—which means *to lend*—and other verbs that indicate an *exchange* of something from one person to another, need both indirect and direct objects. (See the Appendix.) The indirect object is always a person—the person who receives something from the subject. The direct object is the thing that is received. The pattern is as follows:

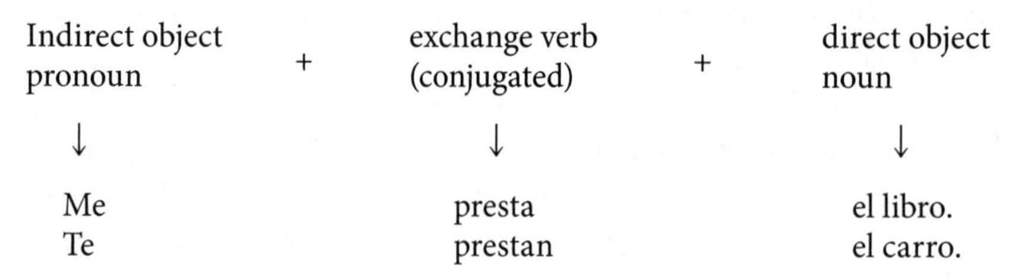

Me	presta	el libro.
Te	prestan	el carro.

He lends the book to me. (To me he lends the book.)
They're lending the car to you. (To you they are lending the car.)

To use a direct object pronoun in place of the noun, put it right after the indirect object pronoun.

Me **lo** presta.	*He lends it to me.*
Te **lo** prestan.	*They're lending it to you.*

If the indirect object is **le** (*to her/to him/to you*) or **les** (*to them/to you all*), it changes to **se** when followed by a direct object pronoun.

Se lo presta (a ella).	*He lends it to her.*
Se lo prestan (a ustedes).	*They're lending it to you all.*

Other exchange verbs include:

dar	*give*	explicar	*explain*
decir	*tell*	mandar	*send*
enseñar	*teach/show*	mostrar	*show*
entregar	*deliver*	ofrecer	*offer*
enviar	*send*		

Ella **me da** muchos regalos.	*She gives me a lot of presents.*
Ella **me los da.**	*She gives them to me.*
Ellos **nos dicen** sus secretos.	*They tell us their secrets.*
Ellos **nos los dicen.**	*They tell them to us.*
Ustedes **nos dicen** la verdad.	*You all tell us the truth.*
Ustedes **nos la dicen.**	*You tell it to us.*
Nosotros **te ofrecemos** los boletos.	*We're offering you the tickets.*
Nosotros **te los ofrecemos.**	*We're offering them to you.*

To borrow can be expressed by using **pedir que** + the subjunctive of **prestar**.

Le pido que me preste su libro.	*I'm asking you to lend me your book.*
¿Me lo presta?	*Will you lend it to me?*

When the indirect-direct object combination is used with an infinitive or a gerund, it can be placed before the conjugated verb in the sentence, or it can be attached to the end of the infinitive or gerund.

Te voy a dar las llaves. — *I'm going to give you the keys.*
Te las voy a **dar.**/Voy a **dártelas.** — *I'm going to give them to you.*

Me está prestando su carro. — *He's lending me his car.*
Me lo está **prestando.**/Está **prestándomelo.** — *He's lending it to me.*

As you can see, these exchange verbs have a very different pattern from the one used in English. Another thing that is different from English is that in Spanish when you use an indirect object pronoun, you can also emphasize it by using the preposition **a** followed by the corresponding pronoun. (See the Appendix.) In English this would be redundant.

Te voy a dar las llaves **a ti.** (no a tu hermano) — *I'm going to give the keys to* ***you.*** *(not to your brother)*
Me está prestando el carro **a mí.** (no a ti) — *He's lending the car to* ***me.*** *(not to you)*

Note that the use of **a** + pronoun is optional, but the indirect object pronoun is necessary.

Apuntes

Apuntes are the *notes* that you take in class. The **nota** that you get at the end of a course is your *grade.*

Mi amigo toma muy buenos **apuntes.** — *My friend takes really good notes.*
Espero sacar una buena **nota** en este curso. — *I hope I get a good grade in this course.*

Es que

Es que and **lo que pasa es que** mean, literally, *It's that . . ./What's happening is that . . .* They are used to indicate that you are about to give an explanation.

Sonia, ¿por qué siempre llegas tarde? — *Sonia, why are you always late?*
Lo siento, señora, **es que** tengo que trabajar antes de venir a clase. — *I'm sorry, Ma'am, it's that I have to work before coming to class.*

Perder

Perder means *to lose,* but it can also mean *to miss* something such as a train or a bus.

Apúrate, no quiero **perder** el tren. — *Hurry up, I don't want to miss the train.*

Perderse means *to fail to experience.*

Es una lástima que **te hayas perdido** la fiesta. — *It's a shame that you missed the party.*

To *miss* a person or a place is expressed by **extrañar** (Latin America) or **echar de menos** (Latin America and Spain).

Te extraño mucho.	*I miss you a lot.*
Echo mucho de menos a mis padres.	*I miss my parents a lot.*

When a part is *missing* from a whole, **faltar** is used.

Faltan tres páginas de la revista.	*Three pages are missing from the magazine.*

Faltar a can mean *to miss work or school.*

Nunca **ha faltado** al trabajo.	*He's never missed a day from work.*
No me gusta **faltar a** clase.	*I don't like to miss class.*

To miss a goal in a game is expressed with **fallar**.

¡Falló!	*He missed!*

Fallar, when used with an indirect object pronoun, means *to let someone down.*

Trabajo duro porque no quiero **fallarte**.	*I work hard because I don't want to let you down.*

To miss an item on a test is expressed with **pasarse (por alto)**.

Se me pasaron (por alto) tres preguntas.	*I missed three questions.*

Quedar con... para

This expression means *to agree to meet someone for.*

Quedé con Alfredo para almorzar.	*I agreed to meet Alfredo for lunch.*

Alternatively, you can use a plural conjugation of **quedar en** + infinitive—*to agree to do something.*

Quedamos en reuinirnos a las ocho.	*We agreed to get together at eight o'clock.*

De acuerdo is a way of saying that you agree to a plan.

Entonces, ¿pasas por mí a las cinco?	*Then will you pick me up at five o'clock?*
De acuerdo.	*OK.*

En cuanto

En cuanto is translated as *as soon as* and is followed by a verb in the subjunctive.

Los llamo **en cuanto** llegue a Bogotá.	*I'll call you (all) as soon as I arrive in Bogotá.*
Dejaré este trabajo **en cuanto** tenga el dinero que necesito para comprar la casa.	*I'll leave this job as soon as I have the money I need to buy the house.*

Por cierto

This expression can be used to insert a new topic—or a new aspect of a topic being discussed—into a conversation. It can be translated as *by the way.*

Ayer vi a Olga con un grupo de sus amigas. **Por cierto,** ¿sigues saliendo con ella?
I saw Olga yesterday with a group of her girlfriends. By the way, do you still go out with her?

No dudar en is an expression that means *not to hesitate to,* usually in command form.

No dudes en contactarme si necesitas algo.
Don't hesitate to contact me if you need anything.

EJERCICIO
7·1

Fill in each blank with the appropriate indirect object pronoun.

1. Amigo, ______ pido que me ayudes.
2. Señor González, ______ rogamos que no nos dé el examen hoy.
3. A sus padres ______ suplica que cambien de opinión.
4. A su novia ______ implora que no llore.
5. ______ voy a pedir a la profesora que me explique la lección.

EJERCICIO
7·2

*Complete the chart with the **yo** form of each verb in the present subjunctive.*

1. bailar ______________
2. cantar ______________
3. comer ______________
4. escribir ______________
5. correr ______________
6. leer ______________
7. estar ______________
8. dar ______________
9. enviar ______________
10. beber ______________

EJERCICIO

7·3

*Complete the chart with the **yo** form of each verb in the present subjunctive.*

1. jugar ______________
2. volver ______________
3. pensar ______________
4. despedir ______________
5. servir ______________
6. pedir ______________
7. divertirse ______________
8. mover ______________
9. cerrar ______________
10. sentirse ______________

EJERCICIO

7·4

*Complete the chart with the **yo** form of each verb in the present subjunctive.*

1. ir ______________
2. ver ______________
3. tener ______________
4. hacer ______________
5. salir ______________
6. haber ______________
7. ponerse ______________
8. decir ______________
9. venir ______________
10. conocer ______________

EJERCICIO
7·5

Change each of the following sentences from English to Spanish.

1. I beg you not to drive so fast.

 ____

2. We're asking them to go with us.

 ____

3. They implore their professor to change the date of the exam.

 ____

4. Are you asking me to leave?

 ____

Express in Spanish the following favors that you might ask of a friend. Use the question form in the present tense.

1. llamar esta noche (a mí) ______________________________
2. llevar a casa (a nosotros) ______________________________
3. ayudar con las maletas (a nosotras) ______________________________
4. mandar una postal (a mí) ______________________________
5. comprar un helado (a mí) ______________________________
6. traer flores (a mí) ______________________________

Change the favors requested in Exercise 7-6 to direct commands. Give two commands for each favor, one in the **tú** *form and one in the* **usted** *form.*

1. ______________________________
2. ______________________________
3. ______________________________
4. ______________________________
5. ______________________________
6. ______________________________

EJERCICIO 7·8

Express in Spanish the following offers that you might make to one person or several people, as indicated.

1. Can I help you? (a ti) ______________________________
2. Can I clean the house for you? (a ustedes) ______________________________
3. Can I take you to the airport? (a vosotros) ______________________________
4. Can I wash your car for you? (a usted) ______________________________

Rewrite each of the following sentences, changing the direct object noun (underlined) into a pronoun.

1. Le estoy enviando un email.

   ____

2. Te doy el dinero la próxima semana.

   ____

3. Nos van a mostrar las fotos de su viaje esta noche.

   ____

4. Él le dice todos sus secretos a su amiga.

   ____

5. Le tengo que entregar la tarea a la profesora mañana.

   ____

6. Les ofrecemos nuestra casa para el verano.

   ____

7. ¿Te presto el dinero?

   ____

8. Ella le enseña español a mi hijo.

   ____

EJERCICIO
7·10

¿Cómo se dice en español? *Express the following in Spanish.*

1. He wants to show you (**tú**) his photos.
2. He wants to show them to you.
3. She's going to teach us the song.
4. She's going to teach it to us.
5. I'm explaining the lesson to her.
6. I'm explaining it to her.
7. I'm going to send him a message.
8. I'm going to send it to him.

¿Cómo se dice en español? *Express the following in Spanish.*

1. Will you lend me your notes?
2. Will you lend them to me?
3. May we borrow your car?
4. May we borrow it?

EJERCICIO
7·12

¿Cómo se dice en español? *Express the following in Spanish.*

1. I miss my friends.

 ____

2. You're going to miss the party.

 ____

3. I don't want to lose my homework.

 ____

4. We're going to miss the bus.

 ____

5. Do you miss your country?

 ____

6. Two books are missing from the list.

 ____

7. She never misses a question.

 ____

8. They're going to lose the game.

 ____

9. They're going to miss the train.

 ____

EJERCICIO
7·13

Circle the most appropriate word or expression to fill in each blank.

1. Te espero a las cinco. ______________.

 Por supuesto   Por cierto   De acuerdo   En cuanto

2. Los llamo ______________ sepa los resultados.

 por supuesto   por cierto   de acuerdo   en cuanto

3. Mira—allí está Diego. ______________, ¿ya sabes que se va a mudar?

 Por supuesto   Por cierto   De acuerdo   En cuanto

4. ¿Me llevas al aeropuerto? ¡______________!

 Por supuesto   Por cierto   Oiga   En cuanto

Express how you would ask five different favors. Ask a Spanish-speaking friend if you have done it correctly.

1. ______________________________
2. ______________________________
3. ______________________________
4. ______________________________
5. ______________________________

Express how you would offer five different favors. Ask a Spanish-speaking friend if you have done it correctly.

1. ______________________________
2. ______________________________
3. ______________________________
4. ______________________________
5. ______________________________

Expressing doubts and uncertainty

·8·

Conversation: Advice to a friend

Gabi: Ema, Estoy muy deprimida. Necesito hablar contigo. Voy a tu casa, si **no te importa**.
Ema, I'm really depressed. I need to talk to you. I'm coming over, if you don't mind.

Ema: Está bien. Te espero.
That's fine. I'll wait for you.

Más tarde:

Ema: Gabi, ¿qué tienes?
Gabi, what's the matter?

Gabi: Es que todo está mal en mi vida. En primer lugar, tengo muchos problemas en el trabajo. Mi jefe se enoja conmigo **cada vez más**. Me regaña por **cualquier** cosa. Estos días no hago nada que le complazca. Me pone tan nerviosa que empiezo a cometer errores innecesarios.
It's just that everything is wrong with my life. In the first place, I have a lot of problems at work. My boss gets madder at me every day. He's on my case for every little thing. Lately I can't do anything that pleases him. He makes me so nervous that I'm beginning to make unnecesary mistakes.

Ema: ¿A qué **se debe** todo eso?
What's the reason for all that?

Gabi: **A lo mejor** es porque él tiene problemas en casa. Pero eso no le da derecho a portarse tan mal conmigo, ¿verdad?
It's probably because he has problems at home. But that doesn't give him the right to take it all out on me, does it?

Ema: Al contrario, es en el trabajo donde debería tener un poco de serenidad para poder solucionar sus problemas personales en casa. **Al menos** es lo que pienso yo.
Quite the contrary, it's at work where he ought to seek a little peace so he can solve his personal problems at home. At least that's what I think.

Gabi: Tengo la impresión que **no hay nadie** que sea realmente feliz. La situación en mi casa **tampoco** me da motivos para alegrarme. ¿Sabes ? Esos dos hombres con quienes comparto la casa **no tienen ni idea** de cómo mantenerla limpia. **No** hacen **nada**. Anoche estuve dos horas limpiando la cocina mientras que ellos comían pizza y veían la televisión. Ya **estoy harta** de sus malas costumbres. Pero eso no es lo peor. **Para colmo**, Roberto ya no quiere hablar conmigo. **A veces** pienso que **no hay nada** en mi vida que realmente valga la pena.
I have the impression that nobody is really happy. The situation at my house doesn't exactly cheer me up either. You know what? Those two guys I share the house with have no idea of how to keep it clean. They don't do anything. Last night I spent two hours cleaning the kitchen while they ate pizza and watched TV. I'm sick of their behavior. But that's not the worst! To top it all off, Roberto refuses to talk to me. Sometimes I think there's nothing truly worthwhile in my life.

Ema: Gabi, tranquilízate y veamos las cosas por orden. **No creo que** las cosas **sean** tan malas como las ves ahora. Para empezar, **te sugiero que hagamos** una lista de las cosas positivas de tu vida. Así, **te darás cuenta** de las ventajas que tienes. Luego haremos un plan para empezar a cambiar las cosas que no te convienen. No deberías deprimirte por lo que tiene solución.

Calm down, Gabi, and let's look at one thing at a time. I don't think things are as bad as they seem right now. For a start, I suggest we make a list of the positive things in your life. That way, you'll realize the advantages that you have. Then we'll make a plan to begin changing the things that aren't working for you. You shouldn't let yourself get depressed.

Gabi: Gracias, Ema. Sabes, ya me siento mucho mejor. Eres una gran amiga.

Thanks, Ema. You know, I already feel much better. You're a great friend.

Ema: **Me importas** mucho. También sé que puedo **contar contigo** para un buen consejo **de vez en cuando.**

I care about you. I also know that I can count on you for good advice from time to time.

Improving your conversation

Importar

Importar can have a number of translations into English. When used with an indirect object, in question form, or as a negative answer, it means *to mind* or *to care,* in the sense of *to be a bother to someone.*

¿**Te importa** si te llamo en la noche?	*Do you mind if I call you at night?*
No **me importa.** Está bien.	*No, I don't mind. It's okay.*

But if it's just a statement, not a response to the question, *Do you mind?,* it means *to not care,* in the sense of *to not be important to someone.*

No me importa si no me llama.	*I don't care if he doesn't call me.*
A él **no le importa** si llueve.	*He doesn't mind if it rains.*

Importar used with an indirect object is also a way to express *to care about/care for something or someone.*

Me importan mucho mis amigos.	*I care a lot about my friends.*
¿Ya no **te importo**?	*Don't you care about me anymore?*

To express *to not matter,* use **importar** without the indirect object.

Está lloviendo.	*It's raining.*
No importa, vamos a jugar de todos modos.	*It doesn't matter. We're going to play anyway.*

To ask someone *what the matter is,* in the sense of *what's wrong,* there are several possible expressions.

¿Qué tiene(s)?
¿Qué te/le pasa?
¿Qué te/le ocurre?

And to tell someone to back off from a private matter, use:

¡Eso **no te/le/les importa**!	*It's none of your business!*

Cada vez más

Cada vez más is a way to express *more and more,* or *gradually getting to be more of a certain quality.*

Me molesta **cada vez más.**	*It bothers me more and more.*
Las lecciones son **cada vez más** complicadas.	*The lessons are more and more complicated.*
El curso es **cada vez más** difícil.	*The course is getting harder and harder.*
La chica es **cada vez más** bonita.	*The girl is getting prettier and prettier.*

Vez is also used in other expressions:

de vez en cuando	*once in a while*
a veces	*sometimes*
una vez	*once*
dos veces	*twice*
tres/cuatro/etc. veces	*three/four/etc. times*
a la vez	*at the same time*
una vez más	*again*
otra vez	*again*
otras veces	*at other times*
la primera vez	*the first time*
la última vez	*the last time*
la próxima vez	*the next time*

No nos vemos con mucha frecuencia, pero ella me llama **de vez en cuando.**	*We don't see each other a lot, but she calls me from time to time.*
A veces nos gusta salir.	*Sometimes we like to go out.*
Ella era mi novia **una vez.**	*She was my girlfriend once.*
Voy a hacer esta tarea solamente **una vez.**	*I'm only going to do this assignment one time.*
Comemos **tres veces** al día.	*We eat three times a day.*
Todas las chicas hablan **a la vez.**	*The girls all talk at the same time/at once.*
Por favor, cántala **una vez más.**	*Please sing it again.*
Por favor, cántala **otra vez.**	*Please sing it again.*
A veces dice que sí; **otras veces** dice que no.	*Sometimes he says yes; other times he says no.*
Esta es **la última vez** que te llamo.	*This is the last time that I'm going to call you.*

Cualquier

Cualquier, generally translated as *any*, is an adjective that has the same form for masculine and feminine nouns.

No dudes en llamarme por **cualquier** cosita.	*Don't hesitate to call me for any little thing.*
Voy a comprar **cualquier** libro que encuentre.	*I'm going to buy any/whatever book I find.*

This adjective changes to **cualquiera** when it occurs *after* a masculine or feminine noun, and has the meaning of *just any old.*

Yo no voy a leer **un libro cualquiera.**	*I'm not going to read just any old book.*
A veces se pone **un vestido cualquiera.**	*Sometimes she puts on just any old dress.*

No

No is used in Spanish before other negative words, unless they are placed at the beginning of a sentence. Some common negative words are:

nada	*nothing*
nadie	*nobody*
nunca	*never*
ninguno, -a	*not a single one*
ni	*not even*
ni... ni	*neither. . . nor*
tampoco	*not either*

¿Qué tienes? — *What do you have?*
Nada. No tengo **nada.** — *Nothing. I don't have anything.*

¿Quién sabe esto? — *Who knows this?*
Nadie. No lo sabe **nadie.** — *No one. No one knows it.*

¿Cuándo te vas a casar? — *When are you getting married?*
Nunca. No me voy a casar **nunca.** — *Never. I'm never getting married.*

¿Quiénes saben la respuesta? — *Who knows the answer?*
No la sabe **ninguno** de los chicos. No la sabe **ninguna** de las chicas. — *None of the boys know it. None of the girls know it.*

Ninguno changes to **ningún** when it is placed *before* a masculine noun, but not before a feminine one.

¿Adónde vas? — *Where are you going?*
No voy a **ningún lugar.**/No voy a **ninguna parte.** — *I'm not going anywhere.*

Ni means *not even.* This can also be expressed with **ni siquiera**.

¿Cuántos amigos tienes en Facebook? — *How many friends do you have on Facebook?*
Ninguno. No tengo **ni** uno. No soy miembro. — *None. I don't have even one. I'm not a member.*
El pobre no tiene **ni siquiera** un lugar donde dormir. — *The poor guy doesn't even have a place to sleep.*

Ni... ni means *neither . . . nor* but can also be translated as *not . . . either.*

El niño no trae **ni lápiz ni cuaderno** a la escuela. — *The child does doesn't bring either a pencil or a notebook to school.*

Tampoco, *not . . . either* is the negative of **también**, *also.*

María no va a la escuela hoy. — *María isn't going to school today.*
Entonces, yo no voy **tampoco.** — *Then I'm not going either.*
Yo **tampoco. Tampoco** va Juan. ¿Va Carlos? — *Me neither. Juan's not going either. Is Carlos going?*
Tampoco. — *(He's not going) either.*

To express *and neither,* use **ni... tampoco.**

Él no baila, **ni su hermano tampoco.**	*He doesn't dance, and neither does his brother.*
Ella no está aburrida, **ni yo tampoco.**	*She's not bored, and neither am I.*

To express that something or somebody does not exist—at least in the opinion of the speaker—the subjunctive is used after a negative expression.

No hay nada en esta tienda que me **guste.**	*There's nothing in this store that I like.*
No conozco a nadie que **cocine** como mi mamá.	*I don't know anybody who cooks like my mother.*
En esta ciudad no hay ningún restaurante que **tenga** pizza como la de Chicago.	*In this city there's not a single restaurant that has Chicago-style pizza.*

Se debe

Se debe indicates *is due to, has been caused by.*

Toda esta destrucción **se debe** al huracán.	*All this destruction is due to the hurricane.*

Deber has a number of functions. You can use it to express *obligation* or *requirement.*

Debemos pagar los impuestos antes del 15 de abril.	*We have to pay our taxes before April 15th.*
Los alumnos **deben** hacer las tareas cada noche.	*The students are required to do the homework every night.*

Speaking of *homework*, remember that both **la tarea** (Latin America) and **el deber** (Spain) refer to *one assignment.* If you have more than one **tarea** or **deber**, then *homework* is expressed as **las tareas** or **los deberes**, which can also be *tasks* or *chores.*

To express *should*, use **deber** in its conditional form, **debería.**

Deberías ir a casa, ya es muy tarde.	*You should go home. It's very late.*

While **deber** can be translated as *to have to,* it is limited to the sense of *being obligated* or *required to.* Other ways of expressing *to have to* include **tener que**, which is more personal.

Debo estar en casa antes de las ocho. Si no, mi mamá se pone nerviosa.	*I have to be home before eight, otherwise my mother gets nervous.*
Tengo que llamar a mi hermana. Le tengo que dar una noticia importante.	*I have to call my sister. I have to tell her some important news.*

Hay que means *have to* or *should* in a very general, impersonal sense.

Hay que tener mucho cuidado en la ciudad por la noche.	*One should be very careful in the city at night./ You should be careful in the city at night.*

A less direct way of giving advice is to use **sugerir**, **aconsejar**, or **recomendar** with an indirect object, followed by **que** and a verb in the subjunctive. The pattern is as follows:

indirect object	+	conjugation of **sugerir /aconsejar/recomendar**	+	**que**	+	subjunctive clause
↓		↓		↓		↓
(A Juan) le		**sugiero**		**que**		**estudie más.**

(To Juan) to him I suggest that he study more.

Le recomiendo que compre estas acciones.	*I recommend that you buy these stocks.*
Les aconsejo que no hagan tanto ruido.	*I advise you all to not make so much noise.*

Expressing doubt

There are a number of ways to express doubt or not being sure of something.

Lo dudo.	*I doubt it.*
Creo que no.	*I don't think so.*
No le creo.	*I don't believe him.*
No lo creo.	*I don't believe it.*
No es posible.	*It's not possible.*
No estoy seguro, -a.	*I'm not sure.*

To express doubt, use a conjugation of **dudar/no creer/no estar seguro, -a** followed by **que** and a subjunctive clause that tells *what you're not sure of* or what you think is *impossible.*

Dudan que esa chica tenga veintiún años.	*They doubt that that girl is twenty-one.*
No creemos que tu hermano esté aquí.	*We don't think your brother is here.*
No estoy segura que él diga la verdad.	*I'm not sure that he's telling the truth.*

Expressions of possibility, impossibility, and probability are also used with a subjunctive verb phrase.

Es posible **que llame** mi amigo.	*My friend might call.*
Es imposible **que salgamos** ahora.	*It's not possible for us to leave now.*
Es probable **que tenga** la gripe.	*She probably has the flu.*

Remember that you use the indicative, rather than the subjunctive, after the expressions **creer que** and **estar seguro, -a que**.

¿Dónde está Miguel?	*Where is Miguel?*
Creo que está en Madrid.	*I think he's in Madrid.*
Estoy seguro que está en Madrid.	*I'm sure he's in Madrid.*

Darse cuenta and realizar

Darse cuenta de que is a common expression that means *to realize* in English.

Me doy cuenta de que tengo que buscar trabajo.	*I realize that I have to look for a job.*

Realizar, on the other hand, means *to carry out, to effect,* or *to make happen.*

El cirujano **realizó** la operación con mucha destreza.	*The surgeon carried out the operation with great skill.*
Por fin **se realizaron** sus sueños.	*Her dreams finally came true.*

A lo mejor

A lo mejor is an expression that means *probably,* or *most likely,* but it is followed by the indicative rather than the subjunctive.

¿Dónde está Roberto?	*Where's Roberto?*
A lo mejor está con sus amigos.	*He's probably with his friends.*

Al menos means *at least.*

Al menos deberías darle la mano.	*You should at least shake his hand.*
Ellos no van a ganar. **Al menos** eso es lo que pienso yo.	*They're not going to win. At least, that's what I think.*

When numbers are involved, it's better to use **por lo menos**.

Existen **por lo menos** tres tipos de nieve.	*There are at least three kinds of snow.*
Vas a necesitar **por lo menos** $200 para el viaje.	*You're going to need at least $200 for the trip.*

In the least, in the sense of *not at all,* is expressed by **en lo más mínimo**.

Eso no me molesta **en lo más mínimo.**	*That doesn't bother me in the least./ I couldn't care less.*

Estar harto

Estar harto, -a de algo/de alguien means *to be fed up with something or somebody.*

¡Vámonos! **Estoy harta de** este lugar.	*Let's go! I'm sick of this place.*
El papá **está harto del** comportamiento de los niños.	*The father is fed up with the children's behavior.*

Para colmo

Para colmo introduces the element that finally causes everything to collapse, like *the straw that broke the camel's back.*

Tengo la gripe, no tengo ningún medicamento, no hay nadie en la casa y **para colmo,** mi teléfono no funciona.	*I have the flu, I don't have any medicine, I'm all alone, and as if that weren't enough, my telephone isn't working.*
¡Esto es **el colmo**!	*That's the last straw!*

Contar

Contar is:

- To count

El niño sabe **contar** de uno a cien.	*The child can count from one to a hundred.*

- To tell a story

Cuéntame de tu juventud.	*Tell me about when you were young.*

- And when followed by **con**, *to count on* or *depend on someone or something.*

Cuenta conmigo. Te voy a llevar la medicina.	*Count on me. I'm going to bring you the medicine.*
Aquí no se puede **contar con** nada. Ahora ni tenemos agua caliente.	*You can't count on anything here. Now we don't even have hot water.*

EJERCICIO 8·1

Match the Spanish expressions in the right column with the English ones in the left column.

1. ______ I don't care. a. No me importa.
2. ______ It doesn't matter. b. ¿Te importa?
3. ______ What's the matter? c. No te importa.
4. ______ That's none of your business. d. Me importas.
5. ______ Do you mind? e. ¿Qué tienes?
6. ______ I care about you. f. No importa.

EJERCICIO 8·2

Fill in each blank with the most appropriate expression using the word **vez**, *in singular or plural form.*

1. El atleta corre ______________ *(faster and faster).*
2. Las dos chicas contestan ______________ *(at the same time).*
3. Esta es ______________ *(the first time)* que te lo pido.
4. ______________ *(Sometimes)* ella va con nosotros, ______________ *(sometimes),* no.
5. ¿Cuántas ______________ *(times)* te lo tengo que repetir?
6. El profesor no da muchos exámenes, pero ______________ *(every once in a while)* nos da una prueba.

EJERCICIO
8·3

*Choose between **cualquier** and **cualquiera** to fill in each blank appropriately.*

1. Ella no se va a casar con un hombre ____________.
2. A mí me gusta ____________ regalo que me dé.
3. No te preocupes, me puedes llamar a ____________ hora.
4. Para la boda, quiero un vestido que valga la pena, no un vestido ____________.

EJERCICIO
8·4

Fill in each blank with the word or expression that most appropriately translates the English words.

1. Estoy completamente solo. No hay ____________ aquí. *(anybody)*
2. Vamos al mercado, pues no tenemos ____________ de comer. *(anything)*
3. ____________ voy a comprender a mi jefe. *(Never)*
4. Yo no estoy de acuerdo, ____________ mi hermano ____________. *(and, neither)*
5. Hoy no vamos a ____________. *(anywhere)*
6. No hay ____________ vendedor de chocolate en el mercado. *(a single)*
7. No hay ____________ un vendedor de chocolate en el mercado. *(even)*
8. ____________ mi mamá ____________ mi papá fuma. *(Neither, nor)*

EJERCICIO
8·5

Complete each sentence from your own personal experience. Ask a Spanish-speaking friend to check your answers.

1. No hay nadie en el mundo que ______________________________.
2. En la ciudad/pueblo donde yo vivo, no existe ______________________________.
3. No conozco a nadie que ______________________________.
4. No quiero comprar nada en la tienda porque no hay nada que ______________________________

   ______________________________.

5. En la habitación donde estoy ahora, no hay ninguna cosa que ______________________

____.

6. En mi trabajo/escuela/casa, no hay ni una persona que ______________________

____.

EJERCICIO 8·6

Using the guidelines below, express the activities that need to be carried out. Use **hay que**, **deber**, **debería**, *or* **tener que** *as appropriate for each category. Ask a Spanish-speaking friend to read your sentences.*

1. What are you obligated or required to do on a regular basis?

____

2. What do you have to do every day?

____

3. What should you do either now or in the near future?

____

4. What is a safety measure required of the general public where you live?

____

EJERCICIO 8·7

Complete the following sentences as directed.

1. A mi mejor amigo le aconsejo que se (olvidar) ______________ de esa chica.
2. El profesor le sugiere a la estudiante que (pasar) ______________ un semestre en el extranjero.
3. Mi amiga me recomienda que (buscar) ______________ otro trabajo.
4. La consejera le recomienda a la chica que (solicitar) ______________ a varias universidades.
5. El médico le aconseja a la mujer que (tranquilizarse) ______________.

EJERCICIO 8·8

Complete each sentence in your own words. Ask a Spanish-speaking friend to read your sentences.

1. A mi mejor amigo le recomiendo que ______________________________.
2. A mi jefe/profesor/padre le sugiero que ______________________________.
3. A las personas que viven en mi barrio les aconsejo que ______________________________
______________________________.
4. Al presidente del país le recomiendo que ______________________________.

EJERCICIO 8·9

Complete the following sentences as directed.

1. El profesor duda que su alumno (poner) ______________ atención en la clase.
2. El alumno cree que (sacar) ______________ muy buenas notas.
3. Nuestros vecinos no dudan que nuestro barrio (ser) ______________ uno de los más seguros de la ciudad.
4. Yo no estoy segura que (ser) ______________ cierto.
5. Mis amigas no creen que sus niños (asistir) ______________ a las mejores escuelas.
6. Es probable que (haber) ______________ mejores escuelas en otras ciudades.
7. A lo mejor el alcalde (estar) ______________ haciendo todo lo posible para mejorar las escuelas.
8. Es probable que nosotros (mudarse) ______________ en julio o agosto.

EJERCICIO 8·10

¿Cómo se dice en español? *Fill in each blank with the Spanish equivalent of the indicated expression.*

1. Él ______________ de la víolencía en esta ciudad. *(is fed up with)*
2. Hay ______________ cinco robos cada día. *(at least)*
3. ______________ deberíamos saludarlo. *(At least)*

4. Primero, pierdo el bus y llego tarde a la oficina, luego mi jefe me despide del trabajo y ______________, mi mejor amiga se enoja conmigo. *(to top it all off)*
5. ______________ sé que puedo ______________ mi esposo. *(At least, count on)*

EJERCICIO
8·11

Imagine that you have an interview with the mayor of your town or city. Use the verbs **aconsejar**, **recomendar**, *and* **sugerir** *to give him or her five suggestions for making improvements to the town or city. Ask a Spanish-speaking friend to read your work.*

____

____

____

____

____

Talking about future events

·9·

Conversation: Seeking a professor's advice

KATY: Profesora Martínez, ¿tiene usted tiempo para hablar un rato conmigo?

Professor Martínez, do you have time to talk to me for a few minutes?

P. MARTÍNEZ: Sí, Katy, **voy a estar** libre hasta mediodía, así que no hay apuro. ¿Qué se te ofrece?

Yes, Katy, I'm going to be free until noon, so there's no rush. What can I do for you?

KATY: Es que me encanta su clase y **estoy pensando especializarme** en la lengua española. ¿Usted cree que tengo el talento suficiente como para **llegar** algún día **a ser** profesora de español?

It's that I love your class, and I'm thinking about majoring in Spanish. Do you think I have the ability to become a Spanish teacher one day?

P. MARTÍNEZ: Claro que lo creo. Me alegra mucho saber que te interesaría especializarte en la lengua española. Te advierto que no te **harás** rica si te dedicas a ser profesora, pero **tendrás** una satisfacción enorme. Para mí, es la mejor profesión.

Of course I think so. I'm so happy to hear that you are interested in majoring in Spanish. I warn you that you probably won't get rich if you devote your life to being a teacher, but you will have enormous satisfaction. I think it's the best profession.

KATY: ¿Qué me recomienda que haga? Estoy en mi segundo año en la universidad y este es mi cuarto semestre de español.

What do you recommend that I do? I'm a sophomore and this is my fourth semester of Spanish.

P. MARTÍNEZ: Mira, después de este semestre, **sabrás** lo básico de la gramática española. Como es imprescindible que estudies por lo menos un semestre en el extranjero, te recomiendo que lo hagas **cuanto antes**, o sea, el próximo semestre. Y si realmente quieres ser profesora de la lengua, te aconsejo que vayas a España durante seis meses y que luego pases otro semestre en uno de los países hispanoamericanos. Así **lograrás ser** completamente bilingüe dentro de un año. Después, **cuando vuelvas**, **completarás** en tu último año los cursos y créditos que hagan falta para tu título.

Look, after this semester, you'll know all the basics of Spanish grammar. Since it's absolutely necessary that you do at least one semester abroad, I recommend that you do it as soon as possible, I mean, next semester. And if you really do want to be a Spanish teacher, I advise you to go to Spain for six months and after that do another semester in one of the Spanish-speaking Latin-American countries. That way, you'll be completely bilingual in just one year. After that, when you come back, you'll finish the courses and credits that you need for your degree in your senior year.

KATY: Todo esto me emociona mucho, pero no sé qué pensarán mis padres sobre estar fuera del país durante un año entero.

I'm so excited about all this, but I don't know what my parents will think about my being out of the country for a whole year.

P. MARTÍNEZ: Deberías hablarlo con ellos. **¿Por qué** no preparas una propuesta formal, en la cual les explicas cuáles son tus **metas** para el futuro y cómo **piensas alcanzar** cada una de ellas? Incluye todos los detalles—lo que **piensas estudiar**, donde e incluso cuánto **va a costar** todo y cómo **vas a ayudar** con los gastos. Eres muy buena estudiante y es probable que consigas una beca.

You should talk it over with them. Why not prepare a formal proposal that explains what your goals are for the future and how you plan to achieve each one? Include all the details—what you're planning to study, where, and even how much it's going to cost, and how you're going to help pay for it. You're an excellent student and you can probably get a scholarship.

KATY: Eso sería fantástico. No se imagina lo emocionada que estoy. Ahora mismo **voy a hablarlo** con mi consejero y luego con la Oficina de Study Abroad. Y **cuando tenga** más información, me gustaría hablar otra vez con usted. Muchísimas gracias por todo.

That would be fantastic. You can't imagine how excited I am. I'm going right now to discuss this with my advisor and then to the Study Abroad Office. And when I have more information, I'd like to talk to you more. Thank you so much for everything.

Improving your conversation

El futuro (the future)

There are a number of ways to talk about the future in Spanish. Since no one knows for sure what the future will bring, the different ways of expressing it reflect the speaker's opinion on how probable it is that something will happen. When it is certain (as certain as it can be) that something is going to happen, then the present tense is used. (This is similar to English.)

La película **empieza** a las 8:10. — *The movie starts at 8:10.*
Las clases **terminan** en mayo. — *Classes end in May.*
Roberto **llega** mañana. — *Roberto arrives tomorrow.*
Nos **vamos** el domingo. — *We're leaving on Sunday.*

Likewise, when you want to make a promise or a commitment to do something, use the present tense. (Look how different this is from English!)

Estoy en tu casa a las ocho. — *I'll be at your house at eight o'clock.*
Te **llamo** esta noche. — *I'll call you tonight.*
Le **prestamos** el dinero. — *We'll lend you the money.*
No se lo **digo** a nadie. — *I won't tell anyone.*

When someone has decided or has made plans to do something, a conjugation of **ir + a +** infinitive is used.

Voy a ir a la casa de Antonio a las ocho. — *I'm going to go to Antonio's at eight o'clock.*
Voy a llamar a mi mamá esta noche. — *I'm going to call my mother tonight.*
Ellos **van a prestarnos** el dinero. — *They're going to lend us the money.*
Vamos a cenar juntos el viernes. — *We're going to have dinner together Friday.*

When someone has not yet decided to do something, but is still thinking about it, a conjugation of **pensar/estar pensando** + infinitive is used.

¿Qué **piensas hacer**?	*What are you planning to do?*
Estoy pensando invitar a Ana a cenar.	*I'm thinking about inviting Ana to dinner.*

The negative of this construction is more decisive, and is equivalent to **no ir + a +** infinitive.

No pienso cenar con él.	*I'm not going to eat with him.*
No pensamos hacer el viaje.	*We're not going to take the trip.*

Note that in English it is common to use the present progressive to express plans for the near future. This is not done in Spanish (except in Argentina, where it is!).

¿Qué **vas a hacer** mañana?	*What are you doing tomorrow?*
Voy a trabajar todo el día mañana.	*I'm working all day tomorrow.*

When the activity is too far ahead to plan for, or if someone is a bit ambivalent or uncertain about doing something, the future tense is used. (See the Appendix.)

¿Qué piensas hacer esta noche?	*What are you planning to do tonight?*
No sé, **iré** al cine o a algún club.	*I don't know, maybe I'll go to the movies or to a club.*
Leeré un libro.	*I'll probably read a book.*
Algún día, **llamaré** a Ángela.	*One of these days I'll call Ángela.*

The future tense can also be used to make predictions—definitely the tense that would be used by the fortune-teller reading your palm or telling you what the crystal ball says—but it is also used for just ordinary feelings we might have about what will happen in the future.

Se casará y **tendrá** cuatro hijos.	*You will get married and have four children.*
Su hijo mayor **será** médico.	*Your eldest son will be a doctor.*
Se eliminarán muchas enfermedades.	*Many diseases will be eliminated.*
Habrá diversas fuentes de energía.	*There will be many different sources of energy.*

A question put in the future tense is the best way to express *I wonder . . .*

¿Qué hora **será**?	*I wonder what time it is?*
¿Cuántos años **tendrá** esa mujer?	*I wonder how old that woman is?*
¿Dónde **estará** mi antigua profesora?	*I wonder where my former teacher is?*

The future tense is also used to express *probably/must be/I guess.*

Juan ya **estará** en su casa.	*Juan must be home by now.*
Ustedes **tendrán** hambre.	*You all must be hungry./I guess you're hungry.*
Mis padres **estarán** preocupados.	*My parents must be worried. /I guess my parents are worried.*

Any of these ways to talk about the future can be used in combination with a subjunctive clause that indicates *when* that future action might happen. Common words that introduce these subjunctive clauses include:

cuando	*as soon as/when*
en cuanto	*as soon as/when*
tan pronto como	*as soon as/when*
siempre y cuando	*if and when*

There are two patterns for these sentences. The subjunctive clause can occur:

- After the future clause.

Te llamo **cuando llegue tu hija.**	*I'll call you as soon as your daughter arrives.*
Pensamos ir a la universidad **tan pronto como nos graduemos de la escuela secundaria.**	*We're planning to go to college as soon as we graduate from high school.*
Van a salir **en cuanto termine el programa.**	*They're going to leave as soon as the show is over.*
Los visitaré **cuando vuelva al Perú.**	*I'll visit them when I go back to Perú.*

- Before the future clause.

Cuando llegue tu hija, te llamo.	*As soon as your daughter arrives, I'll call you.*
Tan pronto como nos graduemos de la escuela secundaria, pensamos ir a la universidad.	*As soon as we graduate from high school, we plan to go to college.*
En cuanto termine el programa, van a salir.	*As soon as the program ends, they're leaving.*
Cuando vuelva al Perú, los visitaré.	*When I go back to Perú, I'll visit them.*

Be very careful not to confuse the **cuando** that indicates a future activity (followed by a subjunctive clause) with the **cuando** that indicates *every time that/whenever*, or simultaneous action (followed by an indicative clause.)

Future activity (subjunctive clause)	Simultaneous activities (indicative clause)
Te llamo **cuando llegue al trabajo.** *I'll call you when I get to work.*	Te llamo **cuando llego al trabajo.** *I (always) call you when I get to work.*
Cuando esté en México voy a comprar ese libro. *When I'm in Mexico I'm going to buy that book.*	**Cuando estoy en México** compro libros. *When (Every time that) I'm in Mexico I buy books.*
Cuando ella vuelva a casa, estará contenta. *When/As soon as she comes back home, she'll be happy.*	**Cuando ella vuelve a casa,** está contenta. *When/Whenever she comes back home, she's (always) happy.*

Si

Si without a written accent mark is unstressed, and usually translates to English as *if*. However, to the English speaker, *if* represents *doubt*, while **si** to the Spanish speaker can represent probability—it really does have a relationship with stressed **sí**—or *yes*! Perhaps this is why **si** is followed by the indicative rather than the subjunctive when it refers to possible future action.

Voy a tu casa **si** no apareces.	*I'm coming to your house if you don't show up.*
Pediremos frijoles **si** no hay carne.	*We'll order beans if there's no meat.*

Unstressed **si** is followed by the *imperfect subjunctive* (see the Appendix) when it means *if something were true.*

Si tú supieras la verdad...	*If you knew the truth . . .*
Si mi papá estuviera aquí...	*If my dad were here . . .*
Si yo tuviera dinero...	*If I had money . . .*

Unstressed **si** is also followed by the imperfect subjunctive to express *if something were to happen.*

Si yo fuera a Argentina...	*If I went to Argentina . . .*
Si ellos nos dieran permiso...	*If they gave us permission . . .*
Si consiguiera ese puesto...	*If I got that job . . .*

These clauses are normally used with a clause using the *conditional* (see the Appendix):

Si tú supieras la verdad, **comprenderías.**	*If you knew the truth, you would understand.*
Si mi papá estuviera aquí, me **enseñaría** a hacerlo.	*If my dad were here, he would show me how to do it.*
Si yo tuviera dinero, **compraría** un coche.	*If I had money, I would buy a car.*
¿Qué **harías** si fueras a Argentina?	*What would you do if you went to Argentina?*
Si yo fuera a Argentina, **hablaría** español todo el tiempo.	*If I went to Argentina, I would speak Spanish all the time.*
Si ellos nos dieran permiso, nos **quedaríamos** un año.	*If they gave us permission, we would stay for a year.*
Si consiguiera ese puesto, **podríamos** comprar una casa.	*If I got that job, we could buy a house.*

Meta

A **meta** is a *goal*—it can even be a *soccer goal*—something we dream about achieving and work hard to reach. *Reaching a goal* is expressed with the verb **alcanzar**.

Voy a trabajar muy duro para alcanzar todas mis **metas.**	*I'm going to work hard to achieve all my goals.*
Su **meta** es ser arquitecto. Lo alcanzará porque es un joven decidido.	*His goal is to be an architect. He'll achieve it because he's a determined young man.*

Alcanzar

Alcanzar can also mean *to reach* a person you've been trying to communicate with, *to reach* something that's up high, or *to catch up with* somebody.

Voy a invitar a Marta si la puedo **alcanzar.**	*I'm going to invite Marta if I can reach her.*
Necesito un libro que está arriba, pero no lo puedo **alcanzar.**	*I need a book that's up there, but I can't reach it.*
Jacinto está bastante alto. Muy pronto **alcanzará** a su papá.	*Jacinto is pretty tall. Soon he'll be as tall as his father.*

Lograr

Lograr is another verb that indicates *achieving*, usually with some struggle.

Espero que **logre** convencerlos.	*I hope she is able to convince them.*
Voy a **lograr** que me paguen el dinero que me deben.	*I'm going to make sure they pay me the money they owe me.*

It can be followed by an infinitive and then means *to manage to.*

Logramos llegar a San Antonio en tres días.	*We managed to get to San Antonio in three days.*

Llegar a ser

Llegar a ser means *to become*, involving a good deal of effort and/or time.

Si te dedicas al trabajo, **llegarás a ser** presidente de la compañía.	*If you devote yourself to the job, you'll become the president of the company.*

Another way to express *become* is **hacerse**, which is more general. It could require effort, but it could also be just what naturally happens.

El hombre **se hizo** rico y famoso.	*The man became rich and famous.*
El hombre **se hizo** viejo.	*The man got old.*

Cuanto antes

Cuanto antes means *as soon as possible.* Other expressions that indicate urgency of action are **lo antes posible** and **en seguida** *(as soon as possible/right away).*

Deberías denunciarlos a la policía **cuanto antes**.	*You should report them to the police as soon as possible.*
Ven a casa **en seguida**.	*Come home right away.*

Por

Por has many functions. It can indicate an exchange of something for something else.

Te doy seis dólares **por** el cuadro.	*I'll give you six dollars for the picture.*

Remember that *please* uses **por**, and *thank you* is followed by **por**:

Por favor, ayúdenos.	*Please help us.*
Gracias **por ayudarnos**.	*Thank you for helping us.*

Por qué

Por qué asks for the *reason* or *motive* of an action (something that has already happened), and **por** indicates the answer.

¿**Por qué** llegaste tan tarde?	*Why were you so late?*
Por la lluvia.	*Because of the rain.*

Para

Para also has many functions, which usually indicate something that is *ahead*, either in time or location.

¿Vas a estudiar **para** un título?	*Are you going to study for a degree?*
Voy **para** la biblioteca.	*I'm going toward the library.*

In the same vein, **para** followed by an infinitive means *in order to.*

Voy a estudiar **para** aprender todo lo que pueda.	*I'm going to study in order to learn everything I can.*

EJERCICIO
9·1

Write the Spanish future tense forms for the following verbs.

1. estar (yo) ________________
2. ser (él) ________________
3. ir (ellos) ________________
4. querer (nosotros) ________________
5. decir (tú) ________________
6. aparecer (ella) ________________
7. escribir (nosotros) ________________
8. poner (ellos) ________________
9. pensar (yo) ________________
10. salir (nosotros) ________________
11. hacer (vosotros) ________________
12. volver (ustedes) ________________
13. venir (él) ________________
14. comer (tú) ________________
15. tener (yo) ________________

EJERCICIO 9·2

Match the English expressions in the left column with the most appropriate Spanish expressions in the right column.

1. ______ Help me.
2. ______ I help you (every day).
3. ______ I'm going to help you (tomorrow).
4. ______ I'll help you (one of these days).
5. ______ I'll help you (tomorrow).

a. Te ayudaré.
b. Ayúdame.
c. Te voy a ayudar.
d. Te ayudo.

Express the following sentences in Spanish.

1. You will get married and have twins.

   ____

2. The party is at three o'clock.

   ____

3. We're leaving tomorrow.

   ____

4. I'll buy a car one day.

   ____

5. I'll call you tonight.

   ____

6. They're going to move to this building next week.

   ____

7. What are you planning to do?

   ____

8. I'm thinking about sending him an e-mail.

   ____

9. I wonder what she's doing.

   ____

10. She's probably working at a hospital.

    ____

EJERCICIO
9·4

Choose between the indicative and the subjunctive to complete the following sentences.

1. Veremos la película en cuanto los niños (estar) _____________ dormidos.
2. Ella siempre me llama si (tener, ella) _____________ un problema.
3. ¿Qué harás si el profesor nos (dar) _____________ un examen mañana?
4. Voy a estudiar tan pronto como (llegar, yo) _____________ a la biblioteca.
5. Los contactaré tan pronto como (salir, yo) _____________ del avión.
6. Te compro un helado si (portarse, tú) _____________ bien.
7. La niña se pone roja cuando la maestra le (hacer, ella) _____________ una pregunta.
8. No vamos en el metro cuando (llover) _____________.
9. Iremos en el carro si (llover) _____________.
10. Abriré el paraguas cuando (empezar) _____________ a llover.

EJERCICIO
9·5

Write the Spanish imperfect subjunctive forms of the following verbs.

1. abrir (ellos) _____________
2. saber (yo) _____________
3. correr (tú) _____________
4. enseñar (ella) _____________
5. dormirse (él) _____________
6. volver (nosotros) _____________
7. traer (yo) _____________
8. ser (usted) _____________
9. ir (ustedes) _____________
10. pensar (tú) _____________
11. poder (ellos) _____________
12. querer (vosotros) _____________
13. leer (yo) _____________
14. comprender (ella) _____________
15. sentirse (él) _____________

EJERCICIO

9·6

Write the Spanish conditional forms of the following verbs.

1. dar (él) ____________________
2. decir (ella) ____________________
3. vender (nosotros) ____________________
4. venir (ustedes) ____________________
5. poder (yo) ____________________
6. hacer (vosotros) ____________________
7. ir (yo) ____________________
8. bailar (tú) ____________________
9. encontrarse (ellos) ____________________
10. conocer (ellas) ____________________
11. deber (nosotros) ____________________
12. pagar (ella) ____________________
13. invitar (él) ____________________
14. enojarse (yo) ____________________
15. aburrirse (él) ____________________

EJERCICIO

9·7

Use the conditional and the imperfect subjunctive to fill in the blanks.

1. Si (tener, yo) ______________ tiempo, te (ayudar, yo) ______________.
2. Si (saber, tú) ______________ la verdad, (enojarse, tú) ______________.
3. Si (estar, nosotros) ______________ en clase, (estar, nosotros) ______________ haciendo el examen.
4. Si (hacer, yo) ______________ un esfuerzo, (ser, yo) ______________ mejor estudiante.
5. Si el profesor (ser, él) ______________ más simpático, no nos (asignar, él) ______________ tanta lectura para el fin de semana.

EJERCICIO
9·8

Fill each blank with **por** *or* **para**, *as appropriate.*

1. ______ favor, enséñame a bailar salsa.
2. Gracias ______ acompañarnos.
3. ______ alcanzar sus metas, tendrá que trabajar duro.
4. Ella pagó cien dólares ______ los zapatos.
5. ¿______ qué pagaste tanto?
6. ¿______ qué quieres ir al banco?
7. Vamos ______ Filadelfia ______ ver la Campana de Libertad.

EJERCICIO
9·9

Write down a possible conversation you might have with a teacher, friend, or relative in which you tell your ideas about your future. Include what is already established (a date of graduation, perhaps), what you are thinking about doing, what you have already planned to do, and what you might do one day. You might add that if something else were true or possible, your plans would be different. You may want to ask this person to help you in some way, and at the end, make a promise to him or her. Be careful not to translate from English, but rather use the guidelines suggested in this chapter for expressing the likelihood of different aspects of your future. Ask a Spanish-speaking friend to read your conversation and comment on your expression.

____

____

____

____

____

____

____

____

Making a case or arguing a point

Conversation: Selecting a company officer

JAVIER: Hoy estamos aquí para hablar de la selección del nuevo director del Departamento de Información y Reclamaciones. Como bien saben ustedes, **actualmente** hay dos candidatas, Marta Gutiérrez e Yvonne Piñeiro. Primero hablaremos de Marta. ¿Qué **opinan** ustedes de su candidatura?	*We're here today to talk about the selection of a new director for the Customer Service Department. As you know, at present there are two candidates, Marta Gutiérrez and Yvonne Piñeiro. First, we'll talk about Marta. What do you think of her candidacy?*
BELÉN: Yo creo que Marta es la persona perfecta para este puesto. Lleva ya veinte años trabajando aquí, **de modo que** conoce bien los negocios de la empresa. Es una persona formal y seria y **además**, se lleva bien con todos los empleados.	*Marta seems to me to be the perfect person for this position. She's been with the company for twenty years, so she knows the business well. She's conservative and serious, plus she gets along well with all the employees.*
CATI: Bueno, **para mí**, si ella es la nueva directora, nada cambiará. Es decir, no veríamos ninguna idea nueva, **por el contrario**, seguiríamos aplicando los mismos programas de siempre. **Es más**, perderíamos los clientes que tenemos, simplemente porque nuestros competidores tienen gente dinámica y programas innovadores.	*Well, in my opinion, if she becomes director, nothing will change. I mean, we wouldn't see any new ideas— just the opposite—we'd keep on implementing the same programs as always. Even more than that, we'd lose our current customer base, simply because our competitors have enthusiastic new people and innovative programs.*
DAVID: Yo estoy de acuerdo con Cati. **Por una parte**, Marta es demasiado conservadora **y por otra**, no despertaría el entusiasmo de los empleados.	*I agree with Cati. In the first place, Marta is too conservative, and furthermore, she wouldn't inspire any enthusiasm among the employees.*
JAVIER: Bien. Ahora díganme qué piensan de Yvonne para este puesto.	*OK. Now tell me what you think of Yvonne for this position.*

Belén: Miren ustedes, si le damos este puesto a Yvonne, sería un desastre para la empresa. En primer lugar, **aunque** ella **tenga** un título de una universidad prestigiosa, no tiene la experiencia necesaria para un puesto tan importante. **Además**, no la conocemos bien, pues sólo trabaja aquí desde febrero de este año. Y **por si fuera poco**, bien saben ustedes que la **despidieron** de su trabajo anterior.

Look, if we give the job to Yvonne, it will be a disaster for the company. In the first place, even though she has a fancy degree, she doesn't have the experience necessary for such an important job. Besides, we don't even know her very well, I mean, she's only been here since last February. And to top it all off, you all know that she was fired from her last job.

Cati: **Por cierto**, he oído que sus colegas piensan que es bastante presumida, que se cree la reina de la oficina. No es muy popular, **que digamos**, entre los empleados. No creo que la acepten como jefa.

As a matter of fact, I've heard that her coworkers think she's a bit too sure of herself, that she thinks she's the queen of the office. She's not exactly popular with the other employees. I don't think they'll be happy with her as the boss.

David: Pues, como la nominé yo, les tengo que decir que la veo como una persona muy inteligente y competente. No obstante, reconozco que le falta experiencia. Y ahora que me dicen que su personalidad podría causar fricciones entre los empleados, apoyaré su decisión en este caso.

Well, since I put her name up, I have to say that I see her as a very bright and competent person. But I do recognize that she lacks experience. And now that you tell me that her personality could cause friction among the employees, then I'll go along with your decision in this case.

Javier: **Evidentemente** no hemos encontrado todavía **la persona indicada** para este puesto. Es posible que tengamos que buscar fuera de la empresa, algo que **en el fondo** no quisiera hacer. Nos reuniremos aquí mañana a la misma hora. Esperaré sus propuestas—¡y **que** sean más esperanzadoras!

Obviously we haven't found the ideal person for this position yet. We may have to look outside the company, which I don't particularly want to do. We'll meet here tomorrow at the same time. I'll expect your suggestions—and they'd better be more promising!

Improving your conversation

Actualmente

This is a true **falso amigo**, as it does not mean *actually*, but rather *right now, at the moment*, or *currently*.

Actualmente, tenemos ciento setenta y cinco empleados. — *Currently, we have a hundred and seventy-five employees.*

Opinar que

Opinar que means *to be of the opinion that.*

Opino que no es una buena idea. — *In my opinion, it's not a good idea.*

Another way to express an opinion is by introducing it with **para** + personal pronoun: **mí/ti/usted/él/ella/nosotros, -as/vosotros, -as/ellos, -as**.

Para mí, no es una buena idea. — *In my opinion, it's not a good idea.*

You could also use **pensar que** or **creer que**.

Pienso que/Creo que es una buena candidata.	*I think she's a good candidate.*

If you use either of these expressions after **no**, the next verb should be in the subjunctive.

No pienso/No creo que **sea** una buena candidata.	*I don't think she's a good candidate.*

De modo que

De modo que is an expression that means *so much so, that . . . .*

Tenía frío, **de modo que** me puse un suéter.	*I was cold, so I put a sweater on./I was so cold that I put a sweater on.*
Era un tipo bastante estudioso, **de modo que** quiso ir a una universidad prestigiosa.	*He was a pretty studious fellow, so he wanted to go to a prestigious university.*

Por una parte... y por otra

This combination is a common way to give two reasons to back up your point. It can be translated as *for one thing . . . and for another* or *in the first place . . . and furthermore/also.*

Debemos ascenderlo. **Por una parte,** lleva años trabajando aquí **y por otra,** es el sobrino del presidente de la empresa.	*We have to promote him. For one thing, he's been working here for years, and for another—he's the nephew of the president of the company.*

Además

This word is used to introduce additional information that helps get a point across. It is usually translated as *plus, in addition,* or *besides.*

Quiero contratarlo. Es inteligente, preparado y **además,** muy trabajador.	*I want to hire him. He's smart, educated, and, in addition, a hard worker.*
No quiero ver esa película. Tiene mucha violencia, es larga y **además,** no tiene ningún actor conocido.	*I don't want to see that movie. It has a lot of violence, it's long, and besides, it doesn't have a single well-known actor.*

Es más

Es más is used to add information to an argument that is more important than the previous information.

Tengo muchas ganas de ver la película. Es una comedia romántica y tiene mi actor favorito. **Es más,** fue nominada para un Óscar.	*I really want to see the movie. It's a romantic comedy and it has my favorite actor. Plus, it was nominated for an Oscar.*

Por si fuera poco

This expression introduces the final, and strongest, reason to support an argument. It can be used for either a positive or a negative argument.

Voy a aceptar el puesto. El trabajo es interesante, paga bien y **por si fuera poco,** me darán seis semanas de vacaciones al año.

I'm going to take the position. The work is interesting, it pays well, and as if that weren't enough, they'll give me six weeks of vacation every year.

In Spain it is also common to use **encima** for the same purposes.

El trabajo es interesante y paga bien. **Encima**, ¡es en París!

The work is interesting and it pays well. To top it all off—it's in Paris!

To introduce a superlative like this for a negative argument, you can use **para colmo**.

Él no es un caballero, que digamos. Llegó tarde para la cita, no se disculpó, pasó todo el tiempo hablando por su celular y **para colmo,** ni se ofreció para llevarme a mi casa después de la fiesta.

He's not exactly a gentleman. He was late for the date, he didn't apologize, he spent the whole time talking on his cell, and to top it all off, he didn't even offer to take me home after the party.

Por el contrario

This expression indicates that what follows is the opposite of what was said before.

No es un buen jugador, **por el contrario**, ni sabe las reglas del juego.

He's not a good player—just the opposite, he doesn't even know the rules of the game.

Bien

Bien is used here to mean *OK* or *understood*—as an acknowledgment of what was previously said. In Spain, **vale** is often used instead.

La decisión está hecha. Ya no hay nada más que hacer.

The decision is made. Nothing else can be done.

Bien/Vale. Vámonos, entonces.

OK. Then let's go.

En primer lugar

En primer lugar introduces a first reason to support an argument, like *in the first place,* or *first of all.*

No voy a quedarme aquí. **En primer lugar,** no hay trabajo para mí aquí.

I'm not staying here. In the first place, there's no work for me here.

Aunque

Remember that **aunque**, which means *even though/although,* is followed by the subjunctive when it introduces information that is already known to the listeners.

Aunque no haya trabajo aquí para ti, yo te puedo mantener.

Although there's no work for you here, I can support you.

Aunque is followed by the indicative when the information is news to the listeners.

Aunque te agradezco la oferta, que es muy generosa, voy a volver a la ciudad.

Although I appreciate your offer, which is very generous, I'm going back to the city.

Ni

This word means *not even*, to point out an unusual example.

Y ¿qué va a hacer José?	*So what's José going to do?*
Ni José sabe la respuesta a esa pregunta.	*Not even José knows the answer to that question.*

Ni siquiera can be used with the same meaning.

Ni siquiera José sabe la respuesta.	*Not even José knows the answer.*

Ni... ni means *neither . . . nor.*

Ni Susana ni su hermana aparecieron en la fiesta.	*Neither Susana nor her sister showed up at the party.*

Despedir

When used without a reflexive pronoun, this verb means *to fire/let go* (from a job). An alternative verb is **correr**, but this is more like *to kick out*—not only from a job, but also from a place.

Me despidieron por faltar tantos días cuando estaba enfermo.	*They fired me for missing so many days when I was sick.*
Y ¿qué haces tú por aquí?	*And what are you doing here?*
Me corrió Lisa.	*Lisa kicked me out.*

Despedirse, used with a reflexive pronoun, means *to say good-bye.*

Ahora tengo que **despedirme** de ti.	*Now I have to say good-bye to you.*
Me sentí muy triste cuando **nos despedimos.**	*I felt really sad when we said good-bye.*

Por cierto

Por cierto is used when you want to insert new information about the topic into the conversation.

Vamos a San Juan para el descanso de primavera.	*We're going to San Juan for spring break.*
Por cierto, yo fui allá el año pasado, y me encantó.	*As a matter of fact, I went there last year, and I loved it.*

Creerse

Creerse, used with a reflexive pronoun, indicates that someone is a little *stuck* on himself or herself.

Ella es simpática, pero su hermano **se cree** mucho.	*She's nice, but her brother is really conceited.*
Ese tipo **se cree** irresistible para las mujeres.	*That guy thinks he's God's gift to women.*

Que digamos

This expression can be inserted after a negative statement to mean *not exactly* in a sarcastic way. It could also be translated as *you might say that.*

Esa profesora no es un genio, **que digamos.**	*That teacher isn't exactly a genius./You might say that that teacher is no genius.*

No obstante

No obstante is an expression that the obstacle to a conclusion that was just stated has been overcome. It is usually translated as *nevertheless* or *still.*

Hacía mal tiempo y llovía durante todo el trayecto. **No obstante,** llegamos a tiempo.	*The weather was awful and it rained throughout the whole trip. Nevertheless, we made it on time.*

Faltar

Faltar (like **gustar**), when used with an indirect object pronoun, indicates *what is lacking to someone.* It is better translated as *to need* or *to not have what's necessary.*

No puedo continuar estudiando, pues **me falta** el dinero.	*I can't keep on studying—I don't have the money (the money is lacking to me).*

Hacerle falta a uno is used in the same way, with the same meaning.

Me hace falta el dinero necesario para seguir estudiando.	*I don't have the money I need to keep on studying.*

Faltar without an indirect object is used to indicate a period of time or an amount of something needed to make up a whole entity.

No podemos participar en el partido, pues **faltan** tres jugadores.	*We can't play the game—we need three more players.*
Tenemos que seguir luchando. Sólo **faltan** dos semanas para las elecciones.	*We have to keep working. There are only two weeks left until the election.*

Evidentemente

Evidentemente is a little bit of a **falso amigo**, as its meaning is closer to *obviously* than *evidently.*

Faltan dos jugadores, así que no vamos a poder jugar.	*We're lacking two players, so we're not going to be able to play.*
¡Evidentemente!	*Obviously!*

Evidently is better translated as **por lo visto.**

Por lo visto, Carlos y Sergio no van a aparecer.	*Evidently, Carlos and Sergio aren't going to show up.*

La persona indicada

La persona indicada is a way of saying *the ideal person for a specific purpose.* It could also be **la mujer indicada, el hombre indicado, el profesor indicado**, and so on.

El pianista tiene mucha paciencia. Parece ser **el maestro indicado** para mi hijo. — *The pianist is very patient. He seems to be the ideal teacher for my son.*

This could also refer to an object or a place that is perfect for a specific purpose.

Este club es muy elegante. Creo que es **el lugar indicado** para la recepción. — *This club is so elegant. I think it's the perfect place for the reception.*

Es posible que

Es posible que as well as **es probable que** are followed by a verb in the subjunctive.

Es posible que llueva mañana. — *It might rain tomorrow.*
Es probable que llueva mucho este mes. — *It will probably rain a lot this month.*

En el fondo

En el fondo can be translated as *basically, as a matter of principle*, or as *down deep*, when it refers to a gut feeling.

En el fondo, no quisiera viajar mucho en el trabajo porque tengo niños pequeños. — *Basically, I'd rather not travel a lot in my job because I have small children.*
En el fondo, creo que es el hombre indicado para ti. — *Down deep, I think he's the right man for you.*

¡Que... !

An expression with **que...** plus a verb in the subjunctive is often used as a final blessing or warning.

Que le vaya bien. — *May all go well with you.*
Que tenga un buen día. — *Have a nice day.*
Que la pases bien./**Que te diviertas.** — *Have a good time.*
¡**Que encuentres** trabajo! — *I hope you get a job!*

Circle the correct verb to complete each sentence.

1. Ahora tenemos que ______________.
   despedir despedirnos
2. Como Pablo no trabaja bien, lo tenemos que ______________.
   despedir despedirse

3. Él es muy presumido, ______________ mucho.

cree   se cree

4. Él es muy presumido, ______________ que es el único chico guapo en toda la escuela.

cree   se cree

5. No puedo terminar la tesis. ______________ el tiempo para hacer la investigación.

Me falta   Falta

6. Es muy tarde para estudiar. ______________ una hora para el examen.

Me falta   Falta

EJERCICIO
10·2

Circle the most appropriate expression for each blank.

1. Creo que es muy listo y ______________, muy simpático.

no obstante   además   por una parte   es más

2. Sólo queda un minuto en el partido. ______________, vamos a ganar.

Por cierto   Aunque   Es más   Evidentemente

3. El curso fue muy difícil para él, ______________, pasó con una buena nota.

no obstante   por el contrario   por lo visto   de modo que

4. El curso fue muy difícil para él, ______________ no sacó una buena nota.

no obstante   por el contrario   por lo visto   de modo que

5. En matemáticas ella es un desastre, pues ______________ sabe sumar y restar.

por cierto   evidentemente   aunque   ni

6. Él no es un experto, ______________, pues no sabía solucionar el problema.

que digamos   no obstante   de modo que   por otra parte

7. ______________, es un experto ______________, está listo para trabajar.

por una parte... y por otra   ni... ni

8. ______________ es un experto, ______________ está listo para trabajar.

por una parte... y por otra   ni... ni

9. Vamos a contratarla, ______________ no tenga experiencia.

aunque   por el contrario   además   es más

EJERCICIO 10·3

Fill in each blank with the most appropriate of the following expressions.

actualmente   de modo que   es más   por el contrario   no obstante

1. Todos estamos muy impresionados con la nueva candidata, ______________ le vamos a ofrecer el puesto.
2. Estamos muy impresionados con la nueva candidata, ______________, no le vamos a ofrecer el puesto.
3. Yo lo apoyo incondicionalmente. Es un hombre responsable y honrado. ______________, es mi mejor amigo.
4. Yo no quiero ascenderlo, ______________, creo que lo deberíamos despedir.
5. Ese señor es ______________ el presidente de la empresa, pero se va a jubilar *(retire)* el próximo mes.

EJERCICIO 10·4

¿Qué opinas de la dieta vegetariana? *Complete the following sentences with your opinion. Ask a Spanish-speaking friend to read your answers.*

1. Opino que ____.
2. No pienso que ____.
3. Creo que ____.
4. Para mí, ____.

¿Cómo se dice en español? *Translate the following sentences into Spanish.*

1. Basically, I think it's a mistake.

   ____

2. We think he's the perfect person for the job.

   ____

3. To be honest with you, I don't think she's the girl for you.

   ____

4. I don't know anybody in this city, I don't have a job or a place to live, and as if that weren't enough, I don't speak the language.

 ___

 ___

5. This isn't exactly the best job in the world.

 ___

6. Have a good day!

 ___

Complete the following sentences in your own words, thinking of a topic about which you care a lot. Do not worry about the order of the sentences at this point, but rather think of them as individual sentences.

1. Opino que ___.
2. Para mí, ___.
3. Por una parte, ___.
4. y por otra, ___.
5. Además, ___.
6. Es más, ___.
7. Aunque ___.
8. Por cierto, ___.
9. No obstante, ___.
10. Por lo visto, ___.
11. Evidentemente, ___.
12. Por el contrario, ___.
13. Ni ___, ni ___.
14. ___ de modo que ___.

EJERCICIO
10·7

Now arrange at least eight of your sentences from Exercise 10-6 into a cohesive paragraph, placing them in a logical order. Make a convincing argument for your cause! Ask a Spanish speaker to comment on the result.

____

____

____

____

____

____

____

____

Narrating a story

·11·

Conversation: A traffic accident

PABLO: Amigo, ¿qué te **pasó**? ¿**Se te rompió** la pierna?	*Hey buddy, what happened to you? Did you break your leg?*
JESÚS: Hola, Pablo. No, no es tan dramático. Sólo **me torcí** el tobillo. **Sin embargo**, me duele bastante y es muy incómodo andar con estas muletas.	*Hi Pablo. No, it's not that drastic. I just twisted my ankle. Still, it hurts a lot and walking with these crutches is so uncomfortable.*
PABLO: ¿Cuándo te **pasó** eso?	*When did it happen?*
JESÚS: **Fue** la noche del campeonato de **básquetbol**. Y **lo peor** es que **perdimos** el partido y las esperanzas de recuperar el título.	*It was the night of the basketball championship. And the worst thing is that we lost the game and all hopes of winning our title back.*
PABLO: Sentémonos aquí un rato y cuéntame cómo **sucedió** todo.	*Let's sit down for a minute and tell me how it all happened.*
JESÚS: Bueno, todo **ocurrió el jueves pasado**. **Era** un día lluvioso y además **hacía** mucho frío. Yo **quería** llegar temprano al gimnasio para estar bien preparado para el partido. **Estaba** un poco preocupado por el partido cuando **salía** de casa, pero **subí** al **carro** y **empecé** a manejar hacia el gimnasio. **De repente sonó** mi celular—**era** mi novia. Ella **estaba** muy entusiasmada por el partido y me **quería** desear buena suerte. **Empecé** a **sentirme** fuerte y preparado para el partido. Mi novia y yo **seguíamos conversando** cuando **de repente me di cuenta** que los carros que **iban** delante **estaban** parados y yo **iba manejando** un poco rápido. **Frené** fuerte, pero ya **era** demasiado tarde. La carretera **estaba** mojada y **choqué** con el carro que **estaba** parado delante. Por la fuerza del frenazo, **me torcí** el tobillo. Me **costó** mucho trabajo salir del carro para hablar con el conductor del otro **carro**, pues me **dolía** mucho el tobillo. La verdad, en ese momento, no **sabía**	*Well, it all happened last Thursday. It was a rainy day and it was also freezing. I wanted to get to the gym early to be ready for the game. I was a little worried about the game when I left home, but I got in the car and started to drive toward the gym. All of a sudden my phone rang—it was my girlfriend. She was all excited about the game and wanted to wish me good luck. I started to feel strong and ready for the game. My girlfriend and I kept on talking when I suddenly realized that the cars in front of me were stopped and I was going a little fast. I slammed on the brakes, but it was too late. The street was wet and I hit the car that was stopped in front of me. That hard braking caused me to twist my ankle. I could hardly get out of the car to talk to the other driver because my ankle hurt so much. To tell you the truth, I didn't know what to do. I was thinking about the game, about my girlfriend, my teammates—it never occurred to me that I wouldn't be able to*

qué hacer. **Estaba pensando** en el partido, en mi novia, en mis compañeros de equipo, **era** imposible **darme cuenta de que** no **iba a poder** jugar esa noche. Pero **por fin llegó** un policía, me **hizo** firmar unos documentos y **luego** una ambulancia me **llevó** al hospital. Allí me **hicieron** una radiografía para averiguar si el tobillo **estaba** roto o no. Gracias a Dios no **estaba** roto, pero **de todos modos** no **iba** a jugar esa noche. Y ahora tengo que usar estas muletas.

play that night. But a policeman finally came and made me sign some documents, and then an ambulance took me to the hospital. They took some X-rays to see if my ankle was broken or not. Thank goodness it wasn't broken, but at any rate I wasn't going to play that night. And now I have to use these crutches.

PABLO: Hombre, ¡qué mala suerte! Lo siento mucho, de verdad.

Man, what bad luck! I'm sorry, really.

Improving your conversation

Narrating in the past

Both the imperfect tense and the preterite tense are used in telling what happened in the past. Each tense has a specific purpose. It is easier to use these tenses correctly if you think about their purposes rather than try to translate from English. Note that the use of the imperfect tense to describe a special period of the past has a very different set of translations into English from those used in a narration. This is reflected in the fact that in a narration (but not in a description) the imperfect progressive tense can be used as an alternative to the imperfect.

Hablaba/Estaba hablando.	*He was talking.*
Comíamos/Estábamos comiendo.	*We were eating.*

Time expressions used with the past tenses:

ayer	*yesterday*
la semana pasada	*last week*
hace dos días	*two days ago*
anteayer	*the day before yesterday*
el año pasado	*last year*
hace diez minutos	*ten minutes ago*
anoche	*last night*
el viernes pasado	*last Friday*
hace cinco años	*five years ago*

To form the imperfect progressive tense, use the following formula:

IMPERFECT OF **ESTAR** + GERUND OF MAIN VERB

(yo) estaba trabajando *I was working*	(nosotros, -as) estábamos pensando *we were thinking*
(tú) estabas durmiendo *you were sleeping*	(vosotros, -as) estabais jugando *you all were playing*
(él/ella/usted) estaba soñando *he/she/you were dreaming*	(ustedes/ellos, -as) estaban escribiendo *you all/they were writing*

Setting the scene with the imperfect tense

To tell the time and place, to describe the weather, and to tell what was already happening when your story began, use the imperfect tense.

Estábamos en San Antonio.	*We were in San Antonio.*
Hacía mucho calor.	*It was hot.*
Eran las dos de la tarde.	*It was two o'clock in the afternoon.*
Yo **nadaba/estaba** nadando.	*I was swimming.*

Telling what happened with the preterite tense

To tell the events of the story, use the preterite tense. Events are often preceded by expressions that indicate the sequence of the action, the time of the action, or that something triggered the action. These are considered preterite signals.

primero	*first*
después/luego	*after that*
de repente/de pronto/súbitamente	*suddenly*
a las ocho	*at eight o'clock*
finalmente	*finally*

Adding details

There are three patterns in a narration:

- Simultaneous actions: imperfect + imperfect
  To tell that two actions were going on at the same time, put both verbs in the imperfect.

Mientras **manejaba, hablaba** por celular.	*While she was driving, she was talking on her cell phone.*
Cuando yo **estudiaba,** mi amigo **veía** la televisión.	*When I was studying, my friend was watching television.*

- Interrupted action: imperfect + preterite
  To tell that one action was already in progress and that another interrupted it, put the first verb—the action in progress—in the imperfect, and the second verb—the action that interrupts—in the preterite.

Mientras **manejaba, sonó** el celular.	*While she was driving, her cell phone rang.*

- A sequence of uninterrupted actions: preterite + preterite
  To tell actions that happened without relating them to any other actions, put all the verbs in the preterite.

Ella **tomó** un vaso de leche y **fue** a su dormitorio.	*She drank a glass of milk and went to her bedroom.*

Querer, saber, poder, tener, and entender

Certain verbs can be tricky to use in the past, simply because they are not used in a progressive form in English. However, when they indicate simultaneous or interrupted action (or feeling) in Spanish, they require the imperfect tense.

Ella no **quería** ir a la fiesta hasta que Juan la invitó.
She didn't want (wasn't wanting) to go to the party until Juan invited her.

Sabíamos que él le gustaba.
We knew (we were knowing) that she liked (was liking) him.

No **podía** abrir la puerta de mi cuarto así que fui a buscar ayuda.
I couldn't (wasn't being able to) open the door to my room, so I went to look for help. (The situation wasn't resolved.)

Tenía que volver a casa y llamé a mi hermano.
I had (was having) to go home and I called my brother.

Since the preterite tense indicates that an action occurred all of a sudden, or that it resolved the question at hand, it can translate into English as a different word.

Quise llamarte, pero mi celular no funcionaba.
I tried (wanted to and failed) to call you, but my cell didn't work (wasn't working).

¡Yo la invité y ella no **quiso** ir!
I invited her and she refused to go (did not want to go, period)!

Él era muy pequeño cuando **supo** la verdad.
He was (was being) very young when he found out (suddenly knew) the truth.

El asistente en el hotel **pudo** abrir la puerta de mi cuarto.
The assistant at the hotel was able (finally managed) to open the door to my room. (The situation was resolved.)

Mi hermano vino por mí y **tuve** que volver a casa.
My brother came to get me and I had to go home.

Rompérsele la pierna

Since no one breaks a bone on purpose, this phrase is used to indicate that *someone's leg got broken*. The construction is as follows:

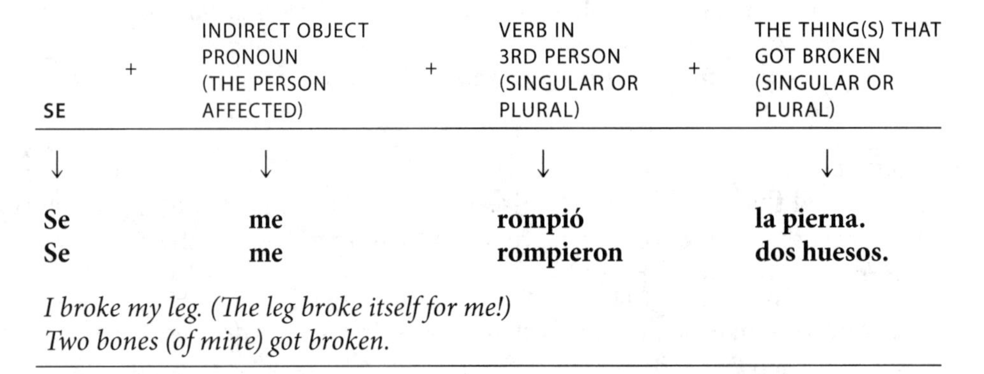

SE	+	INDIRECT OBJECT PRONOUN (THE PERSON AFFECTED)	+	VERB IN 3RD PERSON (SINGULAR OR PLURAL)	+	THE THING(S) THAT GOT BROKEN (SINGULAR OR PLURAL)
↓		↓		↓		↓
Se		**me**		**rompió**		**la pierna.**
Se		**me**		**rompieron**		**dos huesos.**

I broke my leg. (The leg broke itself for me!)
Two bones (of mine) got broken.

Other verbs that blame the accident on the thing rather than on the person include:

- **Quebrársele**, also *to get broken*

  (A mí) se me quebró el brazo. — *My arm got broken.*

- **Olvidársele**, *to have slipped someone's mind/be forgotten*

  (A él) se le olvidó la cita. — *The appointment slipped his mind./He forgot the appointment.*

- **Quemársele**, *to get burned*

  (A ella) se le quemaron los dedos. — *Her fingers got burned./She burned her fingers.*

- **Caérsele**, *to fall from one's hands*

(A nosotros) se nos cayó la caja.	*The box fell from our hands./We dropped the box.*

- **Perdérsele**, *to lose something*

(A usted) ¿se le perdió la tarjeta de crédito?	*Did you lose your credit card?*

- **Quedarse**, *to be left somewhere by mistake*

(A mí) se me quedaron las cartas en el carro.	*The letters were left in the car./I left the letters in the car.*

- **Acabársele**, *to run out of something*

Se me acabó la gasolina.	*I ran out of gas.*

Coche/carro

In Spain, individual automobiles are called **coches**, while in Latin America they are called **carros**. In Spain, *to drive* is **conducir**, while in Latin America **manejar** is used. In Spain, you should never **conducir** while talking on your **móvil**, while in Latin America this wonderful invention is called a **celular**.

Another word in this chapter is different between the two areas: In Spain, they play **baloncesto**. In Latin America, it's **básquetbol**.

Solo

Solo can be used as an alternative for **solamente**, which means *only*.

Solo quería ayudarlo.	*I only wanted to help him.*

Solo can also be a masculine singular adjective. The feminine form is **sola**, and the plural forms are **solos** and **solas**. It can be used to express *only one*, by placing **un solo/una sola** before a noun.

Tenemos **una sola pregunta**.	*We have only one question.*

It can be used to express *all alone/all by oneself.*

El niño está **solo**.	*The little boy is alone.*
Los chicos se fueron y nos dejaron **solas**.	*The boys left and left us alone.*

The expression **dejar (-le a uno) en paz**, literally to leave someone in peace, is usually translated as *to leave someone alone.*

Déjame en paz. Solo quiero estar sola.	*Leave me alone. I just want to be alone.*

When used with the verb **sentir**, **solo** means *lonely.*

Me sentía muy solo.	*I felt really lonely.*

Sin embargo

This expression introduces a statement that is surprising after what was said previously, but takes over in importance. It can be translated as *nevertheless,* or *still.*

No estaba listo para el examen. **Sin embargo,** lo aprobé.	*I wasn't ready for the exam. Still, I passed it.*

Lo peor

This is translated as *the worst thing.* **Lo** can precede an adjective to make it into a noun.

Lo peor de esta clase es que la profesora es terrible.	*The worst thing about this class is that the teacher is terrible.*
Solucionar el problema es **lo importante.**	*Solving the problem is the important thing/ what is important.*

Lo before an adjective can also indicate its strength, and is translated as *how.*

¡No te imaginas **lo contenta** que estoy!	*You can't imagine how happy I am!*

Un rato

This looks like it might be a nasty rodent, but that's actually **una rata**! (And the little one is **un ratón**—which is also the name for the computer mouse.) **Un rato** means *a short period of time, a while.*

Charlamos **un rato** anoche.	*We talked for a while last night.*

Other ways to express time include:

- Una **época**, which isn't an epoch, but rather a period of time where things are or were different from those of other **épocas**. For example, *when I was in high school* is an **época**. When describing an **época** in the past, the imperfect is used.

Cuando estaba en la escuela secundaria, no estudiaba mucho.	*When I was in high school, I didn't study very much.*

- **La hora**, which means *time* in the sense of *time to do something.*

Es **la hora** de comer.	*It's time to eat.*

- **La vez**, which means *the incidence,* as in *the first/second/only/last/etc. time*:

Es la primera vez que estoy en esta ciudad.	*It's the first time I've ever been in this city.*
Fue **la única vez** que lo visité.	*It was the only time I visited him.*
La última vez que lo vi fue en octubre.	*The last time I saw him was in October.*

- **A la (misma) vez** means *at the same time.*
- **A veces** means *sometimes.*
- **El tiempo**, which can refer to *time* in general:

El tiempo vuela.	*Time flies.*
No tengo mucho **tiempo.**	*I don't have much time.*

El **tiempo** can also refer to the weather:

Hace muy buen **tiempo** aquí.	*The weather is great here.*

And *to have a good time* is **divertirse** or **pasarla/pasarlo bien.**

Nos divertimos mucho. **La pasamos muy bien.**	*We had a good time.*

De repente

This means *all of a sudden*, and is a true signal that the verb that follows should be in the preterite tense (if you are telling the story in the past tense).

Estaba caminando por la calle cuando **de repente** oí un sonido muy raro.	*I was walking down the street when all of a sudden I heard a strange noise.*

Other expressions with the same meaning include: **súbitamente/de pronto/de buenas a primeras**.

Sentirse

Sentirse, used with a reflexive pronoun, is followed by an adjective to tell *how someone feels.*

Me siento enfermo.	*I feel sick.*
De repente, **se sintió** mejor.	*Suddenly, she felt better.*

Sentir is used with a direct object to tell *what someone feels.*

Siento un dolor en la espalda.	*I feel a pain in my back.*

A common expression is **lo siento**—literally *I feel it,* but better translated as *I'm sorry.*

Seguir

Seguir, which means *to follow*, can also mean *to keep on doing something* when the verb that follows it is in the gerund (**-ndo**) form.

Seguí manejando.	*I kept on driving.*
Ella **siguió** hablando.	*She kept on talking.*

Continuar can also mean *to keep on doing something*, and it is also followed by a verb in gerund form.

Continuamos discutiendo.	*We kept on arguing.*

Darse cuenta de

This is a very common expression that means *to realize/to suddenly become aware of.*

Ya **me doy cuenta de** que tengo que buscar trabajo.	*Now I realize that I have to look for a job.*
Nos dimos cuenta de que era muy tarde para llegar.	*We realized it was very late to be arriving.*

Es tarde

This means that *the time is late.*

Es muy tarde. Tienes que ir a la cama. — *It's very late. You have to go to bed.*

El examen es mañana y ya **es demasiado tarde** para estudiar. — *The test is tomorrow and now it's too late to study.*

Llegar tarde means *to be late* in the sense of *to arrive late.*

¿Llego tarde? — *Am I late?*

Tu amigo **llegó tarde** y nos perdimos la primera parte de la película. — *Your friend was late and we missed the first part of the movie.*

Estar atrasado means *to be late* in the sense of *to be behind schedule.*

Lo siento, el informe no está listo. **Estoy muy atrasada.** — *I'm sorry, the report isn't ready. I'm really behind.*

Tardar en means *to be late in doing something, to delay.*

No tardes en enviarme la carta. — *Don't be late in sending me the letter.*

Tardé en mandar la solicitud y no me aceptaron en la universidad. — *I was late in sending my application and they didn't accept me at the university.*

Por fin

Por fin indicates relief that something finally happened.

¡**Por fin** estás aquí! — *You're finally here!*

De todos modos

This is an expression that indicates a conclusion that doesn't seem logical in view of what was previously said. It is usually translated as *anyway.*

Yo no invité a Marta a la fiesta, pero vino **de todos modos.** — *I didn't invite Marta to the party, but she came anyway.*

Express in Spanish the following setting for a story.

1. It was three P.M. ____________________
2. It was raining. ____________________
3. I was driving home. ____________________
4. Two friends were with me. ____________________
5. We were all tired. ____________________

EJERCICIO
11·2

Express in Spanish the following simultaneous actions.

1. While I was sleeping, my friends were celebrating. (dormir/celebrar)

    ____

2. She was listening to music while she was studying. (escuchar/estudiar)

    ____

3. He was cleaning the house while the children played outside. (limpiar/jugar)

    ____

4. I was worried when I was taking the test. (estar preocupado/hacer)

    ____

5. The teacher wasn't watching when he was texting his friends. (ver/textear)

    ____

Express in Spanish the following interrupted actions.

1. While I was sleeping, my mother called. (dormir/llamar)

    ____

2. She was listening to music when the phone rang. (escuchar/sonar)

    ____

3. We were having fun when the teacher came in. (divertirse/entrar)

    ____

4. He was talking on his cell when he hit the other car. (hablar/chocar con)

    ____

5. They were playing baseball when it started to rain.

    ____

EJERCICIO 11·4

Express in Spanish the following uninterrupted actions.

1. I got up and got dressed. (levantarse/vestirse)

____

2. We went back home and looked for our books. (volver/buscar)

____

3. He studied a lot and passed the test. (estudiar/aprobar)

____

4. She came to class and sat down. (venir/sentarse)

____

5. They went to the supermarket and bought drinks. (ir/comprar)

____

Circle the appropriate verb form for each blank.

1. No ______________ el problema de matemáticas y fui a hablar con el profesor.
   entendí   entendía
2. El profesor me explicó cómo solucionarlo y luego ______________ completar mi tarea.
   pude   podía
3. ¿Cuándo ______________ que ella mentía?
   supiste   sabías
4. El chico ______________ mucha hambre cuando llegó al restaurante.
   tuvo   tenía
5. ______________ contactarte, pero no contestaste tu celular.
   Quise   Quería

EJERCICIO
11·6

Fill in each blank with the most appropriate form.

1. Ayer, a Antonio ______________ rompió el brazo.
2. A mí no ______________ quemaron los dedos.
3. Al profesor ______________ olvidaron los exámenes.
4. A mis amigos ______________ perdió la llave.
5. A Sarita se le (olvidar) ______________ el nombre del profesor.
6. A Rosita y Mariana se les ______________ (quedar) las tareas en casa.
7. ¿A ti se te ______________ (caer) esta bufanda?

EJERCICIO
11·7

Choose the most appropriate word to fill in each blank.

1. Vamos afuera. Hoy hace muy buen ______________.
   hora   tiempo   época   vez
2. No puedo acompañarte, pues no tengo ______________.
   tiempo   rato   vez   hora
3. Te lo dije muchas ______________.
   épocas   veces   tiempos   horas
4. ¿Qué ______________ es?
   tiempo   hora   horas   rato
5. Mis padres se conocieron en otra ______________.
   tiempo   vez   época   hora
6. ______________ me frustraba mucho.
   A veces   Un rato   La época   Ahora

EJERCICIO
11·8

Fill in each blank with the correct form of the gerund.

1. Estábamos (trabajar) ______________ duro.
2. El padre siguió (caminar) ______________.

3. Los chicos continuaron (correr) ______________.

4. Yo estaba (dormir) ______________.

5. La mesera siguió (servir) ______________ la cena.

6. La niña estaba (pedir) ______________ información.

7. Seguimos (divertirse) ______________.

8. ¿Seguiste (mentir) ______________?

EJERCICIO
11·9

Match the words or expressions in the left column with their meanings in the right column.

1. ______ Tardé en entregárselo.
2. ______ Estaba atrasada.
3. ______ ¡No tardes!
4. ______ Ya era demasiado tarde.
5. ______ Llegué tarde.
6. ______ Es muy tarde.

a. *Don't be late.*
b. *I was behind schedule.*
c. *It was too late.*
d. *It's very late.*
e. *I handed it in late.*
f. *I was late.*

EJERCICIO
11·10

Complete each sentence with an appropriate message.

1. Ella estaba soñando y de repente ______________________________.

2. Quería comprar la casa, pues era bonita, estaba en una vecindad cómoda y ademas, ______

______________________________.

3. No me gustaba este carro, pero de todos modos ______________________________

______________________________.

4. Esperé a mi amigo dos horas y por fin ______________________________.

5. Este apartamento no es perfecto, sin embargo ______________________________.

EJERCICIO 11·11

Put each verb in parentheses in either the imperfect tense or the preterite tense, as appropriate.

Ayer, cuando (1. entrar, yo) ______________ en la clase, (2. ser) ______________ las dos. (3. llover) ______________. (4. querer, yo) ______________ hablar con mi amiga. No (5. estar, yo) ______________ preparada para la clase, pues no me (6. interesar) ______________ el tema. Gracias a Dios, el profesor no (7. estar) ______________ en clase cuando (8. entrar, yo) ______________, y (9. poder, yo) ______________ encontrar un asiento al lado de mi amiga. (10. Empezar, nosotras) ______________ a hablar. (11. hablar, nosotras) ______________ cuando el profesor me (12. hacer) ______________ una pregunta sobre la lección. (13. sentirse, yo) ______________ muy avergonzada. (14. levantarse, yo) ______________ y (15. salir, yo) ______________ del aula. Más tarde, (16. arrepentirse, yo) ______________ y le (17. mandar, yo) ______________ un email al profesor. (18. querer, yo) ______________ disculparme, pero el profesor no me (19. contestar) ______________. Él no (20. querer) ______________ hablar conmigo.

EJERCICIO 11·12

Write a paragraph of eight or nine sentences in which you tell a friend something that happened to you recently. Describe what was going on before the action started, and include at least one example of simultaneous actions, one of interrupted action, and one of uninterrupted action. Use **primero**, **después**, **luego**, **de repente**, *and* **finalmente**. *Ask a Spanish-speaking friend to read your story and comment on your use of the past tenses.*

____

____

____

____

____

____

____

____

____

Retelling a conversation

Conversation 1: Conversation between mother and kindergarten teacher

SRA. MARTÍNEZ: Buenos días, Srta. Sánchez. Es un placer verla de nuevo.

Good afternoon, Miss Sánchez. It's nice to see you again.

SRTA. SÁNCHEZ: Buenos días, Sra. Martínez. Igualmente. El año escolar ha pasado tan rápido, parece mentira que **estemos a punto de** terminar. Creo que Sam ha tenido un buen año y que disfrutará mucho del primer grado.

Good afternoon, Mrs. Martínez. Same here. The school year went so fast, I can't believe it's almost over. I think Sam has had a good year and that he'll enjoy first grade.

SRA. MARTÍNEZ: Me alegro mucho que usted lo diga. Nosotros también creemos que ha hecho muy bien en el kindergarten.

I'm glad to hear you say that. We think he's done well in kindergarten, too.

SRTA. SÁNCHEZ: Sam es un niño que atiende muy bien, algo que me parece muy importante, **ya que** hoy en día hay muy pocos niños—ni hablar de los adultos—que realmente sepan atender. Ustedes lo han educado muy bien, le puedo decir que es **el niño más cortés y considerado de toda** la clase.

Sam is a boy who listens very well, something I think is very special, since these days not very many kids—and few adults—really know how to listen. You have raised him very well; I can tell you he's the best-mannered child in the whole class.

SRA. MARTÍNEZ: Me alegra mucho oírlo, Srta. Sánchez. Nosotros pensamos que Sam lee, escribe y trabaja con los números muy bien **para** su edad. ¿Está usted de acuerdo?

That's music to my ears, Miss Sánchez. We think Sam reads, writes, and works with numbers very well for his age. Do you agree?

SRTA. SÁNCHEZ: Sí, Sra. Martínez. Los exámenes indican que Sam está dentro de los parámetros **para** su edad en lectura, escritura y aritmética. Dibuja bien y es bastante creativo. Y le gusta cantar.

Yes, Mrs. Martínez. The tests show that Sam is within the norms for his age in reading, writing, and arithmetic. He draws well, and he's quite creative. And he likes to sing.

SRA. MARTÍNEZ: Entonces, todo está bien.

Then everything is fine.

SRTA. SÁNCHEZ: La verdad, Sra. Martínez, Sam **sí tiene** un problema bastante serio.

Actually, Mrs. Martínez, Sam has a rather serious problem.

SRA. MARTÍNEZ: ¿Sí? ¿Cuál problema?

Oh? What problem?

SRTA. SÁNCHEZ: Es que no es nada agresivo.	*He's not at all aggressive.*
SRA. MARTÍNEZ: Pero, ¡eso es una buena noticia! Nosotros no somos gente agresiva.	*That's great! We're not aggressive people.*
SRTA. SÁNCHEZ: Nada de bueno, Sra. Martínez. Si no aprende a ser más decidido, a tener más iniciativa, nunca conseguirá un trabajo, ni una pareja. Cuando hago preguntas a toda la clase, Sam nunca levanta la mano, como los otros niños. Si quiero que conteste, tengo que hacerle las preguntas a él en particular.	*There's nothing good about it, Mrs. Martínez. If he doesn't learn to assert himself voluntarily, he'll never get a job, or even a partner in life. When I ask questions to the whole class, Sam never raises his hand like the other children do. If I want him to answer, I have to call on him individually.*
SRA. MARTÍNEZ: Y en ese caso, ¿contesta correctamente?	*And when you do that, does he answer correctly?*
SRTA. SÁNCHEZ: Pues, sí, siempre.	*Well, yes, always.*
SRA. MARTÍNEZ: Eso es todo lo que necesito saber. Muchas gracias, Srta. Sánchez. Que tenga un buen día.	*That's all I need to know. Thank you very much, Miss Sánchez. Have a nice day.*

Conversation 2: Gossip between a mother and daughter

ELENA: Mamá—¡aquí estoy! Tengo que contarte algo sobre la conversación que tuve con la maestra de Sam.	*Mom—here I am! I have to tell you about the conference I had with Sam's teacher.*
MAMÁ: Soy toda oídos. ¿Qué te dijo?	*I'm all ears. What did she say?*
ELENA: Bueno, empezó felicitándome por tener un hijo tan **bien educado** y simpático. Y destacó que era un niño que sabía atender.	*Well, she started off by congratulating me for a boy so well-mannered and nice. She emphasized that he was a child who knew how to listen.*
MAMÁ: ¿Y luego?	*And after that?*
ELENA: Luego dijo que su lectura, escritura y comprensión de aritmética estaban «dentro de los parámetros **para** su edad».	*Then she said that his reading, writing, and math skills were "within the norms for his age."*
MAMÁ: Entonces, no hubo ninguna sorpresa.	*So there were no surprises.*
ELENA: ¡Sí, sí que la hubo! No vas a creer esto. Me dijo que había algo muy importante que tenía que decirme. Cuando le pregunté cuál era el problema, me dijo que Sam no era lo suficientemente agresivo. Yo me quedé aliviada y le contesté que para mí eso era bueno. Pero ella respondió que no era bueno, sino todo lo contrario. Y yo le dije que no éramos gente agresiva y que estaba muy orgullosa de lo que había dicho sobre el comportamiento de Sam. Luego me explicó que él	*Yes, there were! You're not going to believe this. She told me that there was something really important that she had to tell me. When I asked her what the problem was, she told me that Sam wasn't aggressive enough. I was so relieved and I told her that I thought that was good. But she said there was nothing good about it, just the opposite. So I said that we weren't aggressive people and that I was really proud about what she had told me about Sam's behavior. Then she explained to me that he never raised his hand to answer a question like the other kids,*

nunca levantaba la mano como los otros niños para contestar una pregunta, que si quería que respondiera Sam, tenía que dirigirle la pregunta a él individualmente. Y que si él no cambia, nunca conseguirá un trabajo o una pareja.

and that if she wanted him to answer, she had to call on him individually. And that if he doesn't change, that he'll never get a job or a girlfriend!

MAMÁ: Esto es increíble. — *This is unbelievable.*

ELENA: ¿Sabes lo que hice? Le pregunté si Sam respondía correctamente cuando le hacía las preguntas a él. Me contestó que sí. Entonces le di las gracias y le dije que eso era todo lo que necesitaba saber.

You know what I did? I asked her if Sam answered correctly when she asked him a question, and she said yes. So I thanked her and told her that was all I needed to know.

MAMÁ: Bien hecho, hija. — *Good for you, Sweetie.*

Improving your conversation

Direct quotations

Just as in English, in Spanish a conversation can be repeated by quoting exactly what was said using quotation marks (which, as illustrated here, are different from English quotation marks) when the conversation is written. This kind of reported speech is excellent for telling a children's story, and it is also effective for telling the most exciting or dramatic part of something that happened.

Nos escondimos en la cocina y cuando entró Sara, gritamos: **«¡Sorpresa!»** — *We hid in the kitchen and when Sara came in, we shouted, "Surprise!"*

The interlocutor's words are often indicated by placing a dash before the quote, instead of using the quotation marks.

«Tengo mucho miedo», dijo el niño. — *"I'm really scared," said the child.*

—No te preocupes, estoy aquí contigo— respondió el padre. — *"Don't worry, I'm here with you," replied the father.*

Indirect quotations

A longer story, on the other hand, would save the quoted speech (direct discourse) for the most exciting parts, and use reported speech (indirect discourse) to retell all the other things that people said. In reported speech you do not quote a person's exact words, but rather paraphrase what he or she said.

DIRECT QUOTATION	INDIRECT QUOTATION
«Tengo mucho miedo», dijo el niño. *"I'm really scared," said the child.*	El niño **dijo que tenía mucho miedo.** *The child said that he was really scared.*

Formula for indirect quote, or reported speech

subject	+	verb in preterite or imperfect Tense	+	**que**	+	verb in imperfect tense
↓		↓		↓		↓
El niño		**dijo/decía**		**que**		**tenía mucho miedo.**

The child said/was saying (that) he was really scared.

There are two ways to report a question. For a yes-or-no question, use the same formula as shown previously, with **si** instead of **que**.

DIRECT QUESTION	INDIRECT QUESTION
«**¿Estudias español?**» me preguntó la señora. *"Are you studying Spanish?" the woman asked me.*	La señora **me preguntó si estudiaba español.** *The woman asked me if I was studying Spanish.*

To report an answer to a yes-or-no question, use **que sí** or **que no.**

Le contesté **que sí/que no.** *I told her yes/no.*

For an information question, use the same formula as shown, with the question word instead of **que**.

DIRECT QUESTION	INDIRECT QUESTION
«**¿Cuándo estudias?**» me preguntó la señora. *"When do you study?" the woman asked me.*	La señora **me preguntó cuándo estudiaba**. *The woman asked me when I (usually) studied.*
«**¿Adónde van ustedes?**» nos preguntó el señor. *"Where are you going?" the man asked us.*	El señor **nos preguntó adónde íbamos.** *The man asked us where we were going.*

Quoted requests and commands

La niña me pidió: «**Ayúdame con mi tarea, por favor**».	*The little girl asked me: "Help me with my homework, please."*
Los turistas nos rogaban, «**Llévenos a la estación de trenes, por favor**».	*The tourists were begging us, "Please take us to the train station."*
Mi mamá me advirtió: «**No llegues tarde esta noche**».	*My mom warned me: "Don't be late tonight."*
El policía me dijo: «**Baje del auto**».	*The policeman told me: "Get out of the car."*

Formula for reported requests and commands

subject	+	indirect object	+	verb in preterite /imperfect	+	que	+	verb in imperfect subjunctive
↓		↓		↓		↓		↓
La niña		**me**		**pidió**		**que**		**la ayudara con su tarea.**
Los turistas		**nos**		**rogaban**		**que**		**los lleváramos a la estación.**
Mi mamá		**me**		**advirtió**		**que**		**no llegara tarde.**
El policía		**me**		**dijo**		**que**		**bajara del auto.**

The little girl asked me to help her with her homework.
The tourists were begging us to take them to the station.
My mom warned me not to be late.
The policeman told me to get out of the car.

Advanced reported speech

The previous guidelines are for reporting conversations that are in the present indicative tense. When the conversations are in other tenses, use the following formulas. (See the appendix for conjugations.)

Quoted verb	Reported verb
PRESENT SUBJUNCTIVE	IMPERFECT SUBJUNCTIVE
Nos avisó, **«No creo que el director venga»**. *She informed us, "I don't think the director is coming."*	Nos avisó **que no creía que el director viniera**. *She informed us that she didn't think the director was coming.*
FUTURE	CONDITIONAL
Él me dijo, **«Te llamaré»**. *He told me, "I'll call you."*	Él **me dijo que me llamaría**. *He told me (that) he would call me.*
PRETERITE	PRETERITE PERFECT
Isabel dijo, **«Fui a una fiesta»**. *Isabel said, "I went to a party."*	Isabel **dijo que había ido a una fiesta**. *Isabel said that she had gone to a party.*

Ya que

This expression translates to English as *since*, in the sense of *considering the fact that.*

Ya que su hermano está aquí en la oficina, le daré los documentos personalmente.	*Since your brother is here in the office, I'll give him the documents personally.*

Educar

Educar means *to teach good manners to*, and a person who is **bien educado** is one who *has good manners*. A *well-educated person* is **una persona culta**.

La chica es **muy bien educada.**	*The girl has very good manners.*
La chica es **muy culta.**	*The girl is very well educated.*

El más... de todo el grupo

The pattern for expressing a superlative in Spanish is different from the English pattern. Note that the noun is placed before the superlative adjective, and the preposition *in* is expressed as **de**.

Ella es **la chica más alta de la clase.**	*She's the tallest girl in the class.*
Es **el senador más conservador del partido.**	*He's the most conservative senator in the party.*

Sí

When **sí** comes directly after a noun or pronoun, it is translated as an auxiliary verb, such as *does* or *is*, emphasizing contrast to the previous negative statement.

Nadie va a clase hoy.	*Nobody's going to class today.*
¡Nosotros sí!	*We are!*
El chico no habla español.	*The boy doesn't speak Spanish.*
El chico **sí lo habla,** pero es muy tímido.	*The boy does speak it, but he's very shy.*

Estar a punto de

Estar a punto de followed by an infinitive means *to be about to do something.*

Estamos a punto de salir.	*We're about to leave.*
El niño **está a punto de empezar** el primer grado.	*The child is about to start first grade.*

Para

Para can be used to compare someone or something with others of the same category.

Pablo es muy alto **para** su edad.	*Pablo es very tall for his age.*
Para una extranjera, habla muy bien el idioma.	*For a foreigner, she speaks the language very well.*

Por ser

Por ser is used to show that being in a particular category is the reason for a reality.

Por ser tan alto, Pablo fue escogido para el equipo de básquetbol.	*Because he's so tall, Pablo was chosen for the basketball team.*
Por ser extranjera, comete algunos errores cuando habla.	*Because she's a foreigner, she makes some mistakes when she speaks.*

Aconsejar que

Aconsejar que means *to advise* in the sense of *to give advice* and is followed by a verb in the subjunctive.

La profesora **me aconseja que estudie** en el extranjero.	*The teacher advises me to study abroad.*
Le aconsejé que estudiara química.	*I advised her to study chemistry.*

Avisar

Avisar means *to advise* in the sense of *to inform, usually of something important.*

El policía **me avisó** que el registro de mi carro se había caducado.	*The policeman informed me that my car registration had expired.*
La vecina de mi mamá **nos avisó** que mi mamá había salido.	*My mother's neighbor informed us that my mother had gone out.*

Advertir

Advertir is a little stronger than **avisar**, more like *to warn.*

Mi papá **me advirtió** que no manejara si bebía cerveza.	*My dad warned me not to drive if I drank beer.*

Anunciar

Anunciar is *to advertise.*

Hoy **anunciaron** un puesto para un profesor de matemáticas.	*Today they advertised an opening for a math teacher.*

Anunciar can also mean *to announce.*

El jefe **anunció** que se iba a jubilar. *The boss announced that he was going to retire.*

EJERCICIO 12·1

Change the following direct quotes to indirect (reported) speech.

1. El niño dijo: «Estoy contento».
   ____
2. Mi amigo dijo: «Tengo hambre».
   ____
3. Las chicas dijeron: «Nos gusta la clase».
   ____
4. Les dijimos: «Vivimos en esta calle».
   ____
5. Nos dijeron: «Esta es la calle más bonita de toda la ciudad».
   ____

EJERCICIO 12·2

Change the following reported speech to direct quotes.

1. Su mamá me dijo que él no estaba en casa.
   ____
2. Los directores nos dijeron que no había suficiente dinero para el proyecto.
   ____
3. La novia de mi hermano me dijo que ella quería casarse en abril.
   ____
4. Mi hermano me dijo que él no estaba de acuerdo con ese plan.
   ____
5. Su jefe le avisó que no iba a conseguir una subida de sueldo.
   ____

EJERCICIO
12·3

Change the following direct questions to indirect (reported) questions.

1. Nos preguntaron: «¿Ustedes van al cine esta noche?»

____

2. Me preguntó: «¿Cuánto cuesta un vuelo de ida y vuelta a México?»

____

3. Le preguntó, «¿Cuándo te gradúas de la escuela secundaria?»

____

4. Me preguntaron: «¿Qué quieres hacer hoy?»

____

5. Te preguntó, «¿Comes con frecuencia en este restaurante?»

____

Change the following indirect questions to direct (quoted) questions.

1. Él le preguntaba si quería acompañarlo.

____

2. Me preguntó a qué hora comía.

____

3. Nos preguntó dónde estudiábamos.

____

4. Te preguntó con quién andabas.

____

5. Me preguntaron si tenía miedo.

____

EJERCICIO
12·5

Change the following direct requests or commands to indirect (reported) requests or commands.

1. Le pedimos: «Por favor, díganos la verdad».

 ___

2. Le pedí: «Traiga este sobre al director de la compañía».

 ___

3. Le dije: «Venga temprano al trabajo el viernes».

 ___

4. Les dijo: «No lleguen tarde».

 ___

5. Me pidió: «Cómprame un helado, por favor».

 ___

EJERCICIO
12·6

Change the following indirect requests or commands to direct (quoted) requests or commands.

1. Ella le dijo que no la llamara.

 ___

2. Él le pidió que lo pensara.

 ___

3. Yo te aconsejé que vieras esa película.

 ___

4. Me advirtió que no bebiera demasiado.

 ___

5. Ellos le dijeron que saliera temprano.

 ___

EJERCICIO
12·7

Choose **por** *or* **para** *to fill in the blanks in the following sentences.*

1. ______ un estudiante del cuarto año de la universidad, no es muy maduro.
2. ______ no ser muy maduro, tendrá problemas en su trabajo.
3. Lo despideron ______ no ser miembro del partido.
4. ______ un miembro del partido conservador, es bastante liberal.
5. ______ una película ______ niños, era buena.

¿Cómo se dice en español? *Translate the following sentences into Spanish.*

1. She's the best student in the class, since she studies all the time.

   ____

2. He's not well educated, but he has good manners.

   ____

3. He *is* well educated, since he reads constantly.

   ____

4. He has good manners, since his parents were very strict.

   ____

5. She is the best-educated one in her family.

   ____

6. For a well-educated woman, she doesn't seem very bright.

   ____

7. She *is* bright, it's that she doesn't listen.

   ____

8. She lost her job for being late every day.

   ____

¿Cómo se dice en español? *Translate the following sentences into Spanish.*

1. She announced that she was getting married.
2. The doctor warned her not to smoke.
3. She advised him that she was going on vacation.
4. The boss advised her not to leave.
5. They advertised the position.

EJERCICIO 12·10

Listen to a conversation (in English or Spanish) and write down exactly what the two people say. If the conversation is in English, translate it into Spanish. Then change the direct quotes to indirect (reported) discourse. Ask a Spanish-speaking friend to check your work.

APPENDIX

Grammar review

Pronouns

Subject pronouns

SINGULAR	PLURAL
yo	nosotros, nosotras
tú	vosotros, vosotras, ustedes (Uds.)
usted (Ud.)	ustedes (Uds.)
él	ellos
ella	ellas

Indirect object pronouns

(A mí) me	(A nosotros, -as) nos
(A ti) te	(A vosotros, -as) os
(A usted) le	(A ustedes) les
(A él) le	(A ellos) les
(A ella) le	(A ellas) les

Direct object pronouns

me	nos
te	os
lo, la	los, las

Pronouns after prepositions

mí	nosotros, -as
ti	vosotros, -as
usted	ustedes
él	ellos
ella	ellas

After the preposition **con**, use **conmigo** and **contigo**.

Prepositions

a
con
contra
de
en
entre
hacia
para
por
sin
sobre

Adverbs

- That tell *a condition*:

  bien
  mejor
  mal
  peor

- That tell *when*:

  actualmente
  ahora
  anteayer
  antes
  ayer
  después
  hoy
  luego
  mañana
  pronto
  tarde
  temprano
  todavía

- That tell *how often*:

  a menudo
  frecuentemente
  mucho
  nunca
  poco
  siempre

- That tell *where*:

  ahí
  allí/allá
  aquí/acá

- That tell *how much:*

  algo
  bastante
  demasiado
  nada
  poco
  un poco
  mucho
  tanto

- That tell *how* (To form adverbs of manner, begin with the feminine singular form of the corresponding adjective and add -**mente**):

  amablemente
  cuidadosamente
  fácilmente
  lentamente
  rápidamente

- That modify adjectives:

  bastante
  bien
  demasiado
  muy
  poco
  tan

- Certain adverbs of manner use the masculine singular form of the adjective:

  alto
  bajo
  barato
  caro
  claro
  derecho
  despacio
  hondo
  justo
  lento
  rápido
  recto
  seguro

Verbs

Verbs are listed in dictionaries in their infinitive form, which ends in -**ar,** -**er,** or -**ir,** depending on the individual verb.

Present tense

To conjugate regular verbs in the present tense, begin with the stem (the infinitive minus -**ar**/-**er**/-**ir**) and add the following endings to show who is doing the acting.

	-ar	-er	-ir
yo	-o	-o	-o
tú	-as	-es	-es
usted/él/ella	-a	-e	-e
nosotros, -as	-amos	-emos	-imos
vosotros, -as	-áis	-éis	-ís
ustedes/ellos/ellas	-an	-en	-en

Verbs that end in -uir

construir construyo, construyes, construye, construimos, construís, construyen

Verbs that have irregular **yo** forms in the present tense

dar	doy
estar	estoy
ir	voy
decir	digo
hacer	hago
poner	pongo
salir	salgo
tener	tengo
traer	traigo
venir	vengo
oír	oigo

Verbs that end in -cer

conocer	conozco
parecer	parezco

Verbs that end in **-ger/-gir** have an automatic spelling change

recoger	recojo
dirigir	dirijo

Stem-changing verb patterns in the present tense

With these verbs, the last vowel in the stem is replaced by another vowel or vowels in the forms for yo/tú/usted/él/ella/ellos/ellas. The change is indicated in dictionaries by the annotation after the infinitive. The stem does not change in the nosotros, -as/vosotros, -as forms.

-ar verbs

e to **ie** pensar (ie)
p**ie**nso/p**ie**nsas/p**ie**nsa
pensamos/pensáis/p**ie**nsan

o to **ue** alm**o**rzar (ue)
alm**ue**rzo/alm**ue**rzas/alm**ue**rza
alm**o**rzamos/alm**o**rzáis/alm**ue**rzan

u to **ue** j**u**gar (ue)
j**ue**go/j**ue**gas/j**ue**ga
j**u**gamos/j**u**gáis/j**ue**gan

-er verbs

e to **ie**
perder (ie)
p**ie**rdo/p**ie**rdes/p**ie**rde
perdemos/perdéis/p**ie**rden

tener (ie)
tengo/t**ie**nes/t**ie**ne
tenemos/tenéis/t**ie**nen

o to **ue**
poder (ue)
p**ue**do/p**ue**des/p**ue**de
p**o**demos/p**o**déis/p**ue**den

-ir verbs

e to **ie**
sentir (ie, i)
s**ie**nto/s**ie**ntes/s**ie**nte
sentimos/sentís/s**ie**nten

venir (ie, i)
vengo/v**ie**nes/v**ie**ne
venimos/venís/v**ie**nen

o to **ue**
d**o**rmir (ue, u)
d**ue**rmo/d**ue**rmes/d**ue**rme
d**o**rmimos/d**o**rmís/d**ue**rmen

e to **i**
pedir (i, i)
p**i**do/p**i**des/p**i**de
pedimos/pedís/p**i**den

decir (i, i)
digo/d**i**ces/d**i**ce
decimos/decís/d**i**cen

Verbs that are irregular in the present tense

ser	soy/eres/es/somos/sois/son
estar	estoy/estás/está/estamos/estáis/están

Gerunds

To form the gerund, begin with the stem (the infinitive minus **-ar**/**-er**/**-ir**).

-ar verbs

stem + **-ando** (no stem changes)	hablando/pensando/almorzando/jugando

-er verbs

stem + **-iendo**	comiendo/perdiendo/volviendo
stem ending in vowel + **-yendo** (no stem changes)	leyendo/creyendo/cayendo

-ir verbs

stem + **-iendo**	abriendo/partiendo/viviendo
stem ending in vowel + **-yendo**	huyendo/construyendo/oyendo

All **-ir** verbs that have stem changes in the present tense also have stem changes in the gerund. These changes are indicated by the second annotation after the infinitive:

e to **i**	sentir (ie, i)	s**i**ntiendo
	venir (ie, i)	v**i**niendo
o to **u**	dormir (ue, u)	d**u**rmiendo
	morir (ue, u)	m**u**riendo
e to **i**	servir (i, i)	s**i**rviendo
	decir (i, i)	d**i**ciendo

Present progressive tense

To form the present progressive tense, use a present tense conjugation of **estar** plus a gerund.

Estoy escribiendo.	**Estamos** escuchando.
¿**Estás** trabajando?	¿**Están** jugando?/¿**Estáis** jugando?
Está limpiando.	**Están** comiendo.

Preterite perfect tense

To form the preterite perfect tense, use a present tense conjugation of **haber** plus a participle.

Present tense of **haber**

he has ha hemos han habéis

Participles

To form the participle, begin with the stem and add:

-**ar** verbs	-ado
-**er** verbs	-ido
-**ir** verbs	-ido

Irregular participles

abrir	abierto	poner	puesto
cubrir	cubierto	oponer	opuesto
descubrir	descubierto	proponer	propuesto
decir	dicho	ver	visto
predecir	predicho	prever	previsto
escribir	escrito	volver	vuelto
describir	descrito	devolver	devuelto
prescribir	prescrito	revolver	revuelto
hacer	hecho	resolver	resuelto
morir	muerto	romper	roto

Future tense

To form the future tense, begin with the infinitive (all types of verbs) and add:

yo	-é
tú	-ás
usted/él/ella	-á

nosotros, -as	-emos
vosotros, -as	-éis
ustedes/ellos/ellas	-án

Irregular stems in the future tense

1. Drop **e** from infinitive + regular future endings

   haber → habr-
   poder → podr-
   querer → querr-
   saber → sabr-
   caber → cabr-

2. Replace **e/i** with **d** + regular future endings

   poner → pondr-
   salir → saldr-
   tener → tendr-
   venir → vendr-
   valer → valdr-

3. Other + regular future endings

   decir → dir-
   hacer → har-

Conditional tense

To form the conditional tense, begin with the infinitive and add:

yo	-ía
tú	-ías
usted/él/ella	-ía
nosotros, -as	-íamos
vosotros, -as	-íais
ustedes/ellos/ellas	-ían

Conditional forms have the same irregular stems as those of the future tense, followed by regular conditional endings.

Imperfect tense

To form the imperfect tense, begin with the stem minus **-ar**/**-er**/**-ir**, and add the following endings:

-ar verbs	-aba, -abas, -aba, -ábamos, -abais, -aban
-er/**-ir** verbs	-ía, -ías, -ía, -íamos, -íais, -ían

Irregular verbs in the imperfect tense

ser	era, eras, era, éramos, erais, eran
ir	iba, ibas, iba, íbamos, ibais, iban
ver	veía, veías, veía, veíamos, veíais, veían

Preterite tense

There are two distinct regular patterns in the preterite tense.

Type 1 verbs

To form the preterite for most verbs, begin with the stem and add the following endings:

	-ar		-er/-ir			
yo	-é	hablé	-í	comí	escribí	di*
tú	-aste	hablaste	-iste	comiste	escribiste	diste
usted/él/ella	-ó	habló	-ió	comió	esribió	dio
nosotros, as	-amos	hablamos	-imos	comimos	escribimos	dimos
vosotros, -as	-asteis	hablasteis	-isteis	comisteis	escribisteis	disteis
ustedes/ellos, -as	-aron	hablaron	-ieron	comieron	escribieron	dieron

*Dar is an -ar verb with -ir endings in the preterite.

Automatic spelling changes in **yo** form:

-zar → -cé	empezar	empecé
-car → -qué	tocar	toqué
-gar → -gué	jugar	jugué
-guar → -güé	averiguar	averigüé

Automatic spelling changes in **-er/-ir** verbs whose stem ends in a vowel:

leer	-ió → yó	leyó	-ieron → -yeron	leyeron
construir	-ió → yó	construyó	-ieron → -yeron	construyeron

Stem changes

-ar verbs — no stem change
-er verbs — no stem change
-ir verbs — 2nd stem change in usted/él/ella and ustedes/ellos/ellas forms

pedir (i, i)	dormir (ue,u)
pedí	dormí
pediste	dormiste
pedisteis	dormisteis
p**i**dió	d**u**rmió
p**i**dieron	d**u**rmieron

Type 2 verbs

The following verbs change in the stem for all persons and have a different set of endings from Type 1 verbs.

Stem changes

andar → anduv-	hacer → hic-
tener → tuv-	querer → quis-
estar → estuv-	venir → vin-
poder → pud-	decir → dij-*
saber → sup-	traer → traj-*
pon → pus-	
haber → hub-	

*Third-person plural forms ending in -j drop the **i**: **dijeron, trajeron.**

Type 2 verb endings

yo	-e	nosotros	-imos
tú	-iste	vosotros	-isteis
usted/él/ella	-o	ellos	-ieron

Irregular verbs in the preterite tense

The verbs **ir** and **ser** have the same form in the preterite tense.

fui	fuimos
fuiste	fuisteis
fue	fueron

Present subjunctive

To form the present subjunctive, start with the **yo** form of the present indicative minus **-o**, then add the following conjugations:

	-ar VERBS	**-er/-ir** VERBS
yo	-e	-a
tú	-es	-as
usted/él/ella	-e	-a
nosotros, -as	-emos	-amos
vosotros, -as	-éis	-áis
ustedes/ellos/ellas	-en	-an

Verbs whose infinitives end in **-car/-gar/-zar/-ger** have automatic spelling changes in the present subjunctive:

-car	-que, -ques, -que, -quemos, -quéis, -quen	busque/etc.
-gar	-gue, -gues, -gue, -guemos, -guéis, -guen	largue/etc.
-zar	-ce, -ces, -ce, -cemos, -céis, -cen	empiece/etc.
-ger	-ja, -jas, -ja, -jamos, -jáis, -jan	recoja/etc.

Verbs that end in **-ar** and **-er** with stem changes in the present tense have the same changes in the present subjunctive:

piense mueva

Verbs that end in **-ir** with stem changes in the present tense have the same changes in the present subjunctive, except in the **nosotros** and **vosotros** forms. There they use the second stem-change:

dormir (ue,u)	duerma, duermas, duerma, durmamos, durmáis, duerman
servir (i,i)	sirva, sirvas, sirva, sirvamos, sirváis, sirvan
mentir (ie,i)	mienta, mientas, mienta, mintamos, mintáis, mientan

Three verbs have irregular forms in the present subjunctive:

ir	vaya, vayas, vaya, vayamos, vayáis, vayan
haber	haya, hayas, haya, hayamos, hayáis, hayan
ver	vea, veas, vea, veamos, veáis, vean

Command forms

Affirmative commands in the **tú** form are the same as the **usted** indicative form:

habla
come
escribe

There are a number of irregular forms:

decir	di
hacer	haz
poner	pon
tener	ten
venir	ven
ir	ve
ser	se

Negative commands in the **tú** form use the present subjunctive form:

no hables
no comas
no escribas

Affirmative commands in the **vosotros** form are like the infinitive, with a **d** replacing the final **r**:

hablad
comed
escribid

Negative commands in the **vosotros** form are like the negative **tú** commands, with an **i** added before the **s**:

no habléis
no comáis
no escribáis

Both affirmative and negative commands in the **usted** and **ustedes** forms use the subjunctive:

hable	hablen
coma	coman
escriba	escriban
no hable	no hablen
no coma	no coman
no escriba	no escriban

When object pronouns are added to affirmative commands, they are attached to the end:

Cuéntame.	Cuéntamelo.
Díganos.	Díganoslo.
Esperemos.	Esperémoslo.

When object pronouns are added to negative commands, they go between **no** and the verb:

No me cuentes./No me lo cuentes.
No nos diga./No nos lo diga.
No lo esperemos.

Imperfect subjunctive

To form the imperfect subjunctive, begin with the third-person plural (**ellos**) form of the preterite tense, minus **-ron**:

hablaron → habla-
comieron → comie-
escribieron → escribie-
durmieron → durmie-
tuvieron → tuvie-
fueron → fue-

Then add the following endings:

yo	-ra
tú	-ras
usted/él/ella	-ra
nosotros, as	-ramos
vosotros, as	-rais
ustedes/ellos/ellas	-ran

Examples

-ar verbs

hablar	hablara/hablaras/hablara/habláramos/hablárais/hablaran

-er verbs

comer	comiera/comieras/comiera/comiéramos/comiérais/comieran
leer	leyera/leyeras/leyera/leyéramos/leyérais/leyeran

-ir verbs

escribir	escribiera/escribieras/escribiera/escribiéramos/escribiérais/escribieran

-ir stem-changing verbs

dormir	d**u**rmiera/d**u**rmieras/d**u**rmiera/d**u**rmiéramos/d**u**rmiérais/d**u**rmieran

Pattern 2 verbs

tener	tuviera/tuvieras/tuviera/tuviéramos/tuviérais/tuvieran
ir/ser	fuera/fueras/fuera/fuéramos/fuerais/fueran

Spanish-English glossary

A

a to
a la vez at the same time (See Chapter 8.)
a lo mejor probably (See Chapter 8.)
a ninguna parte nowhere (See Chapter 8.)
a propósito on purpose; speaking of which (See Chapter 2.)
a veces sometimes (See Chapters 8 and 11.)
a ver let's see (See Chapter 1.)
abrigarse to bundle up; put on a coat
abuela grandmother
aburrido, -a, -os, -as bored
aburrirse to get bored (See Chapter 6.)
acabar de to have just (See Chapters 3 and 10.)
acción action
aceptar to accept
acompañar to accompany; go with
aconsejar to advise (See Chapter 8.)
actor actor
actriz actress
actualmente now; currently (See Chapter 10.)
además also (See Chapter 10.)
adentro inside
adiós good-bye (See Chapter 4.)
aficionado, -a, -os, -as enthusiastic fan; supporter
afuera outside
agosto August
agresivo, -a, -os, -as agressive
agua water
ahora now
al menos at least (See Chapter 8.)
alcalde mayor
alcanzar to reach (See Chapter 9.)
alcohol alcohol
alegrarse to be happy
algo something
algún, alguna, -os, -as some; a certain
aliviar to alleviate; relieve
allí over there
almorzar to eat lunch (See Chapter 4.)
alquilar to rent
alquiler rent amount
alrededor around
alto, -a, -os, -as tall
alumno, -a pupil; student
amar to love
ambulancia ambulance
amigo, -a friend
amistoso, -a, -os, -as friendly
andar to go; walk; wander
animal animal
año year
anoche last night
anteayer the day before yesterday
anterior previous
antes before
antiguo, -a, -os, -as very old; ancient
aparecer to appear
apartamento apartment
aplicación coat (of paint, glue) (See Chapter 6.)
aplicar to apply (paint, glue) (See Chapter 6.)
aplicarse to pertain to (See Chapter 6.)
apoyar to support (See Chapter 2.)
apreciar to appreciate; esteem
aprender to learn
aprobar to pass (test, course)
apropiado, -a, -os, -as appropriate
apuntes notes taken during a lecture or meeting
apuro hurry
aquí here
aritmética arithmetic
arte art
ascender to go up
asegurarse to make sure
así es that's right
así que so (See Chapter 1.)
asiento seat
asignar to assign
asistir to attend
asociación association

atender to listen
atleta athlete
atlético, -a, -os, -as athletic
atrás behind
atrasado, -a, -os, -as late; behind (See Chapter 11.)
aula classroom
aunque even though (See Chapter 3.)
auténtico, -a, -os, -as authentic
averiguar to find out
ayudar to help

B

bailar to dance
baile a dance
balcón balcony
banco bank; bench
baño bathroom
barato, -a, -os, -as cheap
basado, -a, -os, -as based
base base
básico basic; fundamentally
básquetbol basketball
bastante rather; quite (See Chapter 5.)
basura trash
beca scholarship
béisbol baseball
beisbolista baseball player
bello, -a, -os, -as fine; beautiful
beso kiss
biblioteca library
bien fine; well; OK; quite (See Chapters 3, 4, and 10.)
bilingüe bilingual
biología biology
boca mouth
boda wedding
bueno actually; well (See Chapters 1 and 4.)
bueno, -a, -os, -as good
bufanda scarf
buscar to look for; go get (See Chapter 6.)

C

cada vez más more and more (See Chapter 8.)
caer fall (See Chapter 10.)
café coffee, café
calcetín sock
calefacción heating
cambiar to change
cambiar de opinión change one's mind
camiseta tee-shirt
campeonato championship
candidato, -a candidate
candidatura candidature
cansado, -a, -os, -as tired
cantar to sing
cantidad amount
caribeño, -a, -os, -as Caribbean
cariño affection
carne meat
carretera highway
carro car (See Chapter 10.)
carta letter
casa house; home
casarse to get married
casi almost
caso case; instance
causar to cause
celular cell phone
cenar eat dinner (See Chapter 4.)
céntrico central
centro center
cerca near
cerveza beer
chao bye
charlar to chat
chica girl
chico boy
chico, -a, -os, -as small; little
chisme gossip
chocar to bump into
cine movie theater
ciudad city
claro of course (See Chapter 3.)
claro, -a, -os, -as clear; light in color
clase class; kind; type
clásico, -a, -os, -as classic; classical
cliente client; customer
club club
coche car; automobile (See Chapter 10.)
cocina kitchen; cuisine
colega colleague; coworker
colmo limit; last straw (See Chapter 8.)
color color
comedor dining room
cometer to commit; make (an error)
comida food
cómo how; what
como like; as (See Chapters 1 and 2.)
como si fuera as if it were (See Chapter 4.)
compañero, -a de cuarto roommate
compartir to share
compatible compatible
competente competent
competidor, -a competitor
complacer to please; make happy
completamente completely
completar to finish
componente component
comportamiento behavior
comprar to buy
compras purchases
comprender to understand
con razón no wonder (See Chapter 5.)
concierto concert

condominio condominium
congreso conference
conocer to become acquainted with; know
conseguir to get; acquire
conservador, -a conservative
considerado, -a, -os, -as considerate
contabilidad accounting
contacto contact
contador, -a accountant
contar to count; tell; relate (See Chapter 8.)
contento, -a, -os, -as happy
contestar to answer
continuar to continue; keep on (See Chapter 11.)
contratar to hire
contrato contract
convenir to be suitable for
conversar to talk
convertir en to change into; transform
correctamente correctly
correcto, -a, -os, -as correct
correr to run
cortés polite; courteous
costar cost
costumbre custom
creativo, -a, -os, -as creative
crédito credit
creer to believe; think
creerse to be conceited (See Chapter 10.)
cuaderno notebook
cuál which; that
cualquier any (See Chapter 8.)
cualquiera any (See Chapter 8.)
cuándo when
cuando when (See Chapter 9.)
cuánto how much
cuanto antes as soon as possible (See Chapter 9.)
cuarto bedroom
cuarto, -a, -os, -as one fourth/fourths; quarters
cuenta account; bill
cuidado care
curar to cure

D

darse cuenta de to realize
dato fact
de of; from (See Chapter 4.)
de acuerdo con in agreement with (See Chapters 4 and 7.)
de hecho (See Chapter 2.)
de modo que so (See Chapter 10.)
de repente suddenly (See Chapter 11.)
de todos modos anyway (See Chapter 11.)
de vez en cuando once in a while (See Chapter 8.)
deber to be obligated to
deber assignment; task (See Chapter 8.)
decente decent
decidido, -a, -os, -as determined
decir to say; tell
decisión decision
decoración decoration
dedicarse to work as; devote oneself to (See Chapter 3.)
dejar to leave (See Chapter 5.)
del of the; from the
delante ahead
delincuencia crime (criminal activity)
demasiado extremely (See Chapter 5.)
dentro de within
depender to depend
deporte sport
deportista athlete
deprimido, -a, -os, -as depressed
deprimirse to get depressed
derecho right
desafortunadamente unfortunately
desastre disaster
desayunar to eat breakfast (See Chapter 4.)
descansar to rest
describir to describe
desde since; from (See Chapter 2.)
desde cuándo since when (See Chapter 1.)
despacio slow; slowly
despedir to fire (See Chapter 10.)
despedirse to say good-bye to (See Chapter 10.)
despertar to awaken
despertarse to wake up
después afterward (See Chapter 4.)
destacar to emphasize
destrucción destruction
detallado, -a, -os, -as detailed
detalle detail
día day
dibujar to draw
dieta diet
diez ten
difícil difficult; hard
dinámico, -a, -os, -as dynamic
director, -a director
dirigir direct
discoteca discotheque
disfrutar to enjoy
disponible available
dispuesto, -a, -os, -as willing
distancia distance
diverso, -a, -os, -as diverse
divertirse to have fun
doble double
documentación documentation; official papers
dólar dollar
doler to hurt; ache
dónde where
dormir to sleep
dormitorio bedroom
dos two

dramático, -a, -os, -as dramatic; drastic
dudar to doubt (See Chapter 8.)
durante during
duro, -a, -os, -as hard (surface/work)

E

edificio building
educar to raise; rear (See Chapter 12.)
efectivamente exactly that; really (See Chapter 4.)
egoísta selfish
el the
él he
elegante elegant
eliminar to eliminate; get rid of
ella she
ellos, -as they
emborracharse to get drunk (See Chapter 6.)
emocionado, -a, -os, -as excited
emocionante exciting
emocionarse to get excited (See Chapter 6.)
empezar to begin; start
empleado, -a employee
empresa company; corporation
en in; on; at (See Chapter 4.)
en común in common
en cuanto as soon as (See Chapters 7 and 9.)
en efecto exactly (See Chapter 4.)
en el fondo basically; down deep (See Chapter 10.)
en general in general
en lo más mínimo in the least (See Chapter 8.)
en particular in particular
en primer lugar in the first place (See Chapter 10.)
en serio seriously
encantado, -a, -os, -as charmed; enchanted; delighted
encantar to charm; delight
enchilada enchilada
encontrar to find
encontrarse to meet up
enérgico, -a, -os, -as energetic
enfadarse to get mad; get angry (See Chapter 6.)
enfermedad sickness; disease
enfocar to focus on
engordarse to get fat (See Chapter 6.)
enojarse to get mad; get angry (See Chapter 6.)
enorme huge; enormous
enseñar to teach; show (See Chapter 7.)
ensuciar to get dirty
entender to understand
entero, -a, -os, -as whole; entire
entonces so (See Chapter 4.)
entrada entrance
entre between; among
entregar to hand in; hand over (See Chapter 7.)
entusiasmo enthusiasm
enviar to send (See Chapter 7.)
equipo team
error error; mistake
es decir that is (See Chapter 5.)
es importante que it's important that (See Chapter 6.)
es más more to the point (See Chapter 10.)
es que it's just that (See Chapter 7.)
escolar scholastic
esconder to hide
escribir to write
escritura writing
escuchar to listen
escuela school
esencialmente essentially; effectively
esfuerzo effort
eso, -a, -os, -as that; those
espacioso, -a, -os, -as roomy; spacious
especializarse to specialize; major
espectador, -a spectator
esperanza hope; wish
esperanzador, -a, -os, -as promising
esperar to wait; hope
esposa wife
esposo husband
esquina corner (outside)
estacionamiento parking
estar a punto de to be about to (See Chapter 12.)
estudiante student
estudiar to study
estudio office; study
evidentemente obviously (See Chapter 10.)
examen exam; test
excelente excellent
excesivamente too; more than desirable
exigente strict; demanding
existir to exist
experiencia experience
experto expert
explicar to explain
explorar to explore
extra extra
extranjero, -a, -os, -as foreign

F

fácil easy
fallar to fail; let down (See Chapter 7.)
falso, -a, -os, -as incorrect; false
faltar to be lacking (See Chapter 7 and 10.)
familia family
fantasma ghost
fantástico, -a, -os, -as fantastic
fascinar to fascinate
favor favor
favorito, -a, -os, -as favorite
febrero February
felicitar to congratulate

feliz happy
fiesta party
fíjate que notice that (See Chapter 3.)
fin end
fin de semana weekend
firmar to sign
flojo, -a, -os, -as lazy; loose
flor flower
forma shape; form; way
formal formal
formulario form; application
foto(grafía) photo
fotocopia photocopy
frecuencia frequency
fregadero kitchen sink
frenar to brake
frenazo slammed brake
fricción friction
frijol bean
frío cold
frustrarse to get frustrated (See Chapter 6.)
fuente fountain; source
fuera de outside of
fuerte strong
fumar to smoke
futuro future

G

ganar to win; earn; gain
ganas desires (See Chapter 4.)
gasto expense
gimnasio gym
gracias thanks
grado grade (year in school)
graduarse to graduate
gramática grammar
gran great
grande big; large
gritar to yell; shout
grupo group
guerra war
gustar to be pleasing to (See Chapter 2.)
gusto taste; pleasure

H

haber to have (auxiliary verb)
habitación room
hablar to talk; speak
hacer to do; make
hacer falta to be missing (See Chapter 10.)
hambre hunger
harto, -a, -os, -as fed up (See Chapter 8.)
hasta until; even
hasta luego until later (See Chapter 4.)
hay there is; there are
hay que one must (See Chapter 8.)
herirse to get hurt; wounded (See Chapter 6.)
hermana sister
hermano brother
hispanoamericano, -a, -os, -as Hispanic
hola hello; hi
honrado, -a, -os, -as honorable; honest
hora hour; time
horrible horrible
hospital hospital
hoy today
huracán hurricane

I

idea idea
ideal ideal
igualmente equally; same here
imaginarse to imagine
implorar to beg (See Chapter 7.)
importante important
importar to be important to (See Chapter 8.)
imposible impossible
imprescindible absolutely necessary
impresión impression
impresionado, -a, -os, -as impressed
impuesto tax
incluso including; actually; even (See Chapters 3 and 5.)
incluyendo including
incómodo, -a, -os, -as uncomfortable; inconvenient
incondicionalmente unconditionally
increíble unbelievable
increíblemente unbelievably
indicado, -a, -os, -as (See Chapter 10.)
individualmente individually; personally
información information
informática computer programming
ingeniero engineer
inglés English
iniciativa iniciative
innecesario, -a, -os, -as unnecessary
innovador, -a, -os, -as novel; unique; innovative
inquilino tenant; renter
instrucciones instructions; directions
interesante interesting
internacional international
investigación research; investigation
ir to go; come (See Chapter 6.)
irresponsable irresponsible
irse to leave (See Chapter 5.)

J

jefe, jefa boss
jubilarse to retire
jugador, -a player
jugar to play

julio July
juntos, -as together

L

lado side
lástima misfortune; shame
lavar to wash
lección lesson
lectura reading selection
leer to read
lejos far away
lengua tongue; language
levantar to raise
levantarse to get up
ley law
libre free
libro book
listo, -a, -os, -as ready; smart
llamarse to be called (See Chapter 1.)
llave key
llegar to arrive
llegar a ser to become (See Chapter 9.)
llevar to carry; bring; take (See Chapter 1.)
llevarse to get along (See Chapter 5.)
llorar to cry
llover to rain
lluvioso, -a, -os, -as rainy
lo it; that (See Chapters 1, 6, and 11.)
loco crazy
lograr to achieve (See Chapter 9.)
luego then; later (See Chapter 4.)
lugar place
lunes Monday
luz light; electricity

M

maestro, -a teacher; master
mamá mother
mañana tomorrow; morning
mandar to send (See Chapter 7.)
manejar to drive
manera way
mano hand
mantener to keep; maintain (See Chapter 2.)
mar sea
marcharse to leave (See Chapter 5.)
más more
matemáticas mathematics
mayor larger; older
medicina medicine
médico doctor
mediodía noon
medir to measure
mejor better
mejorarse to get better (See Chapter 6.)
menos less; minus
mensualmente monthly
mentir to tell a lie
mentira falsehood; lie
merengue merengue (a dance)
mes month
mesera waitress
mesero waiter
meta goal (See Chapter 9.)
metro subway; meter
miedo fear
mientras while
mientras tanto meanwhile
milla mile
mío, -a, -os, -as mine
mira look (See Chapter 5.)
mirar to look
mismo, -a, -os, -as same
moderno, -a, -os, -as modern
modo way
mojado, -a, -os, -as wet
momento moment
mostrar to show (See Chapter 7.)
motivo motive; reason
mover to move (See Chapter 3.)
moverse to move around (See Chapter 3.)
muchacha girl
muchacho boy
mucho a lot
mudarse to move one's residence (See Chapter 3.)
muleta crutch
mundo world
muñeca doll
música music
muy very

N

nacer to be born
nada nothing (See Chapter 8.)
nada que ver nothing like (See Chapter 5.)
nadar to swim
nadie nobody (See Chapter 8.)
natural natural
necesitar to need
negocio business; shop
nervioso, -a, -os, -as nervous
ni not even (See Chapters 8 and 10.)
ni hablar to say nothing of (See Chapter 5.)
ni siquiera not even (See Chapter 10.)
ni... ni neither . . . nor (See Chapter 8.)
niñera, -o babysitter
ninguno, -a not one (See Chapter 8.)
niño, -a child
no no, not (See Chapter 8.)
no dudar en to not hesitate to (See Chapter 7.)
no obstante nevertheless (See Chapter 10.)
no... ni not . . . or (See Chapter 5.)
noche night
nombre name

nota memo; grade (on schoolwork); musical note
noticia news item
novela novel
novia girlfriend; fiancée
novio boyfriend; fiance
nuestro, -a, -os, -as our
nuevo, -a, -os, -as new
número number
nunca never (See Chapter 8.)

O

o sea that is (See Chapter 2.)
obtener to get; obtain
ocupado, -a, -os, -as busy
ofrecer to offer (See Chapter 7.)
oiga listen (See Chapter 7.)
ola wave
olvidar to forget (See Chapter 10.)
opinar to be of the opinion (See Chapter 10.)
orgulloso, -a, -os, -as proud
oscuro, -a, -os, -as dark
otra vez again (See Chapter 8.)
oye listen (See Chapter 7.)

P

paciencia patience
pagar to pay
país nation; country
pájaro bird
papá father
para for (See Chapters 9 and 12.)
para colmo to top it all off (See Chapter 8.)
paraguas umbrella
parámetros parameters
parar to stop
parecer to seem
parecer mentira to not seem possible (See Chapter 1.)
parecerse to be like (See Chapter 5.)
pared wall
pareja partner
parque park
parte part
partido game
partir to leave (See Chapter 5.)
pasado, -a, -os, -as previous
pasar to go by
pedir to ask for; request (See Chapter 7.)
película movie; film
peligro danger
pensar to think
peor worse
pequeño, -a, -os, -as little; small
perder to lose; miss (See Chapter 7.)
perderse to get lost (See Chapters 6 and 7.)
perdido, -a, -os, -as lost
perfecto, -a, -os, -as perfect
pero but
personal personal
personalidad personality
picante hot (spicy)
pie foot
pierna leg
pintar to paint
piscina swimming pool
placer pleasure
plan plan
planchar to iron
planear to plan
plato plate; dish
poder to be able to
policía police officer; police force
ponerse enfermo, -a, -os, -as to get sick (See Chapter 6.)
popular popular
por (See Chapters 4 and 9.)
por cierto by the way (See Chapters 7 and 10.)
por el contrario on the contrary (See Chapter 10.)
por fin finally (See Chapter 11.)
por lo menos at least (See Chapter 8.)
por orden in the correct order
por otra parte also; furthermore (See Chapters 2 and 10.)
por qué why (See Chapter 9.)
por ser (See Chapter 12.)
por si fuera poco as if that weren't enough (See Chapter 10.)
por supuesto naturally; of course (See Chapter 7.)
por una parte for one thing (See Chapter 10.)
porque because
portarse to behave
posibilidad possibility
posible possible (See Chapter 10.)
positivo, -a, -os, -as positive
postre dessert
practicar to practice
precioso, -a, -os, -as adorable; precious; cute
preferencia preference
preferir to prefer
pregunta question
preocuparse to worry (See Chapter 6.)
preparar to prepare
prestar to lend (See Chapter 7.)
prestigioso, -a, -os, -as prestigious
presumido, -a, -os, -as conceited; stuck-up; presumptuous
presumir to presume
presupuesto budget
primero, -a first
primo, -a cousin
principal main
probable probable (See Chapter 10.)
probar to try out; try on
problema problem

profesión profession
profesional professional
profesor, -a professor; teacher
programa program
prometer to promise
pronto soon
propio, -a, -os, -as own
proponer to propose
propósito purpose
propuesta proposal
proteger to protect
protesta protest
próximo, -a, -os, -as next
pueblo town
pues then; well; because (See Chapters 2 and 3.)
puesto job; position
pulcro, -a, -os, -as neat; tidy
pulgada inch
punto point

Q

que (See Chapter 10.)
que digamos (See Chapter 10.)
qué tal (See Chapter 3.)
que that, which, who
quebrar to break (See Chapter 11.)
quedar con... para to commit to (See Chapter 7.)
quedarse to stay; remain (See Chapter 5.)
quemar to burn (See Chapter 10.)
querer to want; care for; love
quién, -es who
quisiera would like (See Chapter 2.)

R

radiografía x-ray
raro, -a, -os, -as strange
rato a short time (See Chapter 11.)
realmente really
reclamación claim
recomendar to recommend (See Chapter 8.)
reconocer to recognize
recuperar to recover
recurso source
regalar to give as a gift
regalo gift
regañar to scold
regresar to return
reina queen
relativo, -a, -os, -as relating to
rellenar to fill out; complete
reparación repair
repasar to review
repetir to repeat
requerido, -a, -os, -as required
responder to respond; answer
responsable responsible
respuesta answer
restar to subtract
restaurante restaurant
reunión meeting
reunir to invite to meet
reunirse to meet again
rico, -a, -os, -as rich; delicious
ridículo, -a, -os, -as ridiculous
robo robbery
rogar to beg (See Chapter 7.)
rojo, -a, -os, -as red
romper to break
ropa clothing

S

saber to know
sacar to take; take out
salir to leave; go out (See Chapter 5.)
salón large room; hall
salsa sauce; salsa (a dance)
saludar to greet; say hello
sano, -a, -os, -as healthy
satisfacción satisfaction
se debe (See Chapter 8.)
secretario, -a secretary
seguir to continue; follow (See Chapter 11.)
seguro, -a, -os, -as secure; safe
seis six
selección choice; selection
semana week
semestre semester
sentarse to sit down
sentirse to feel (See Chapter 11.)
serenidad calm; serenity
serio, -a, -os, -as serious
setecientos seven hundred
si if; indeed
sí yes (See Chapter 12.)
siempre always
siempre y cuando if and when (See Chapter 9.)
simplemente simply
sin embargo nevertheless (See Chapter 11.)
sincero, -a, -os, -as honest; sincere
sino but rather (See Chapter 1.)
sistema de SPG GPS system
situación situation
sobre about; over; on top of
solicitud application (See Chapter 6.)
sólo only (See Chapter 11.)
solo, -a, -os, -as alone (See Chapter 11.)
solución solution
solucionar to solve
sonar to ring
soñar to dream
soportar to tolerate (See Chapter 2.)
sorpresa surprise

sostener to hold
suave soft
subir to go up
suceder to happen
sucio, -a, -os, -as dirty
suerte luck
suficiente enough
suficientemente sufficiently
sugerir to suggest
sumar to add
suplicar to beg (See Chapter 7.)
suyo, -a, -os, -as yours; his; hers; theirs

T

taco taco
talento talent
tamal tamale
también also
tampoco not either (See Chapter 8.)
tan pronto como as soon as (See Chapter 9.)
tanto... como as much as
tardar to delay (See Chapter 11.)
tarde late; afternoon (See Chapter 11.)
tarea assignment; task (See Chapter 8.)
teatro theater
teléfono telephone
televisión television program
televisor TV set
tener to have
tener en común to have in common (See Chapter 5.)
tenis tennis
terminar to finish; end
tesis thesis; academic paper
textear to text
tiempo time; weather (See Chapters 1 and 11.)
tímido, -a, -os, -as shy; timid
tipo type; kind (See Chapter 5.)
tirar to throw
título title; master's degree
tobillo ankle
todo lo contrario just the opposite (See Chapter 5.)
todo, -a, -os, -as all
tomar to take; drink
tono tone
torcer to twist
trabajar to work
traer to bring (See Chapter 6.)
tráfico traffic
tranquilizarse to calm down
tranquilo, -a, -os, -as calm; quiet
tratar de to try to (See Chapter 7.)
tratarse de to be about
triángulo triangle
triste sad
tú you
tuyo, -a, -os, -as yours

U

ubicación location
una vez once (See Chapter 8.)
una vez más one more time (See Chapter 8.)
universidad university
un/una/unos/unas some
usar to use
usted, -es you; you all

V

valer la pena to be worthwhile (See Chapter 6.)
vamos come on (See Chapter 5.)
vecindad neighborhood
vegetariano, -a, -os, -as vegetarian
veinte twenty
vendedor, -a seller; salesman
venir to come (See Chapter 6.)
ventaja advantage
ver to see; watch
verano summer
verdad truth (See Chapter 5.)
verde green
verdura vegetable
vez time; instance (See Chapter 11.)
viajar to travel
vida life
videojuego videogame
viejo, -a, -os, -as old
viernes Friday
vigilancia surveillance
vino wine
visitar to visit
vivir to live
volver to return
volver a to do again (See Chapter 5.)
vosotros, -as you all

Y

y and
ya yet; already; now (See Chapter 1.)
ya que since (See Chapter 12.)
ya sea whether (See Chapter 2.)
yo I

English-Spanish glossary

A

a lot mucho
about sobre
accept, to aceptar
accompany, to acompañar
accountant contador, -a
accounting contabilidad
achieve, to lograr
action acción
actor actor
actress actriz
add, to sumar
adorable adorable; precioso, -a, -os, -as
advantage ventaja
advertise, to anunciar
advise, to aconsejar
affection cariño
after después de
afternoon tarde
afterward después
again otra vez; de nuevo
aggressive agresivo, -a, -os, -as
alcohol alcohol
all todo, -a, -os, -as
almost casi
alone solo. -a, -os, -as
already ya
also también; además; por otra parte
although aunque
always siempre
ambulance ambulancia
among entre
amount cantidad
ancient anciano, -a, -os, -as
and y
animal animal
ankle tobillo
announce, to anunciar
answer, to contestar; responder
answer respuesta
any cualquier
anyway de todos modos
apartment apartamento; piso
appear, to aparecer
application (for a job, college entrance, etc.) solicitud
apply, to (paint, glue, makeup, etc.) aplicar
appreciate, to apreciar
appropriate apropiado, -a, -os, -as
arithmetic aritmética
around alrededor
arrive, to llegar
art arte
as much as tanto como
as soon as tan pronto como; en cuanto
as soon as possible lo antes posible
ask for, to pedir
assign, to asignar
assignment tarea; deber; asignatura
association asociación
at en
at least al menos; por lo menos
athlete atleta; deportista
athletic atlético, -a, -os, -as
attend, to asistir
authentic auténtico, -a, -os, -as
available disponible

B

babysitter niñera
balcony balcón
bank banco
base base
baseball béisbol
baseball player beisbolista
based basado, -a, -os, -as
basic básico; fundamental
basically en el fondo
basketball básquetbol; baloncesto
bath baño
bathroom baño
be able, to poder
be about, to tratarse de
be about to, to estar a punto de
be alike, to parecerse a
be born, to nacer

be called, to llamarse
be devoted to, to dedicarse a
be important to, to importar
be late, to llegar tarde; tardar
be obligated to, to deber
be pleasing to, to gustar
be presumptuous, to presumir
be suitable, to convenir
be worthwhile, to valer la pena
bean, frijol
beautiful bello, -a, -os, -as; bonito, -a, -os, -as; hermoso, -a, -os, -as; lindo, -a, -os, -as
because porque
become, to llegar a ser
bedroom dormitorio; cuarto
beer cerveza
before antes de
beforehand antes
beg, to pedir; rogar; suplicar; implorar
begin, to empezar; comenzar
behave, to portarse; comportarse
behavior comportamiento
behind atrás; atrasado, -a, -os, -as
believe, to creer; pensar; opinar
bench banco
better mejor
between entre
big grande
bigger mayor; más grande
bilingual bilingüe
bill cuenta
biology biología
bird pájaro
book libro
bored aburrido, -a, -os, -as
boss jefe; jefa
boy muchacho; chico
boyfriend novio
brake, to frenar
break, to romper; quebrar; descomponer
bring, to traer; llevar
brother hermano
budget presupuesto
building edificio
bump into, to chocar con
burn, to quemar
business negocio
busy ocupado, -a, -os, -as
but pero
buy, to comprar
by the way por cierto
bye chao; adiós; hasta luego

C

café café
calm tranquilidad; serenidad; tranquilo, -a, -os, -as
calm down, to tranquilizarse; calmarse
candidacy candidatura
candidate candidato, -a
car coche; carro; automóvil
care cuidado
Caribbean caribeño, -a, -os, -as
carry, to llevar
case caso
cause, to causar; motivar
cause motivo
cell phone celular; móvil
center centro
championship campeonato
change, to cambiar
change one's mind, to cambiar de opinión
chat, to charlar
cheap barato, -a, -os, -as
child niño, -a
choice selección
city ciudad
claim, to reclamar
class clase
classic clásico, -a, -os, -as
classroom aula; salón de clase
clear claro, -a, -os, -as
client cliente
clothing ropa
club club
coat (of paint) aplicación; mano
coffee café
cold frío
colleague colega
color color
come, to venir; ir
commit to quedar con... para
company compañía; empresa
compatible compatible
competent competente
competitor competidor, -a
complete completar; terminar; acabar
completely completamente
component componente
computer programming informática
conceited presumido, -a, -os, -as
concert concierto
condominium condominio; piso
conference congreso
congratulate, to felicitar
conservative conservador, -a
considerate considerado, -a
contact, to contactar
continue, to seguir; continuar
contract contrato
central céntrico, -a, -os, -as
corner (outside) esquina
corner (inside) rincón
corporation empresa

correct correcto, -a, -os, -as
correctly correctamente
cost costo
count, to contar
country país
cousin primo, -a
coworker colega
crazy loco, -a, -os, -as
creative creativo, -a, -os, -as
credit crédito
crime delincuencia
crutch muleta
cry, to llorar
cuisine cocina
cure, to curar
currently actualmente
custom costumbre
customer cliente

D

dance, to bailar
dance baile
danger peligro
dark oscuro, -a, -os, -as
day día
day before yesterday anteayer
decent decente
decision decisión
decoration decoración
delicious rico, -a, -os, -as; sabroso, -a, -os, -as; delicioso, -a, -os, -as
delight, to encantar
delighted encantado, -a, -os, -as
demanding exigente
depend, to depender
depressed deprimido, -a, -os, -as
describe, to describir
dessert postre
destruction destrucción
detail detalle
detailed detallado
determined decidido, -a, -os, -as
diet dieta
difficult difícil
dining room comedor
direct directo, -a, -os, -as
directions instrucciones
director director, -a
dirty sucio, -a, -os, -as
disaster desastre
discotheque discoteca
disease enfermedad
dish plato
distance distancia
diverse diverso, -a, -os, -as
do, to hacer
do again, to volver a...
doctor médico; doctor, -a
documentation documentación
doll muñeca
dollar dólar
double doble
doubt, to dudar
dramatic dramático, -a, -os, -as
draw, to dibujar
dream, to soñar
dream sueño
drink, to tomar; beber
drive, to manejar; conducir
during mientras
dynamic dinámico, -a, -os, -as

E

earn, to ganar
easy fácil
eat breakfast, to desayunar
eat dinner, to cenar
eat lunch, to almorzar
effectively esencialmente
effort esfuerzo
elegant elegante
eliminate, to eliminar
emphasize, to destacar
employee empleado, -a
end, to terminar; acabar
end fin
energetic enérgico, -a, -os, -as
engineer ingeniero, -a
enjoy, to disfrutar; gozar de
enough suficiente
enthusiasm entusiasmo
entrance entrada
essay tesis; ensayo
even incluso; hasta
exactly efectivamente; en efecto
exam examen
exasperated harto, -a, -os, -as
excellent excelente
excessively excesivamente
excited emocionado, -a, -os, -as
exciting emocionante
exist, to existir
expense gasto
experience experiencia
expert experto
explain, to explicar
explore, to explorar
extra extra
extremely demasiado; extremadamente

F

fact dato
fail, to fallar; suspender
fall, to caer

false falso, -a, -os, -as
family familia
fan (supporter) aficionado, -a; fanático, -a
fantastic fantástico, -a, -os, -as
far away lejos
fascinate, to fascinar
father padre; papá
favor favor
favorite favorito, -a, -os, -as
fear miedo
fed up harto, -a, -os, -as
feel, to sentirse
fill out, to rellenar
film película
finally por fin
find, to encontrar
find out, to averiguar
fine bien
fine bello, -a, -os, -as
finish, to completar; terminar; acabar
fire (from a job), to despedir
first primero
flower flor
focus on, to enfocar
follow, to seguir
food comida
foot pie
foreign extranjero, -a, -os, -as
forget, to olvidar; olvidarse de
form formulario
formal formal
fountain fuente
free (of control) libre
free (of charge) gratis
frequency frecuencia
friction fricción
friend amigo, -a
friendly amistoso, -a, -os, -as
from de
furthermore además; por otra parte; es más
future futuro

G

game partido; juego
get, to conseguir; obtener
get along, to llevarse
get better, to mejorarse
get bored, to aburrirse
get depressed, to deprimirse
get dirty, to ensuciar
get drunk, to emborracharse
get excited, to emocionarse
get fat, to engordarse
get frustrated, to frustrarse
get happy, to alegrarse
get hurt, to herirse
get lost, to perderse
get mad, to enojarse; enfadarse
get married, to casarse
get ready, to prepararse
get sick, to enfermarse; ponerse enfermo, -a, -os, -as
get together, to reunirse
get up, to levantarse
ghost fantasma
gift regalo
girl muchacha; chica
girlfriend novia
go, to ir; andar
go by, to pasar
go get, to buscar
go out, to salir
go up, to subir; ascender
go with, to acompañar
goal meta
good bueno, -a, -os, -as
good-bye adiós; chao; hasta luego
gossip chisme
GPS sistema de posicionamiento global (SPG)
grade (in school) grado
grade (on schoolwork) nota
graduate, to graduarse
grammar gramática
grandmother abuela
great gran
green verde
greet, to saludar
group grupo
gymnasium gimnasio

H

hand mano
hand in, to entregar
hand over, to entregar
happen, to pasar; suceder; ocurrir
happy contento, -a, -os, -as; feliz
hard (test, problem) difícil
hard (work, surface) duro, -a, -os, -as
have, to tener
have fun, to divertirse
have in common, to tener en común
have just, to acabar de
he él
healthy sano, -a, -os, -as
heating calefacción
hello hola
help, to ayudar
here aquí
hi hola
hide, to esconder
highway carretera
hire, to contratar
Hispanic hispano, -a, -os, -as
hold, to sostener

home casa
honest sincero, -a, -os, -as; honrado, -a, -os, -as; honesto, -a, -os, -as
hope, to esperar
hope esperanza
horrible horrible
hospital hospital
hot (in temperature) caliente
hot (in spice) picante
hour hora
house casa
how cómo; como
how much cuánto
huge enorme
hunger hambre
hurricane huracán
hurry apuro
hurt, to doler
husband esposo

I

idea idea
ideal ideal
if si
if and when siempre y cuando
imagine, to imaginarse
imperative imprescindible
important importante
impossible imposible
impressed impresionado, -a, -os, -as
impression impresión
in en
in common en común
in front delante
in general en general
in particular en particular
inch pulgada
including incluyendo; incluso
incorrect incorrecto, -a, -os, -as
individually individualmente; personalmente
information información
iniciative iniciativa
innovative innovador, -a
inside of dentro de
instance vez; caso
instructions instrucciones
interesting interesante
international internacional
iron, to planchar
irresponsible irresponsable

J

job trabajo; puesto

K

keep, to mantener; quedarse con
key llave
kiss beso
kitchen cocina
know, to (information) saber
know, to (a person or place) conocer

L

lack, to faltar; hacer falta
language idioma; lengua
large grande
last último, -a, -os, -as
last night anoche
last straw colmo
late tarde
later más tarde; después; luego
law ley
lazy flojo, -a, -os, -as; perezoso, -a, -os, -as
learn, to aprender
leave, to salir; partir; irse; dejar
leg pierna
lend prestar
less menos
lesson lección
let down, to fallar
let know, to avisar
letter carta
library biblioteca
lie, to mentir
life vida
lift, to levantar
light (noun) luz
light (in color) claro, -a, -os, -as
like como
like, to apreciar; querer; gustar
limit límite; colmo
listen, to escuchar; atender; oír
little pequeño, -a, -os, -as; chico, -a, -os, -as
live, to vivir
location ubicación
look, to mirar
look at, to mirar
look for, to buscar
lose, to perder
lost perdido, -a, -os, -as
love, to querer; amar; encantar
love amor
luck suerte

M

main principal
maintain, to mantener
major in, to especializarse en
make, to hacer
make (a mistake), to cometer
make happy, to alegrar
make sure, to asegurarse
master's degree título
mathematics matemáticas

mature maduro, -a, -os, -as
mayor alcalde
meanwhile mientras tanto
measure, to medir
meat carne
medicine medicina
meeting reunión
meet up, to reunirse
memo nota
mile milla
mine mío, -a, -os, -a
minus menos
miss perder; extrañar; echar de menos
mistake error; falla
modern moderno, -a, -os, -as
moment momento
month mes
monthly mensualmente
more más
more and more cada vez más
morning mañana
mother mamá; madre
mouth boca
move, to mover; moverse; mudarse; trasladarse
movie película
movie theater cine
music música

N

name nombre
natural natural
naturally por supuesto
near cerca
neat pulcro, -a, -os, -as
need, to necesitar
neighborhood vecindad; barrio
neither . . . nor ni... ni
nervous nervioso, -a, -os, -as
never nunca
nevertheless sin embargo; no obstante
new nuevo, -a, -os, -a
news item noticia
next próximo, -a, -os, -as
night noche
no no
no wonder con razón
nobody nadie
none ninguno, -a
noon mediodía
not no
not either tampoco
not even ni siquiera
not hesitate to, to no dudar en
not seem possible, to parecer mentira
notebook cuaderno
notes (to help one remember) apuntes
nothing nada
notice noticia
now ahora; actualmente
nowhere en ninguna parte
number número

O

obtain, to obtener; conseguir
obviously evidentemente
of de
of course claro; por supuesto
offer, to ofrecer
office oficina; estudio; despacho
OK bien; de acuerdo
old viejo, -a, -os, -as; antiguo, -a, -os, -as
older mayor; más viejo, -a, -os, -as
on en
on purpose a propósito
once una vez
one uno, -a
one-fourth cuarto, -a
only solo
ordinary corriente; ordinario, -a, -os, -as
our nuestro, -a, -os, -as
outside afuera
outside of fuera de
over there allí
own propio, -a, -os, -as

P

paint, to pintar
paint pintura
park parque
parking estacionamiento
part parte
partner pareja
party fiesta
pass, to pasar
pass (a test), to aprobar
patience paciencia
pay, to pagar
perfect perfecto, -a, -os, -as; indicado, -a, -os, -as
personal personal
personality personalidad
pertaining to relativo, -a, -os, -as
photo foto(grafía)
photocopy fotocopia
place lugar
plan plan
plate plato
play, to jugar
player jugador, -a
please, to gustar; complacer
pleasure gusto; placer
point punto
police force policía
police officer policía
polite cortés; bien educado, -a, -os, -as

popular popular
positive positivo, -a, -os, -as
possibility posibilidad
possible posible
practice práctica
precious precioso, -a, -os, -as
prefer, to preferir
preference preferencia
prepare, to preparar
prestigious prestigioso, -a, -os, -as
presume presumir
previous previo, -a, -os, -as; anterior; pasado, -a, -os, -as
principal (main) principal
probable probable
probably probablemente
problem problema
profession profesión; carrera
professional profesional
professor profesor, -a
program programa
promise, to prometer
promising esperanzador, -a
proposal propuesta
propose, to proponer
protect, to proteger
protest, to protestar
proud orgulloso, -a, -os, -as
pupil alumno, -a
purchases compras
purpose propósito

Q

queen reina
question pregunta
quiet tranquilo, -a, -os, -as
quite bastante; bien

R

rain lluvia
rainy lluvioso, -a, -os, -as
raise, to levantar
raise (children), to educar
rather bastante
reach, to alcanzar
read, to leer
reading selection lectura
ready listo, -a, -os, -as
realize, to darse cuenta de
really realmente; muy
reason razón; motivo; causa
recognize, to reconocer
recommend, to recomendar
recover, to recuperar
red rojo, -a, -os, -as
relieve, to aliviar
remain, to quedarse
rent, to alquilar
rent (amount) alquiler
repair, to reparar
repeat, to repetir
request, to pedir
required requerido, -a, -os, -as
research, to investigar
respond, to responder
responsible responsable
rest descansar
restaurant restaurante
retire, to jubilarse
return, to regresar; volver
review, to repasar
rich rico, -a, -os, -as
ridiculous ridículo, -a, -os, -as
right derecho
ring, to sonar
rise, to subir
robbery robo
room habitación
roommate compañero, -a de cuarto
round trip ida y vuelta
run, to correr

S

sad triste
safe seguro, -a, -os, -as
salesman/saleswoman vendedor, -a
same mismo, -a, -os, -as
satisfaction satisfacción
sauce salsa
say, to decir
say good-bye, to despedirse
scarf bufanda
scholarship beca
scholastic escolar
school escuela
scold, to regañar
sea mar
seat asiento
secretary secretario, -a
secure seguro, -a, -os, -as
see, to ver
seem, to parecer
selection selección
selfish egoísta
semester semestre
send, to mandar; enviar
serious serio, -a, -os, -as
seriously en serio
shame lástima; vergüenza
shape forma
share, to compartir
she ella

shop tienda; negocio
should debería
shout, to gritar
show, to mostrar; demostrar; enseñar
shy tímido, -a, -os, -as
sickness enfermedad
side lado
sign, to firmar
simply simplemente
sincere sincero, -a, -os, -as
sing, to cantar
sink (kitchen) fregadero
sink (bathroom) lavabo
sister hermana
sit down, to sentarse
situation situación
six seis
sleep, to dormir
slow lento, -a, -os, -as
slowly despacio; lentamente
small pequeño, -a, -os, -as; chico, -a, -os, -as
smart inteligente; listo, -a, -os, -as
smoke, to fumar
so así que
sock calcetín
soft suave
solution solución
solve, to resolver
some algún, -a, -os, -as
something algo
sometimes a veces; de vez en cuando
soon pronto
source fuente
spacious espacioso, -a, -os, -as
speak, to hablar
specialize, to especializarse
spectator espectador, -a
sport deporte
start, to empezar; comenzar
stay, to quedarse
stop, to parar
strange raro, -a, -os, -as
strict exigente
strong fuerte
stuck-up presumido, -a, -os, -as
student estudiante; alumno, -a
study, to estudiar
subtract, to restar
subway metro
suddenly de repente
sufficiently suficientemente
suggest, to sugerir
summer verano
support, to apoyar; sostener; mantener
sure seguro, -a, -os, -as
surprise sorpresa
surveillance vigilancia
swim, to nadar
swimming pool piscina

T

take, to llevar; traer; sacar
talent talento
talk, to hablar; conversar; charlar
tall alto, -a, -os, -as
task tarea; deber
taste, to probar
taste gusto
tax impuesto
teach, to enseñar
teacher maestro, -a; profesor, -a
team equipo
tee-shirt camiseta
telephone teléfono
television program televisión
television set televisor
tell, to decir; contar
tell a lie, to mentir
ten diez
tenant inquilino, -a
tennis tenis
test examen
text, to textear
thanks gracias
the el; la; los; las
theater teatro
there is/there are hay
thesis tesis
think, to pensar; creer; opinar
throw, to tirar; echar
tidy pulcro, -a, -os, -as
time tiempo; hora; vez
timid tímido, -a, -os, -as
tired cansado, -a, -os, -as
title título
to a
today hoy
together juntos, -as
tolerate tolerar; soportar
tomorrow mañana
tone tono
town pueblo
traffic tráfico
trash basura
travel, to viajar
triangle triángulo
truth verdad
try on, to probar
try out, to probar
try to, to tratar de
turn into, to convertirse en
twist, to torcer

two dos
type tipo; clase

U

umbrella paraguas
unbelievable increíble
unbelievably increíblemente
uncomfortable incómodo, -a, -os, -as
unconditionally incondicionalmente
understand, to entender; comprender
unfortunately por desgracia; desafortunadamente
university universidad
unnecessary innecesario, -a, -os, -as
until hasta
use, to usar; utilizar

V

vegetable verdura
vegetarian vegetariano, -a
very muy
videogame videojuego
visit, to visitar

W

wait for, to esperar
waiter mesero; camarero
waitress mesera; camarera
wake up, to despertarse
wall pared
want querer
war guerra
warn, to advertir; avisar
wash, to lavar
watch, to ver
water agua
wave (ocean) ola
way modo; manera; forma
weather tiempo
wedding boda
week semana
weekend fin de semana
well bien; bueno
wet mojado, -a, -os, -as
what qué; que
when cuándo; cuando
where dónde; donde
while mientras
who quién; quien
whole entero, -a, -os, -as
why por qué
wife esposa
willing dispuesto, -a, -os, -as
win, to ganar
wine vino
within dentro de
work, to trabajar
world mundo
worry, to preocuparse
worse peor
would like quisiera
write, to escribir
writing escritura

X

x-ray radiografía

Y

year año
yell, to gritar
yes sí
you tú; usted
you all ustedes; vosotros, -as
yours tuyo, -a, -os, -as; suyo, -a, -os, -as

Answer key

1 Introducing yourself and others

1·1 1. es 2. soy 3. somos 4. eres 5. son 6. sois 7. son 8. es

1·2 1. sé 2. Sabe 3. Conoces 4. encontramos 5. se reúne

1·3 1. Me llamo 2. Se llama 3. Nos llamamos 4. Nos llamamos 5. Se llama

1·4 1. que 2. Quién; que 3. que/quien 4. Quiénes 5. Qué

1·5 1. Hace cuatro años que vivimos en este país./Llevamos cuatro años viviendo en este país. 2. Trabajamos juntos desde el once de febrero. 3. Llevo treinta minutos nadando./Hace treinta minutos que estoy nadando. 4. Hace tres meses que no veo a mi familia./Llevo tres meses sin ver a mi familia. 5. Llevo dos semanas sin fumar./Hace dos semanas que no fumo.

1·6 1. e 2. j 3. c 4. g 5. h 6. i 7. d 8. f 9. b 10. a

1·7 1. Es 2. Se llaman 3. Mi nombre es 4. Encantada 5. De dónde son 6. no es así 7. sino de 8. sino 9. Llevo... estudiando 10. parece mentira

1·8 1. seamos 2. estés 3. tenga 4. haga 5. trabajemos 6. corran 7. escriba 8. piensen 9. conozcáis 10. duerman

1·9 1. así que 2. sino 3. Bueno 4. estén

1·10 1. ¿Cómo se llaman ustedes?/¿Cómo os llamáis? 2. Son/Sois de/l Ecuador, ¿verdad?/¿no es así?/¿no? 3. No, no somos de/l Ecuador, sino de El Salvador. 4. ¿Hace cuánto tiempo que están aquí?/¿Cuánto tiempo llevan (viviendo) aquí? 5. Hace dos años que vivimos aquí./Llevamos dos años viviendo aquí. 6. ¿Conoce/s a nuestra hermana, ¿verdad?/¿no es así?/¿no? 7. Parece mentira que no la conozca.

1·11 Individual answers will vary.

2 Expressing opinions, likes, and dislikes

2·1 1. vuelvan 2. te vayas 3. estudie 4. comamos 5. haga 6. ayude

2·2 1. ir 2. que yo vaya 3. que trabajemos 4. trabajar 5. bailar 6. que él baile 7. descansar 8. descansar

2·3 1. desde 2. Como 3. como 4. Cómo 5. Desde 6. cómo 7. como 8. Desde 9. Como 10. como

2·4 1. hoy o mañana 2. aquí o en tu país 3. con un hombre o con una mujer 4. para ti o para tu amiga

2·5 1. de hecho 2. para serte sincero 3. por otra parte 4. A propósito 5. o sea

2·6 1. me 2. te 3. les 4. nos 5. les 6. os 7. les 8. le

2·7 1. encantan 2. parece 3. gustan 4. parecen 5. gustan 6. gustas 7. importas 8. importo

2·8 1. a, b, c, e, j, l 2. d, i 3. d, i 4. a, b, c, e, h, j, l 5. g 6. d, i 7. a, b, c, e, h, j, l 8. k 9. f

2·9 1. His attitude bothers me. 2. They love to play basketball. 3. What do you think?/How do you like it? 4. Do you like to go to the movies? 5. Children annoy him. 6. The news makes me sad/The news saddens me. 10. The class bores us. 11. You're important to me./I care about you.

2·10 1. Me encanta ir a la playa. 2. Le fascinan sus ideas. 3. No le gusta el ruido. 4. Le gustas tú. 5. Le aburren sus clases. 6. Me encanta la música de la guitarra. 7. Nos gustan las películas de horror. 8. Les encanta ir de compras. 9. Me parece feo. 10. Nos gusta.

2·11 1. mantienen 2. sostienen 3. apoyan 4. soporto

2·12 1. ¿Te gusta bailar? 2. ¿Te gustaría bailar? 3. Me encantaría bailar contigo. 4. Nos gustaría descansar ahora. 5. Les gusta escuchar música. 6. Les encantaría ir a un concierto. 7. ¿Le gusta jugar (al) fútbol? 8. No, no le gusta jugar (al) fútbol. 9. ¿Les gustaría ir al circo? 10. Sí, nos encantaría.

2·13 Individual answers will vary.

3 Striking up a conversation

3·1 1. Estoy 2. Está 3. están 4. Estamos 5. está enferma 6. están cansados 7. estoy contento, -a/ emocionado, -a 8. estamos nerviosos, -as

3·2 1. se 2. te 3. se 4. dedican 5. Nos 6. -as 7. -o 8. se... -a

3·3 1. Dime 2. No me digas 3. ¡Escucha! 4. ¡No te muevas! 5. Dígale 6. Escriba una carta 7. Espérenme/Esperadme 8. ¡No olviden!/¡No olvidéis!

3·4 1. suavecito(a) 2. chiquita 3. loquito 4. boquita 5. animalito 6. casita 7. pajarito 8. florecita 9. Dieguito 10. Carmencita

3·5 1. Bien. 2. Acabo de comprar un carro. 3. ¿En serio? 4. ¡Qué bueno! 5. ¡Claro!

3·6 1. h 2. c 3. i 4. g 5. j 6. b 7. a 8. d, f 9. k 10. f 11. e 12. l

3·7 1. ¿A qué se dedica tu novio? 2. Es profesor. 3. Es un profesor excelente. 4. Elena se dedica a limpiar la casa. 5. Por favor, no te mudes. 6. ¡No te muevas! Quiero sacar una foto. 7. Acabamos de hacer el examen. 8. ¿Qué acabas de decir? 9. ¡Imagínate!/¡Fíjate que me mudo la próxima semana!

3·8 1. no conoce a mis otros amigos. 2. el profesor es muy bueno. 3. ya la ha visto dos veces. 4. nos encanta esta ciudad. 5. prefiero los pueblos pequeños.

3·9 1. no asista a nuestra escuela. 2. el profesor sea excelente. 3. nadie quiera ir con él. 4. esté muy lejos de aquí. 5. haya más tráfico aquí que en un pueblo pequeño.

3·10 Individual answers will vary.

4 Making dates and appointments

4·1 1. el sábado 2. por la noche 3. a las ocho 4. de la noche 5. los jueves 6. el jueves

4·2 1. Soy Margarita./Habla Margarita./Te llama Margarita. 2. Te llamo 3. La fiesta es el domingo por la noche. 4. Es a las ocho de la noche. 5. ¿Dónde es la fiesta? 6. Es en mi casa.

4·3 1. la cerveza 2. nos encanta 3. en el cine 4. Quiero 5. En efecto 6. estudiar 7. desayunar

4·4 1. h 2. v 3. f 4. n 5. u 6. a 7. g 8. w 9. c 10. j 11. r 12. p 13. o, p 14. s 15. i 16. t 17. e 18. d 19. k 20. q, l 21. a 22. e, m 23. b

4·5 1. Me encanta la cocina/comida peruana. 2. ¿Me quieres?/¿Me amas? 3. Te gusta mi hermana, ¿verdad?/¿no?/¿no es así? 4. En efecto./Efectivamente. 5. ¿Te gustaría/Quisieras hablar con ella? 6. Sí, me encantaría. 7. ¿Tienes ganas de ir al cine? 8. No, no tengo ganas de ir.

4·6 1. ¿Dónde está? 2. ¿Dónde están? 3. ¿Dónde está? 4. ¿Dónde son? 5. ¿Dónde estamos? 6. ¿Dónde es? 7. ¿Dónde estoy? 8. ¿Dónde es?

4·7 1. Soy yo. 2. ¿Tienes ganas de almorzar? 3. Bueno, estoy ocupado(a) ahora. 4. Bien/Vale. Te llamo el sábado. 5. Entonces, ¿no estás enojado(a)? 6. No. Hasta luego/Nos vemos luego.

4·8 1. ¿Qué quieres? 2. Me encantaría verte esta noche. 3. Voy al cine con Sara. 4. Entonces, ¿no puedes cenar conmigo? 5. En efecto/Efectivamente. 6. Bien/Vale/De acuerdo. Hasta luego.

4·9 1. Hola, soy Miguel. 2. Te llamo a ver si puedes cenar conmigo esta noche. 3. Bien/Vale. ¿A qué hora? 4. ¿A las siete? 5. Bien. /Vale. 6. Marta no me quiere. 7. Entonces, ¿por qué no sales con Patricia? ¡(A ella) le gustas mucho! 8. Bueno, entonces, ¿por qué no?

4·10 Individual answers will vary.

5 Describing people, places, and things

5·1 1. irresponsable 2. buenos 3. amistosa 4. exigente

5·2 1. estoy 2. está 3. están 4. son 5. son 6. es 7. son 8. son

5·3 1. más alto que Diego 2. más bajo que Arturo 3. tan alto como Arturo 4. más de 5. menos de 6. mas... que 7. tan... como 8. más libros que Ana 9. tantos libros como Berta

5·4 1. bastante 2. demasiado 3. muy/bien 4. muy/bien

5·5 1. tan... como 2. la más lista de todas 3. tan lista como 4. más lista que

5·6 1. dejar 2. sales 3. dejes 4. se van/se marchan 5. parte/sale 6. deja

5·7 1. Mira 2. es decir 3. La verdad 4. Vamos 5. ni hablar 6. Con razón 7. todo lo contrario

5·8 Individual answers will vary. Sample answer: 1. ¡Con razón está tan orgullosa su mamá!

5·9 1. cantaba 2. cocinaba 3. pensábamos 4. comía 5. perdían 6. debías 7. hacíamos 8. estaban 9. escribía 10. iba 11. conocía 12. miraban 13. caminábamos 14. jugaban 15. disfrutaba 16. corrían 17. podía 18. tenía 19. éramos 20. veíamos 21. salía 22. dejábamos 23. parecía 24. mentían

5·10 1. Eran pequeños. 2. Estábamos contentos. 3. ¿Eras responsable? 4. Estaba aburrida. 5. Leía muy bien. 6. Íbamos a la playa. 7. Se divertían mucho. 8. No conocía a nadie. 9. Me gustaba el chocolate. 10. Te quería. 11. Ellos no me dejaban salir. 12. Se parecía a su mamá.

5·11 1. They were small/little. 2. We were happy. 3. Were you responsible? 4. I/She was bored. 5. I/He/She read/used to read very well. 6. We used to go/would go/always went to the beach. 7. They used to/would always have/always had a good time. 8. I/He/She didn't know anybody. 9. I liked chocolate. 10. I loved/cared about you. 11. They never/would never/never used to let me go out. 12. She looked like her mother.

5·12 1. Cuando ella tenía cuatro años, era muy tímida. 2. Le gustaba jugar sola. 3. Tenía dos muñecas favoritas. 4. Se llamaban/sus nombres eran Barbie 1 y Barbie 2. 5. Sus padres la comprendían/entendían. 6. Le hablaban mucho. 7. No la dejaban ver televisión todos los días. 8. Iban juntos al parque. 9. Ahora, no es tímida. 10. Tiene muchos amigos y ya no juega con muñecas.

5·13 Individual answers will vary.

5·14 Individual answers will vary.

6 Expressing wants and needs

6·1 1. sea 2. tenga 3. conozca 4. ofrezca 5. comprenda 6. aconseje

6·2 1. sepa 2. sabe 3. hacer 4. aprecie 5. pueda 6. pintar 7. esté 8. tenga 9. tiene 10. sirva

6·3 1. Queremos un(a) compañero(a) de cuarto que no fume. 2. Busco a mi primo, que trabaja aquí. 3. Ella busca a alguien que trabaje aquí. 4. Quieren un carro/coche que no use mucha gasolina. 5. Necesitamos un vendedor que hable español. 6. Ellos tienen un vendedor que habla español.

6·4 1. conseguir/obtener 2. se pone 3. engordar 4. consigue/obtiene 5. me pongo 6. enriquecerse 7. te enfermas/te pones enfermo(a) 8. te pierdes

6·5 1. ¡No te enfermes!/¡No te pongas enfermo(a)! 2. Espero/Ojalá que no se enoje/enfade. 3. Quiere casarse. 4. ¡Mejórate/Mejórese/Mejoraos pronto! 5. Ella se frustra fácilmente. 6. Nos aburrimos en esa clase. 7. No quiero que te preocupes/se preocupe. 8. Se emocionan cuando piensan en el viaje.

6·6 1. haya 2. se den cuenta 3. se enoje 4. preservemos 5. te portes 6. pierda

6·7 1. ¿Puedes venir a mi casa? 2. ¿Vas al mercado? 3. ¿Vas a nuestra boda? Es en el Jardín Botánico. 4. ¿Va él al cine con nosotros? 5. ¿Vienes acá/aquí mucho/frecuentemente/a menudo? 6. ¿Van ustedes a clase?/¿Vais a clase? 7. ¿Vienen ustedes a clase mañana/¿Venís a clase mañana? 8. ¿A qué hora viene/ vienes/vienen/venís?

6·8 1. Sí, voy./No, no puedo ir. 2. Sí, voy./No, no voy. 3. Sí, voy./No, no voy. 4. Sí, va./No, no va. 5. Sí, vengo a menudo/frecuentemente/mucho./No, no vengo... 6. Sí, vamos./No, no vamos. 7. Sí, venimos./ No, no venimos. 8. Venimos a las _______.

6·9 1. incluyendo 2. incluso 3. incluso 4. solicitud 5. formulario 6. formas 7. solicitar 8. aplicarse 9. asegurarnos 10. vale la pena

6·10 Individual answers will vary.

7 Making requests and offers

7·1 1. te 2. le 3. les 4. le 5. Le

7·2 1. baile 2. cante 3. coma 4. escriba 5. corra 6. lea 7. esté 8. dé 9. envíe 10. beba

7·3 1. juegue 2. vuelva 3. piense 4. despida 5. sirva 6. pida 7. me divierta 8. mueva 9. cierre 10. me sienta

7·4 1. vaya 2. vea 3. tenga 4. haga 5. salga 6. haya 7. me ponga 8. diga 9. venga 10. conozca

7·5 1. Te ruego que no manejes/conduzcas tan rápido. 2. Les pedimos que vayan con nosotros. 3. Le imploran a su profesor(a) que cambie la fecha del examen. 4. ¿Me pides/estás pidiendo que me vaya?

7·6 1. ¿Me llamas esta noche? 2. ¿Nos llevas a casa? 3. Nos ayudas con las maletas? 4. ¿Me mandas una postal? 5. ¿Me compras un helado? 6. Me traes flores?

7·7 1. Llámame/Llámeme esta noche. 2. Llévanos/Llévenos a casa. 3. Ayúdanos/Ayúdenos con las maletas. 4. Mándame/Mándeme una postal. 5. Cómprame/Cómpreme un helado. 6. Tráeme/Tráigame flores.

7·8 1. ¿Te ayudo? 2. ¿Les limpio la casa? 3. ¿Os llevo al aeropuerto? 4. ¿Le lavo el carro/coche?

7·9 1. Se lo estoy enviando./Estoy enviándoselo. 2. Te lo doy la próxima semana. 3. Nos las van a mostrar./ Van a mostrárnoslas. 4. Se los dice a su amiga. 5. Se la tengo que entregar mañana./Tengo que entregársela mañana. 6. Se la ofrecemos para el verano. 7. ¿Te lo presto? 8. Ella se lo enseña a mi hijo.

7·10 1. Quiere mostrarte sus fotos. 2. Te las quiere mostrar./Quiere mostrártelas. 3. Ella nos va a enseñar la canción. 4. Nos la va a enseñar./Va a enseñárnosla. 5. Le estoy explicando la lección. 6. Se la estoy explicando./Estoy explicándosela. 7. Voy a enviarle un mensaje. 8. Se lo voy a enviar./Voy a enviárselo.

7·11 1. ¿Me presta(s) sus/tus apuntes? 2. ¿Me los presta(s)? 3. ¿Nos presta(s) su/tu carro/coche? 4. Nos lo presta(s)?

7·12 1. Extraño/Echo de menos a mis amigos. 2. Te vas a perder la fiesta. 3. No quiero perder mi tarea. 4. Vamos a perder el autobús. 5. ¿Extrañas/Echas de menos tu país? 6. Faltan dos libros de la lista. 7. Nunca se le pasa (por alto) una pregunta. 8. Van a perder el juego. 9. Van a perder el tren.

7·13 1. De acuerdo 2. en cuanto 3. Por cierto 4. Por supuesto

7·14 Individual answers will vary.

7·15 Individual answers will vary.

8 Expressing doubts and uncertainty

8·1 1. a 2. f 3. e 4. c 5. b 6. d

8·2 1. cada vez más rápido 2. a la vez 3. la primera vez 4. A veces... otras veces 5. veces 6. de vez en cuando

8·3 1. cualquiera 2. cualquier 3. cualquier 4. cualquiera

8·4 1. nadie 2. nada 3. Nunca 4. ni... tampoco 5. ninguna parte/ningún lugar 6. ningún 7. ni/ni siquiera 8. ni... ni

8·5 Individual answers will vary. Sample answer: 1. No hay nadie en el mundo que prepare pollo frito como mi abuela.

8·6 Individual answers will vary. Sample answer: 1. Debo sacar la basura cada día.

8·7 1. olvide 2. pase 3. busque 4. solicite 5. se tranquilice

8·8 Individual answers will vary. Sample answer: 1. A mi mejor amigo le recomiendo que estudie más.

8·9 1. ponga 2. saca 3. es 4. sea 5. asistan 6. haya 7. está 8. nos mudemos

8·10 1. está harto 2. por lo menos 3. Al menos 4. para colmo 5. Al menos... contar con

8·11 Individual answers will vary.

9 Talking about future events

9·1 1. estaré 2. será 3. irán 4. querremos 5. dirás 6. aparecerá 7. escribiremos 8. pondrán 9. pensaré 10. saldremos 11. haréis 12. volverán 13. vendrá 14. comerás 15. tendré

9·2 1. b 2. d 3. c 4. a 5. d

9·3 1. Te casarás/Se casará/Se casarán/Os casaréis y tendrás/tendrá/tendrán/tendréis gemelos. 2. La fiesta es a las tres. 3. Nos vamos mañana. 4. Compraré un carro/coche algún día. 5. Te llamo esta noche. 6. Van a mudarse/Se van a mudar a este edificio la próxima semana. 7. ¿Qué piensas/piensa hacer? 8. Pienso/Estoy pensando mandarle un email. 9. ¿Qué estará haciendo (ella)? 10. Estará trabajando en un hospital.

9·4 1. estén 2. tiene 3. da 4. llegue 5. salga 6. te portas 7. hace 8. llueve 9. llueve 10. empiece

9·5 1. abrieran 2. supiera 3. corrieras 4. enseñara 5. se durmiera 6. volviéramos 7. trajera 8. fuera 9. fueran 10. pensaras 11. pudieran 12. quisiérais 13. leyera 14. comprendiera 15. se sintiera

9·6 1. daría 2. diría 3. venderíamos 4. vendrían 5. podría 6. haríais 7. iría 8. bailarías 9. se encontrarían 10. conocerían 11. deberíamos 12. pagaría 13. invitaría 14. me enojaría 15. se aburriría

9·7 1. tuviera... ayudaría 2. supieras... te enojarías 3. estuviéramos... estaríamos 4. hiciera... sería 5. fuera... asignaría

9·8 1. Por 2. por 3. Para 4. por 5. Por 6. Para 7. por... para

9·9 Individual answers will vary.

10 Making a case or arguing a point

10·1 1. despedirnos 2. despedir 3. se cree 4. cree 5. me falta 6. Falta

10·2 1. además 2. Evidentemente 3. no obstante 4. de modo que 5. ni 6. que digamos 7. Por una parte... y por otra 8. ni... ni 9. aunque

10·3 1. de modo que 2. no obstante 3. Es más 4. por el contrario 5. actualmente

10·4 Individual answers will vary. Sample answer: 1. Opino que sería difícil vivir sin carne.

10·5 1. En el fondo creo que es un error. 2. Pensamos/Creemos que es la persona indicada para el puesto. 3. Para serte sincero(a), no creo que sea la chica indicada para ti. 4. No conozco a nadie en esta ciudad, no tengo trabajo ni dónde vivir y por si fuera poco no hablo el idioma/la lengua. 5. Este no es el mejor trabajo del mundo, que digamos. 6. Que tengas un buen día.

10·6 Individual answers will vary.

10·7 Individual answers will vary.

11 Narrating a story

11·1 1. Eran las tres de la tarde. 2. Llovía/Estaba lloviendo. 3. Yo manejaba/estaba manejando/conducía/estaba conduciendo a casa. 4. Dos amigos estaban conmigo. 5. Todo estábamos cansados.

11·2 1. Mientras yo dormía/estaba durmiendo, mis amigos celebraban/estaban celebrando. 2. Ella escuchaba/estaba escuchando música mientras estudiaba/estaba estudiando. 3. Él limpiaba/estaba limpiando la casa mientras los niños jugaban/estaban jugando afuera. 4. Yo estaba preocupado(a) mientras hacía/estaba haciendo el examen. 5. El profesor/La profesora no veía cuando él texteaba/estaba texteando a sus amigos.

11·3 1. Mientras yo dormía/estaba durmiendo, mi mamá/madre llamó. 2. Ella escuchaba/estaba escuchando música cuando sonó el teléfono. 3. (Nosotros) nos divertíamos/nos estábamos divirtiendo cuando entró la profesora/el profesor. 4. Él hablaba/estaba hablando por celular/móvil cuando chocó con el otro carro/coche. 5. Jugaban/Estaban jugando (al) béisbol cuando empezó a llover.

11·4 1. (Yo) me levanté y me vestí. 2. Volvimos a casa y buscamos nuestros libros. 3. Estudió mucho y aprobó el examen. 4. Vino a clase y se sentó. 5. Fueron al supermercado y compraron bebidas.

11·5 1. entendía 2. pude 3. supiste 4. tenía 5. Quise

11·6 1. se le 2. se me 3. se le 4. se les 5. olvidó 6. quedaron 7. cayó

11·7 1. tiempo 2. tiempo 3. veces 4. hora 5. época 6. A veces

11·8 1. trabajando 2. caminando 3. corriendo 4. durmiendo 5. sirviendo 6. pidiendo 7. divirtiéndonos 8. mintiendo

11·9 1. e 2. b 3. a 4. c 5. f 6. d

11·10 Individual answers will vary.

11·11 1. entré 2. eran 3. Llovía/Estaba lloviendo 4. quería 5. estaba 6. interesaba 7. estaba 8. entré 9. pude 10. Empezamos 11. Hablábamos/Estábamos hablando 12. hizo 13. Me sentía (if that's how she felt/was feeling when the next action occurred)/Me sentí (if that's how she suddenly felt) 14. Me levanté 15. salí 16. me arrepentí 17. mandé 18. Quería 19. contestó 20. quería (if that's how he was feeling when the phone rang)/quiso (if he simply refused to answer it)

11·12 Individual answers will vary.

12 Retelling a conversation

12·1 1. El niño dijo que estaba contento. 2. Mi amigo dijo que tenía hambre. 3. Las chicas dijeron que les gustaba la clase. 4. Les dijimos que vivíamos en esa calle. 5. Nos dijeron que esta era la calle más bonita de toda la ciudad.

12·2 1. Su mamá me dijo: «Él no está en casa». 2. Los directores nos dijeron: «No hay suficiente dinero para el proyecto». 3. La novia de mi hermano me dijo: «Quiero casarme en abril». 4. Mi hermano me dijo: «No estoy de acuerdo con ese plan». 5. Su jefe le avisó: «No vas a conseguir una subida de sueldo».

12·3 1. Nos preguntaron si íbamos al cine esta/esa noche. 2. Me preguntó cuánto costaba un vuelo de ida y vuelta a México. 3. Le preguntó cuándo se graduaba de la escuela secundaria. 4. Me preguntaron qué quería hacer hoy/ese día. 5. Te preguntó si comías con frecuencia en ese restaurante.

12·4 1. Él le preguntaba: «¿Quieres acompañarme?» 2. Me preguntó: «¿A qué hora comes?» 3. Nos preguntó: «¿Dónde estudian/estudiáis?» 4. Te preguntó: «¿Con quién andas?» 5. Me preguntaron: «¿Tienes miedo?»

12·5 1. Le pedimos que nos dijera la verdad. 2. Le pedí que trajera ese sobre al director de la compañía. 3. Le dije que viniera temprano al trabajo el viernes. 4. Les dijo que no llegaran tarde. 5. Me pidió que le comprara un helado.

12·6 1. Ella dijo: «No me llames». 2. Él le pidió: «Piénsalo». 3. Yo te aconsejé: «Ve esta/esa película». 4. Me advirtió: «No bebas demasiado». 5. Ellos le dijeron: «Sal temprano».

12·7 1. Para 2. Por 3. por 4. Para 5. Para, para

12·8 1. Ella es la mejor estudiante de la clase, ya que estudia todo el tiempo. 2. No es culto, pero es bien educado. 3. Él sí es culto, ya que lee constantemente. 4. Es bien educado, ya que sus padres eran muy exigentes. 5. Ella es la más culta de su familia. 6. Para una mujer culta, no parece muy lista. 7. Ella sí es lista, es que no escucha. 8. Ella perdió su trabajo por llegar tarde todos los días.

12·9 1. Ella anunció que se iba a casar/que iba a casarse. 2. El médico le advirtió que no fumara. 3. Ella le avisó que se iba de vacaciones. 4. El jefe le aconsejó que no se fuera. 5. Anunciaron el puesto.

12·10 Individual answers will vary.